# Musical Creativity
# in Twentieth-Century China

# Eastman Studies in Music

# Musical Creativity
# in Twentieth-Century China

## Abing, His Music, and
## Its Changing Meanings

by

Jonathan P. J. Stock

University of Rochester Press

First published 1996

University of Rochester Press
34–36 Administration Building, University of Rochester
Rochester, New York, 14627, USA
and at PO Box 9, Woodbridge, Suffolk IP12 3DF, UK

IBSN 1-878822-76-4
ISSN 1071-9989

**Library of Congress Cataloging-in-Publication Data**

Stock, Jonathan P. J., 1963–
    Musical creativity in twentieth-century China : Abing, his music,
and its changing meanings / by Jonathan P. J. Stock.
        p.    cm. — (Eastman studies in music, ISSN 1071-9989;6)
    Includes bibliographical references and index.
    ISBN 1-878822-76-4 (alk. paper)
    1. A-bing, 1893–1950. 2. Musicians—China—Biography. 3. Music—
China—20th century—History and criticism. I. Series.
ML419.A67S76   1996
781.62'951'0092—dc20                        96-28056
                                               CIP
                                             MN

**British Library Cataloguing-in-Publication Data**
A catalogue record for this book is available from the British Library.

This publication is printed on acid-free paper.
Printed in the United States of America

# Acknowledgments

I have benefited on frequent occasions from the kindness, support, interest, and advice of a large number of individuals and institutions during the periods of both fieldwork and writing. Among these, the insights of Robert Provine and Michael Spitzer have been plundered particularly mercilessly. I also wish to thank Carlton Benson, Margaret Birley, Chen Yingshi, Dai Shuhong, Dai Xiaolian, Christopher Evans, Stephen Jones, Frank Kouwenhoven, Terence Liu, John Myers, Kimiko Ohtani, Peng Benle, Hélène La Rue, Antoinet Schimmelpenninck, Martin Stokes, Tang Yating, Wolfgang Wiese, Rembrandt Wolpert, Wu Ben, Wu Zhimin, and Su Zheng, all of whom have provided guidance, material, or detailed feedback at one stage or another. I am obliged also to Sean Culhane and Ralph Locke for their assistance with many aspects of finishing the manuscript, and for their support throughout the publication process. Institutional acknowledgments are due to the Shanghai Conservatory of Music, where the bulk of this research was carried out, and to the British Academy and British Council for fieldwork grants. The British Academy also provided a postdoctoral fellowship, held at the University of Durham, which granted the opportunity to write up this material. The Horniman Museum in London and Pitt Rivers Museum, Oxford, generously allowed access to their collections of historical instruments, and the Recording Archive of the Shanghai Library allowed access to historical sound recordings. An earlier version of chapter 2 appeared in the journal *Ethnomusicology*, while a preliminary form of chapter 4 appeared in *Asian Music*. I am grateful to, respectively, the Board of Trustees of the University of Illinois and to Martin Hatch, editor of *Asian Music*, for permission to present new versions here and also to the readers and editors whose feedback helped me focus the initial versions of those two essays.

For assistance with the preparation of the accompanying recording, I would like to thank Bernadine Blake, Anna Burleigh, Ding Shande, Hana Grisdale, Peter Manning, Rebecca Letts, Susie Winkworth, and Wu Zhimin. Tracks 1–4 were originally recorded by the Music Research Institute, Beijing, and subsequently issued by China Record Company. Unfortunately, and despite numerous letters, telephone calls, and faxes to these institutions, it has proven impossible to discover the identity of the copyright-holder (if any) for these tracks.

A special acknowledgment is due to my wife, Joo-Lee; she wishes to forego the long-suffering spouse characterization, at least as far as it is related to the preparation of this study. Her true sufferings, she insists, result from my more mundane shortcomings and foibles, and these, she notes with regret, have remained disconcertingly consistent throughout the completion of this work. To her, with love, I dedicate this book.

# Contents

# Abing CD Contents

Track 1  *The Moon Reflected on the Second Springs,* performed by Abing (*erhu*) (rec. Music Research Institute, 1950, Wuxi. China Record Company, 51189).

Track 2  *Listening to the Pines,* performed by Abing (*erhu*) (rec. Music Research Institute, 1950, Wuxi. China Record Company, 51191).

Track 3  *Great Waves Washing the Sand,* performed by Abing (*pipa*) (rec. Music Research Institute, 1950, Wuxi. China Record Company, 51191).

Track 4  *Zhaojun Crosses the Border,* performed by Abing (*pipa*) (rec. Music Research Institute, 1950, Wuxi. China Record Company, 51190).

Track 5  *Partridges Flying,* performed by Zhang Lisheng *(erhu)* and an unnamed *ban* player (rec. date [1930s] & place [Shanghai?] not given. Pathé Baidai, 33937).

Track 6  *The Moon Reflected on the Second Springs,* performed by an unnamed street musician (*leiqin*) (rec. Jonathan Stock, April 1990, Beijing).

Track 7  *The Moon Reflected on the Second Springs,* performed by Wu Zhimin (*erhu*) and Zhang Liduo (harp) (rec. 1982, Shanghai).

Track 8  *The Moon Reflected on the Second Springs,* arranged by Chu Wanghua, performed by Rebecca Letts (piano) (rec. Jonathan Stock, May 1996, Durham).

Track 9  *The Moon Reflected on the Second Springs,* arranged by Ding Shande, performed by Hana Grisdale and Anna Burleigh (violins), Bernadine Blake (viola), and Susie Winkworth (cello) (rec. Jonathan Stock, May 1996, Durham).

# List of Maps, Figures, and Photographs

# Musical Creativity
## in Twentieth-Century China

A

**• 阿炳**(1893—1950)　民间音乐家。原名华彦钧、江苏无锡东亭人。当地雷尊殿道士华清和之子。华清和号雪梅，擅长演奏各种民间乐器，尤精于琵琶。阿炳自幼从其父学习音乐。四岁丧母，二十一岁患眼病，三十五岁双目失明。在无锡市以沿街卖唱和演奏各种乐器为生，经常演唱当日新闻。

抗日战争时期，编唱过《汉奸的下场》等曲；抗战胜利后，又编唱“前走狼，后走虎，世上猫子吃老鼠”和“金圆券满天飞”等歌词，对国民党反动统治进行揭露、抨击。阿炳的器乐演奏深为群众欢迎爱好。其超群技艺，早在十八岁时已被当地道教音乐界所公认。曾广泛学习各种民间音乐，能超脱狭窄的师承和模仿，根据自己对现实生活的感受，创作、演奏各种器乐曲。著名的有二胡曲*《二泉映月》、*《听松》、*《寒春风曲》；琵琶曲*《大浪淘沙》、*《昭君出塞》、*《龙船》等。1950 年曾将他所演奏的六首乐曲录音，并由中央音乐学院民族音乐研究所将其记录整理，编成《阿炳曲集》(音乐出版社 1956)。

**• 阿茨**　哈尼族民歌的一种。也称阿栖或洒子必阿。阿茨是情歌的统称，并有歌曲的意思。在云南红河县一带，又分为大声唱的阿茨(见谱例)、小声唱的阿茨等若干种。长篇抒情歌有《装烟歌》、《吸烟歌》、《邀约出外》等数

Abing, as presented in
a leading Chinese music dictionary.
Although the quality of his image is poor,
this is the only photo of Abing known to exist.
*Source:* Zhongguo yishu yanjiuyuan yinyue yanjiusuo,
Editors, *Zhongguo yinyue cidian,*
(Beijing: Renmin yinyue chubanshe, 1985), 1.

# Introduction

## The Individual in Ethnomusicology

While ethnomusicologists experience a great deal of face-to-face contact with individual informants or teachers in the field and specialize in concentration on a particular person, the literature of the field provides surprisingly little information about the individual in music.                                         Bruno Nettl.[1]

Biographical work is rare, though not unheard of, in the discipline of ethnomusicology.[2] Partly this is because ethnomusicologists have desired to paint broad pictures of musical activity in specific cultures or societies. To some, the concentration on one particular musician would be premature when whole musical repertories, genres, and styles remain unknown. On another level, as social scientists, ethnomusicologists are fascinated by "music as culture" and "music cultures"; we seek to expose, understand, and relate—in both senses of the word—a given culture's accepted norms of musical thought, sound, and behavior. Theoretically at least, this would provide a foundation for the cross-cultural comparison of what Nettl refers to as "total music systems," supposedly one of ethnomusicology's primary aims.[3] But there is a danger in concentrating too exclusively on musical norms. Nettl warns that in its most extreme form this notion approaches:

> [A] belief in the homogeneity of non-Western cultures, resulting in the idea that members of whole cultures do not possess much individuality, and that a picture of musical life in the population at large gives one, *ipso facto*, a picture of music in the life of each individual.[4]

Notwithstanding this caveat, Nettl notes in a later work that the ethnomusicologist remains more interested in what is "typical" of a music culture than "the personal, the idiosyncratic, [or] the exceptional."[5] Since publication of Nettl's book, however, the topic of individuality has become more prominent in the field of ethnomusicology. For instance, Thomas Turino has called for ethnomusicologists to pay greater attention to the "multiplicity of subjective cultural positions" espoused by "individuals who typically would be thought of as belonging to the same 'culture,' the same ethnic group, or at least the same society." Culture, for Turino, is a process involving "individual variation and agency" applied by concrete actors at specific historical moments to resources including "ideas, dispositions, practices, material objects, and modes of expression and behavior."[6] As his study of contrasting uses for rural Conimeño music in the cities and villages of contemporary Peru demonstrates, the appearance of cultural coherence disguises a composite of multiple individual positions. The personal, the idiosyncratic, and the exceptional, then, are very much part of the collective, the typical, and the ordinary.

Similar concerns were articulated in the discipline of social anthropology by John Blacking more than a decade earlier. Introducing an account of Venda dance, Blacking comments as follows:

> Social anthropologists are heirs to a long tradition of examining general human problems in the most specific and limited of contexts. But their enthusiasm for a properly constituted science of culture and society has led them to contradict their traditional method of enquiry by writing in the ethnographic present and explaining social action as the result not of individual decisions made in historical situations, but of factors such as social and economic forces and cultural imperatives.[7]

Other ethnomusicologists, too, have discussed the role of the historically situated individual. Tim Rice, proposing a new, interrogative disciplinary model, gave new emphasis to the realm of the personal (and the diachronic) by asking: "How do people historically construct, socially maintain, and individually create and experience music?"[8] In this study, I examine how one individual's experience of music was structured by the historical and social contexts of which he was part; how he functioned as a creative musician, both as a performer and a composer; and how the performance of his musical works and content of his biography are reinterpreted by members of the newer conservatory tradition in contemporary China. As such, I am slightly recasting Rice's question to read: how did one individual historically experience and create music, and how has this music been socially maintained?

Naturally, an inquiry which opens with the stated aim of examining the personal, the idiosyncratic, and the exceptional will differ in presentation from such models of ethnomusicological study as, say, Steven Feld's account of Kaluli sound culture.[9] Nonetheless, a deeper similarity may also be seen. Ethnomusicologists, as anthropologists and specialists in many other disciplines, are used to abstracting from specific examples. A discussion of Kaluli musical aesthetics is useful well beyond the forests, waterfalls, and clearings of Papua New Guinea because lessons learned there provide a perspective from which other traditions may be viewed. So it is, too, with the study of an individual musician; such answers as emerge offer a foundation for more general, cross-cultural considerations and a point of reference for the study of a musical tradition as it unfolds through time.

Intriguingly, the Kaluli themselves illustrate a second potential justification for lending individual focus to an ethnomusicological account. Receiving a copy of the first edition of his book *Sound and Sentiment* while revisiting the Kaluli in 1982, Steven Feld showed the volume to his friends. Translating certain passages for discussion with them led to a process Feld called dialogic editing, or "negotiations of what Kaluli and I said to, about, with, and through each other, juxtapositions of Kaluli voices and my own."[10] Results of this process were published as a Postscript to the second edition of the book, and include the following observation:

> One of the most interesting outcomes of dialogic editing with the Kaluli was the way my [Kaluli] readers essentially reconstituted portions or versions of source materials in my field notes upon hearing them summarized, capsuled, or stripped of their situated details. . . . To do that they worked generalizations back to an instance, an experience, a remembered activity or action.[11]

Thus, although the compressed and combined published accounts tried to encapsulate an overall picture of Kaluli sound and sentiment, Steven Feld's local acquaintances sometimes found greater meaning by considering specific, socially situated musical activities and positions. Of course, they had a personal interest in identifying who had said what within their cultural group, but I suspect this tendency to find significance in stories about individuals is operative cross-culturally as well. Intellectually speaking, we may feel it is important first to discover why and how Chinese in general create and employ music; however, we may find the life and compositions of an individual musician both easier to reckon with and more meaningful.

## Blind Abing

There must also be some practical advantages in focusing on individual musicians when they are recognized and treated as such by their own society. The Chinese musician Abing provides a case in point. A household name in China, Abing and his music are widely known across much of the nation. Apart from the dissemination of a plethora of biographical articles, musical analyses, a film, and an eight-part television series, transcriptions of his pieces are performed, recorded, and broadcast with great frequency by conservatory-trained Chinese musicians, and widely studied by amateur instrumentalists. All these points set Abing apart from the "typical" folk musician. Yet were we to ignore him, we would risk compromising our understanding of Chinese music making, since Abing occupies a central place in the affections of Chinese listeners and in the minds of the musicologists and performers who explain and re-create his music. Through the study of an individual such as Abing, then, the ethnomusicologist does not so much lose sight of the "music culture" as approach it from another side.

Surprisingly little is actually known about Abing. Born in the 1890s and given the name Hua Yanjun, he was brought up as a Daoist musician in the city of Wuxi, Jiangsu Province in East China (see maps 1 and 2). In early adulthood his sight declined and he took to performing songs and instrumental pieces in the streets, now using the name *xiazi* Abing, Blind Abing or, perhaps more suggestive of the senses in which such a name might be used, "Blindman" Abing. In 1950, the year of his death, six of his performances were recorded: on three he played the *erhu* (two-stringed fiddle) and on the other three the *pipa* (four-stringed lute). Four of these recordings are reproduced on the accompanying CD (tracks 1–4). These were later published in transcription as instrumental solos to be performed by new generations of conservatory-trained musicians. Beyond this thumbnail sketch, little can be said of Abing with any degree of confidence. Nevertheless, what makes him a fascinating subject for study is that a great deal more *has* been said about him, and often with considerable confidence. To some he represents the archetypal Chinese folk musician, to others an oppressed revolutionary, to yet more a romantic visionary, and to still others again a dubious figure connected with urban subcultures of drug abuse and prostitution. Similarly, his music for *pipa* and, even more, for *erhu* has been variously interpreted as nationalist tone painting and as revolutionary autobiography.

## Ethnomusicology and History

In reassessing such interpretations this study is ultimately less concerned with establishing historical or musicological "truth" than with examining how different explanations of a single life and set of musical products have arisen and operate.[12] In order to do this it is necessary to engage with a hundred years of Chinese history, from the final years of the nineteenth century to the closing decade of the twentieth. According to the Chinese historical world view, this is contemporary stuff indeed, but, unlike their musicological counterparts, ethnomusicologists have only quite recently begun to include substantial historical material within their studies of living musical traditions.[13]

Recognition of the historical dimension reflects a reappraisal of the role of history within ethnomusicology. Daniel Neuman, in the Epilogue to a volume specifically concerned with this issue, identifies three distinct historical orientations which concerned his co-contributors. These are "reflexive music history," or the history of music history, prepared by those involved in that history; "interpretive music history," externally created historical accounts of music cultures written to support present-day arguments; and "immanent music history," the representation by music of the history of its creators and consumers.[14] In other words, ethnomusicologists have become interested not only in the histories of those whom they study but also in the ways in which "history" (or "tradition") is manipulated by present-day

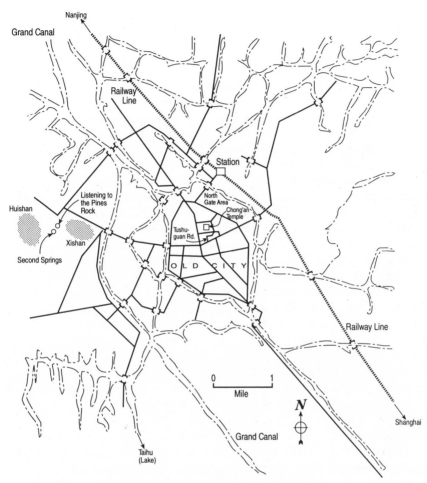

Map 1. Wuxi in the Early Twentieth Century.

individuals and the manner in which musical sound itself invokes real or imagined historical pasts.

The presentation in this study of historical detail is thus primarily intended to inform subsequent discussion of contemporary Chinese interpretations of Abing and his music. Although Abing died more than forty years ago, histories of his life and music (what I choose to call "the Abing tradition") have continued to be created, both by Chinese conservatory-trained musicians and among their audiences in general. There are two reasons why it is worth analyzing the processes through which those affected by this system envisage their cultural heritage. First, the Chinese conservatory system has only rarely received serious scholarly attention. Nonetheless, it has been a dominant force in music making throughout much of the twentieth century. If we are to understand the present-day Chinese music culture, we need to come to terms with this important tradition. Second, ethnomusicologists have of late become increasingly interested in the organization of modern, urban musical practices. While the situation necessarily differs from one nation to another, there is often enough in common to provide fruitful opportunities for cross-cultural comparison.

## Chinese Music Research

Alan Thrasher has traced the indigenous tradition of music research in China back 2500 years to the creation of Confucian theoretical texts concerned with music philosophy and the regulation of pitch.[15] Later, the codification of court ritual was added, together with the classification of musical instruments and description of their construction. More recently again, collections of notations were made, most usually of what may be considered elite genres. Song and drama texts were assembled, and published together with theoretical annotations. Twentieth-century Chinese academic research in music largely continued to focus on these subjects, paying less regard to the study of regional folk musics as actually performed today. As Lawrence Witzleben states, "Unlike in the West, anthropology has had virtually no impact on musicology in China. Although some Chinese scholars have conducted extensive fieldwork, contextual data and informants' perspectives are rarely included."[16] On the other hand, there was a great amount of collection and compilation of regional folk musics for applied ends. For instance, scholars transcribed and studied regional opera tunes in order to understand how to compose new music with folk elements. They recorded and memorized instrumental repertories for their own revision and use in urban and broadcast performances, and many assembled folk materials to use in their own teaching. It is only from the mid–1980s that a new trend has begun to appear, following the gradual dissemination in mainland China of ethnomusicological theory.[17]

The establishment of Chinese music conservatories since the 1920s led to the training of many musicians in the performance and study of newer styles of "national music." This music was inspired by Western models of musical context, composition, and technique. Among its new emphases were "modernized," "scientific," and virtuoso performance skills; concert hall performance; the concept of the pre-composed "artwork"; and equal-tempered intonation. Despite these changes, an equally crucial part of the rise of the new conservatory tradition was its appropriation of indigenous musical styles. Conservatory musicians, although they receive a large element of Western classical music theory in their training, typically speak of themselves as the inheritors and refiners of older, regional folk styles.[18] When reflecting upon their own music making, they tend to maintain a positive attitude toward changes introduced by themselves ("improvements," "modernizations"), and deprecate more conservative modes of performance ("reactionary," "out of tune," "unscientific," "crude").[19]

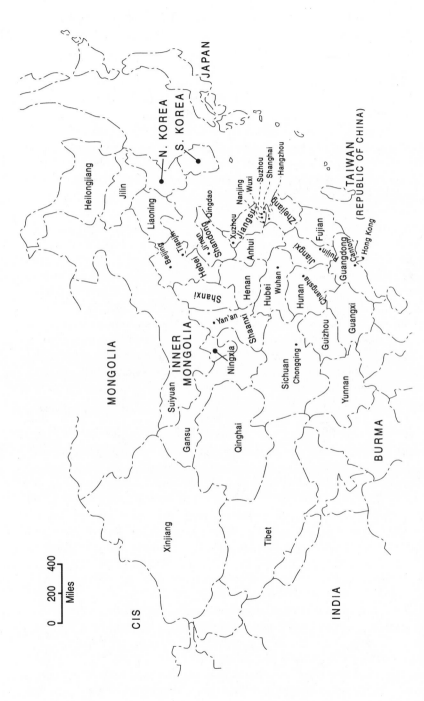

Map 2. Chinese Provinces and Cities.

Until perhaps 1985, then, Chinese academic music scholarship made little reference to social or cultural issues.[20] For many a Chinese author, these were non-issues: the definition of an extant music culture, the introduction of its musical thought, and the description of its actual musical behavior were beyond the purview of musical study.[21] Chinese musicology can probably tell us how many varieties of spike fiddle are performed by members of the southwestern minority races, or detail precisely the calculation by Zhu Zaiyu (1536–c.1610) of what, with hindsight, we recognize as equal-tempered semitones. But it would have great difficulty in explaining the appeal of *karaoke* to urban youth, or assessing an individual folk singer's musical aesthetics. The point is not, however, to criticize Chinese musicology for being the way it is; after all, it is a special discourse designed primarily for other Chinese musicologists. Instead, my argument is that, although indigenous scholarship is an important source of information and opinion, the ethnomusicological researcher needs to engage critically with much of this scholarship in light of the observation and analysis of actual musical sounds and their broader social contexts.

Western (including Western-trained and -located Chinese) scholars of Chinese music have published a wide range of material concerned with Chinese music culture. Some, necessarily including those active when access to mainland China was impossible or difficult, have chosen to focus on historical issues: organology, aesthetics, the place of music in court rituals, the reconstruction of ancient repertories, opera scripts, and drama history. Others have taken a single genre as their focus, perhaps including some discussion of contemporary performance practice and informants' perspectives. A final type of Western study looks primarily at the organization, negotiation, or experiencing of musical activity within the present-day Chinese context, centering less on specifics of musical sound than on issues of social or cultural context.[22]

The present study draws inspiration and material from each of these trends: it opens with a historical approach, incorporates a detailed examination of instrumental solos performed by Abing, and looks at the envisioning of Abing and his music in contemporary Chinese society. In terms of emphasis, this last aspect forms the ultimate aim of the book. Ethnomusicologically motivated approaches to music making have much to contribute to the understanding of Chinese musical culture, and appear underutilized in that field at present. Yet, this is neither a Feldian "ethnography of sound" nor a "musical anthropology" in the manner of Anthony Seeger;[23] there are dauntingly many Chinese, Chinese sounds, and Chinese opinions, past and present, for anything so broad to be assayed by any but the boldest and most experienced ethnomusicologist. I am quite unable to explain "Why Chinese sing," but I do aim to furnish for the Abing tradition a musical ethnography, in Seeger's sense of "the writing down of how sounds are conceived, made, appreciated and influence other individuals, groups, and social and musical processes."[24]

## Ethnography and Fieldwork

In some respects, however, this is an unusual musical ethnography. Ideally, a book presenting Abing's music would begin with an analysis of his own views and activities, both musical and otherwise. However, Abing died some thirty-nine years before this would-be ethnographer arrived in China, thus rendering impossible the kind of interactive fieldwork normally favored by ethnomusicologists. Much hard evidence has disappeared, and it is now difficult to follow up some clues.[25] Instead, I have needed to construct a historical and musical profile of Abing's life and the ensuing four decades from a plethora of written and oral sources and from my own observations of the contemporary situation. Work effectively began during the course of an academic year enrolled at the Shanghai Music Conservatory (1989–90), although this particular project was not my main area of inquiry at that time.[26] Two subsequent periods of postdoctoral research, each of a few months (1992, 1993), helped focus my mind on this subject, and also on local opera, a style I hope to write about next. During my sojourns in Shanghai, I was able to learn to play (badly) Abing's fiddle music; to listen to more expert performances; to hold formal and informal discussions with Chinese academics, instrumental teachers, professional and amateur performers, students, and non-musicians; and to collect written and recorded material pertaining to Abing and his music. I also visited Wuxi, Abing's birthplace, to interview researchers and musicians there, and met further scholars at conservatories, research institutes, and arts institutes in Beijing and Nanjing.

The very density of available written material (scores and texts) marks out a second peculiarity of this study: it is very much the ethnography of a literate tradition. Chinese musicians and scholars were often quick to refer me to preferred articles, to employ written schemes, and to notate musical examples. Not only this, but in many instances they saw these as privileged media of information. Scholars would begin, "In my article this is treated more fully," before giving me a spoken outline of what they had written. At the same time, although those whom I met were typically very open and generous with their information and interpretations, some were anxious not to be directly named as the sources. Such reserve is understandable given fairly recent occurrences in China's past; during the Cultural Revolution to volunteer any sort of personal opinions to a foreigner was a dangerous activity indeed. As a result, fully aware that this will disappoint readers hoping for a richer feel of how I interacted with specific Chinese informants, such remarks are reported or summarized without reference to their source.

My own interest in Abing developed out of historical and musical research into the *erhu*. Noting that modern fiddle players seemed to perform and record Abing's solo *The Moon Reflected on the Second Springs* more often than any other composition, I soon found that academics and teachers appeared to have produced more articles about this piece and its creator than about all other *erhu* pieces and composers put together. Every conservatory teacher had his or her own—strongly held—opinion about who exactly Abing was and what his music meant. Yet this mass of written and spoken data produced strikingly little consensus. At first, I decided to look more closely into the variety of views that centered around Abing, thinking it might be possible to uncover a more accurate picture of the life of this musician. Also, noting certain musical relationships between all three of Abing's surviving *erhu* solos, which contemporary *erhu* players seemed not to have considered, I wished to understand more completely the original creative context of this music. Were these pieces three individual creations, all portraying quite different subjects, as their contrasting titles appeared to suggest, or were they three related workings of the same musical material, as preliminary musical analysis seemed to infer?

In attempting to answer these questions, the first effectively biographical, the second musicological, I stumbled across others which struck me as being of potential interest to ethnomusicologists in general, rather than just to those studying Chinese music. As a result, my research outline gradually developed away from "Who was Abing, and what was his music originally like?" to the more complex, "How and why has the interpretation of Abing and his music changed over the decades since his death?" The original queries became subsumed within a broader inquiry, their resolution forming the grounding for further analysis.

## Ethnomusicology and Music Analysis

In common with many other ethnomusicologists, Anthony Seeger has argued against the analysis of musical products, maintaining that such studies "rarely relate their musical analysis to other aspects of the social and cultural environment of which music is always a part."[27] This view is clearly part of what Jean-Jacques Nattiez has identified as a larger disciplinary trend, in which it was held that an appropriate analysis of a society's music making could only proceed from the examination of social and cultural context:

> [O]ne must remember that since the 1960s ethnomusicology had become increasingly an "anthropology of music" under the influence of Merriam . . . and Blacking. . . . No doubt this seemed quite justified after the often ethnocentric armchair ethnomusicology that characterised the beginnings of the discipline. However, because of the widespread assumption that only a knowledge of the cultural environment would permit a true understanding of the music from an oral tradition, all analytical activity, which, it was suspected, substituted the tools of the Western researcher for the values and concepts of the native musician, began to disappear gradually from ethnomusicological monographs.[28]

Analysis, it was believed, as far as it concentrated on specific sound structures as opposed to musical processes, risked ignoring the thoughts and practices of the subjects themselves.[29] And it was these thoughts and practices, and their organization into systems and processes, that became the primary focus of ethnomusicological work. In his essay, Nattiez goes on to review the "musicological" analysis of Central African polyphonic music by Simha Arom, commending especially the "cultural *relevance*" of Arom's work (my emphasis).[30] In fact, such a concern is also articulated in Seeger's above-cited comment on music analysis, now given more fully: "Detailed musical analysis can produce highly competent descriptions of musical forms from around the world, but rarely *relate* their musical analysis to other aspects of the social and cultural environment of which music is always a part" (again, my emphasis).[31] Whether or not they agree that music should be related to social and cultural environment, or society and culture to musical structure, it appears that both analyst and anthropologist are preoccupied with the detailing of those instances when music impinges directly upon life and life upon music.[32] Ethnomusicologists are, I believe, generally fascinated by the interaction of the "musical" and the "non-musical," however these domains are defined in specific cases. The challenge for music analysis within ethnomusicology, then, is not whether to analyze sound structures but whether or not an analysis can be termed in such a way that its results speak directly to questions encountered during the remainder of the ethnomusicological study.

Returning to Abing, do his six surviving musical structures contain any clues as to how they were created? If so, how do Abing's creative process and context compare with those by and in which his music is re-created today? If there are observable differences, are they acknowledged by contemporary Chinese musicians themselves, and what do they reveal about the present-day performance tradition? When music analysis supplies even tentative answers to such questions as these, it is beginning to act as a bridge back to the long-deceased composer. As such, analysis should be able to play a vital role in situations where cultural change, political atmosphere, or the simple passing of time makes first hand, ethnographic immersion less effective.

A second role for product-based music analysis might be found among music cultures where particular musical products are reified, where "compositions" are habitually identified as the fixed creations of a specific individual and disseminated and re-created as such in recorded and written form. In these cultures, including modern China, an approach which is able to consider musical "products" may dovetail quite closely with the views of the tradition bearers themselves.[33] When this occurs, the process of relating cultural insights to musical features should be accomplished all the more directly.

In this book I develop a form of music analysis that seems particularly suited to the analysis of monodic modal music. The analytic format is essentially reductive, adapting Schenkerian format to illustrate fundamental melodic motion within a specific piece or fragment. This analysis rests upon a number of suppositions that are worth briefly examining, both for the adept musicological analyst, who will need to resist the temptation to hear the examples as tonal unfoldings replete with harmonic resonance, and for the music anthropologist, who may wonder how these analytical insights compare with those arising from folk evaluation.

Three basic aspects of Chinese music make this form of analysis effective. First, Chinese music has a well-articulated theoretical tradition as regards modal structure.[34] The individual degrees of each mode were believed, by Chinese theorists, to fall into a hierarchy with certain modal degrees (placed at phrase ends) treated as melodic goals. Melodic goals were patterned and alternated to build up larger musical structures.[35] Second, in many genres there exists an ornamental practice sometimes referred to as *jia hua*, "adding decorations": the insertion between important pitches of manually- or vocally-convenient decorative notes and patterns. Very often, these are a mixture of grace notes and melodic auxiliary, passing, and escape tones. Third, in many traditional Chinese musical styles, different metrical forms of the same underlying melodic progression are recognized and performed. Metrical expansion is accompanied by the slowing down of performance tempo and increase of note density through the *jia hua* process. In certain expanded forms of a melody it is possible to find as many as sixteen notes in the position occupied by one or two notes in a fast, contracted version. Metrical positioning and note duration are other factors of significance in the recognition of melodic targets, as indeed are fingering patterns in the case of instrumental music, where ornamentation is often confined to those pitches readily at hand.

The form of analysis employed here uses an awareness of Chinese modal theory and ornamentation-expansion practices to strip away less essential layers of decorative filling in order to reveal a more fundamental series of melodic goals. Goals of primary importance are notated, as in Schenkerian analysis, with hollow note heads; those of secondary importance as filled note heads. The stems of such pitches are commonly connected by a beam, especially when doing so clarifies phrase structure. Notes of progressively diminishing structural weight are incorporated as unbeamed stemmed notes and as unstemmed note heads. Those deemed without structural consequence are simply omitted.[36]

There are several distinctions from more classic forms of Schenkerian analysis. Most importantly, no underlying *Urlinie* is presupposed. Melodic lines are not considered redolent with harmonic implication, although the relative stability of each modal degree provides melodic direction. Furthermore, multiple versions of a theme may be aligned, as in paradigmatic analysis, with the reduction forming a kind of "average" reading of these specific tunes, and it is generally themes that are reduced in this manner rather than complete compositions. These are quite central departures from Schenkerian orthodoxy, departures that I believe are necessary to tailor the analytical method to the musical material in question.

In fact, such a hybrid analytical means has precedent not only in Chinese musical theory and practice but also in more general ethnomusicological and analytical writing. A number of scholars have, at different times, proposed the application of various systems of reductive analysis to non-Western musical structures. Particularly stimulating examples include John Blacking's analysis of Venda children's songs and V. Kofi Agawu's study of Northern Ewe vocal music.[37] In writings on Indonesian music, mention of "nuclear" melodies is commonplace. Moving to the field of East Asian zither music, more strictly reductive accounts include David Loeb's rigorous analysis of Japanese *koto* zither music and Joseph Lam's evaluation of modes of analysis as applied to Chinese *qin* zither music.[38]

There remains the final possibility that this analytical form might be discredited through its association (in its classic form) with increasingly embattled notions of organicism and economy.[39] Having introduced what it is that these analyses are intended to show, and why it is I believe they are an appropriate means of achieving this, it is perhaps also necessary in this self-conscious age to take a moment to clarify what these analyses are not. The analytic reductions endeavor to show where a particular melodic theme is going and how an accustomed listener might make sense of the soundstream in context. The reductions do not claim to demonstrate why one particular theme is "better" than another, or that one piece is a masterwork while another is not. Value judgment is already implicit in the whole scholarly process of selection of topic, consideration of approach, assemblage of material, and filtering of examples. But, having acknowledged this, I have made no attempt to employ the analyses to what might be called directly critical ends.

## Structure

This study is divided into six chapters. The first of these introduces the historical, social, economic, and political contexts within which Abing operated as a musician. With recourse to recent historical research, I question the popular misconception of early twentieth-century China as a stagnant and depressed society, and suggest that the sometime commonplace notion of folk musician as anonymous musical craftsman existing in splendid isolation from urban, national, and international currents was never an appropriate image for the city-dwelling Abing.[40] Instead, processes of urbanization; the expansion of international communications through mechanized transportation, newspaper, and radio; and violently marked realignments of government policy all locate this individual Chinese musician within a specific historical time and place.

In chapter 2, I look more closely at the sense that later Chinese commentators have made of the life of Abing. With the aid of theoretical positions developed by scholars in the fields of literary criticism, music sociology, musicology, and ethnomusicology, I investigate the creation of biographical narrative and its reliance upon specific social ideologies. Illustrating biographers' endowment of Abing with particular psychological, patriotic, or revolutionary traits, I show how political change in China and the rise of fresh biographical and musicological evidence has led to conflict between contrasting interpretations of the musician and his compositions.

Chapter 3 forms in certain respects a musical parallel to the historical account provided in chapter 1. The instruments that Abing played, most prominently the *erhu* (or *huqin*) and the *pipa*, are introduced, and the role of musical notation in the transmission of Chinese traditional music is discussed. Music making in Abing's home, the city of Wuxi, is then examined, with attention given to the genres and styles prevalent during the first half of the twentieth century, including Daoist ensemble music, local dramatic music, and early Chinese popular music as broadcast over the new radio stations and played on private gramophones. This music analysis affords an opportunity to draw out basic principles of Chinese traditional composition and performance, principles also employed by Abing. Overall, the chapter forms an introduction to the general musical situation within which Abing's specific creative acts took place. Although this discussion is primarily aimed at the general musical or sinological reader, Chinese music experts will, I hope, also find some unfamiliar material in this chapter and a convenient summary of the old.

The following two chapters analyze in more detail the six performances by Abing recorded in 1950. Chapter 4 focuses on the three *erhu* pieces, arguing that it may be more profitable to consider these as three improvisatory reworkings of related material than as independent and immutable compositions. Through a study of the use of common melodic material in all three solos, certain fundamental aspects of Abing's improvisatory style are identified, a process that leads to a more general reconsideration of the relationship between composition, recall, and improvisation. Chapter 5 looks specifically at the three *pipa* solos and their relationships to other Chinese pieces and repertories. Again, similar material is found among the three *pipa* solos, and Abing's technique of structuring this material and preexisting folk tunes into finished performances is examined. From this pair of chapters, a detailed impression emerges of Abing's techniques as composer and performer.

Finally, in chapter 6, focus shifts to the re-creation of Abing's music in present-day China. Study of the rise of the conservatory system in mainland China, taking the specific example of the adoption and re-envisioning of Abing's music by conservatory-trained musicians, reveals much about the changing conditions of music making in the world's most populous nation during the past half century. The historical approach initiated in chapter 1 is brought up to date, and the rise of contrasting biographical and musicological explanations of Abing's life and music are worked into this narrative.

## Note on Romanization and Translation

The Western reader of a book on Chinese history or culture faces a twofold problem in the area of romanization. Firstly, numerous systems of romanization have been adopted at various times, some based more closely on regional pronunciations than on the "standard" pronunciations of contemporary Mandarin Chinese, some showing speech tone and others not. Secondly, inconsistent and inaccurate usages abound, leading the innocent reader to take alternative transliterations of the same personal name, place, or term as indicating two distinct items.

The romanization of Chinese characters in this book follows, with very few exceptions, the *pinyin* system, that used officially in mainland China today. Exception is made for the city of Hong Kong, more familiar to non-Chinese in this transliteration of its Cantonese pronunciation than in its Mandarin form, Xianggang. Likewise, Canton is retained in place of Guangzhou, and Tibet preferred to Xizang. Other obsolete romanizations familiar to the Western reader are placed in brackets behind the equivalent *pinyin* reading on the first appearance of that name or term. Examples include Qing (Ch'ing) Dynasty, Sun Zhongshan (Sun Yat-sen), and Jiang Jieshi (Chiang Kai-shek).[41] Also, I consistently employ Beijing (Peking) throughout, ignoring its temporary change of name to Beiping during the first half of the twentieth century. When quoting passages from other writers I follow their romanization, adding *pinyin* within square brackets only if required: "Wusih [Wuxi]," for instance. The names of Chinese authors of Western-language sources follow their appearance on the publications in question, even if misromanized there.

Chinese personal names are written with family name first, as in Chinese usage, and, where available, I give dates of birth and death at the first mention of each person. Unlike some writers, I write the two syllables of Abing as a single word rather than separately as A Bing. The name was more a nickname than a full, formal title; he would never have been addressed simply as A or Mr. A, a possibility which division of the name into two parts appears to allow.

Titles of compositions are translated wherever possible, *pinyin* appearing at the first mention of each title. However, where translation would result in a title meaningless to the non-Chinese reader, a *pinyin* transliteration is employed instead. Musical instruments and genres are normally romanized rather than translated, though in the case of homophonic names additional elaboration is made, and generic instrumental terms sometimes appear: for example, fiddle is used as a synonym for the bowed *erhu* and lute signifies the plucked *pipa*. Also, literal translations of Chinese terms appear when these evoke the flavor of the original. A glossary of the principal names, terms, and titles mentioned in this study, including the simple form Chinese characters now standard in mainland China, is presented towards the end of the book.

The pronunciation of the majority of *pinyin* symbols is broadly similar to their English equivalents (Abing: "A" as in "car," "bing" as in "Bing Crosby"). A few consonants requiring special attention are listed below, together with commensurate English pronunciations and examples:

| *pinyin* | English | example | approximate pronunciation |
|:---:|:---:|:---:|:---:|
| c | ts | Cao | nuTS & hOW |
| q | ch | qin | CHIN |
| x | sh | xia | SHE & cAr |
| zh | j | zhi | Job & dIRt |

## Periodization of Chinese History

It has long been customary to divide Chinese history into periods delineated by the rise and fall of major dynasties. Naturally, Chinese history is far more fragmented than these periods suggest, and major cultural developments do not always coincide with the passing of the "mandate of heaven" from one ruling family to another. Nonetheless, through dint of custom, these dynastic time periods are convenient as aids to historical orientation. Those referred to in this book are:

| | | |
|---|---|---|
| Song Dynasty | 960–1279 | |
| Northern Song | 960–1127 | |
| Southern Song | 1127–1279 | |
| Yuan Dynasty | 1271–1368 | (Mongols) |
| Ming Dynasty | 1368–1644 | |
| Qing Dynasty | 1644–1911 | (Manchus) |
| Republic | 1912–1949 | (continuing in Taiwan) |
| People's Republic | 1949 onwards | |

## Notes

1. Bruno Nettl, *The Study of Ethnomusicology: Twenty-Nine Issues and Concepts* (Urbana: University of Illinois Press, 1983), 278.

2. See, for instance, Bruno Nettl, "Biography of a Blackfoot Singer," *Musical Quarterly* 54 (1968): 199–207; Jeff Todd Titon et al., *Worlds of Music: An Introduction to the Music of the World's Peoples* (New York: Schirmer, 1984); Judith Vander, *Songprints: The Musical Experience of Five Shoshone Women* (Urbana: University of Illinois Press, 1988); Charles Capwell, "Marginality and Musicology in Nineteenth-Century Calcutta: The Case of Sourindro Mohun Tagore," in Bruno Nettl and Philip V. Bohlman, eds., *Comparative Musicology and the Anthropology of Music: Essays on the History of Ethnomusicology* (Chicago: University of Chicago Press, 1991), 228–43. On the contrary, biography is a standard approach in musicology, for which the nearest ethnomusicological equivalent is the book devoted to a single culture. For a stimulating perspective on the ethnomusicology of the individual, and further use of a biographical approach, see Timothy Rice, *May It Fill Your Soul: Experiencing Bulgarian Music* (Chicago: University of Chicago Press, 1994).

3. Nettl, *Study of Ethnomusicology*, 9.

4. Bruno Nettl, "Biography," 199. For further discussion of change in scholarly attitudes towards individuality and the folk musician, see Philip V. Bohlman, *The Study of Folk Music in the Modern World* (Bloomington: Indiana University Press, 1988), 69–86.

5. Nettl, *Study of Ethnomusicology*, 9.

6. Thomas Turino, *Moving Away from Silence: Music of the Peruvian Altiplano and the Experience of Urban Migration* (Chicago: University of Chicago Press, 1993), 8–9.

7. John Blacking, "Movement, Dance, Music, and the Venda Girls' Initiation Cycle," in Paul Spencer, ed., *Society and the Dance: The Social Anthropology of Process and Performance* (Cambridge: Cambridge University Press, 1980), 64–91 (64).

8. Timothy Rice, "Towards a Remodeling of Ethnomusicology," *Ethnomusicology* 31 (1987): 469–88 (473).

9. Steven Feld, *Sound and Sentiment: Birds, Weeping, Poetics, and Song in Kaluli Expression*, 2nd ed. (Philadelphia: University of Pennsylvania Press, 1990).

10. Feld, *Sound*, 241.

11. Feld, *Sound*, 251.

12. In this sense, this study is unlike the standard "life and works" books of Western musicology. Typically, these collect and codify knowledge about an individual composer and his works but pay less attention to social issues underlying rival interpretations.

13. The exception is perhaps the specialist field of historical ethnomusicology, but, at least with reference to China, work of this sort has tended to focus upon the reconstruction of long-lost musical traditions through the decipherment of rare and ancient manuscript notations.

14. Daniel M. Neuman, "Epilogue: Paradigms and Stories," in Stephen Blum, Philip V. Bohlman, and Daniel M. Neuman, eds., *Ethnomusicology and Modern Music History* (Urbana: University of Illinois Press, 1991), 268–77 (269).

15. Alan R. Thrasher, "China," in Helen Myers, ed., *Ethnomusicology: Historical and Regional Studies* The New Grove Handbooks in Music (London: Macmillan, 1993), 311–44 (311).

16. J. Lawrence Witzleben, "*Jiangnan Sizhu* Music Clubs in Shanghai: Context, Concept and Identity," *Ethnomusicology* 31 (1987): 240–60 (257).

17. Du Yaxiong discusses the introduction of ethnomusicology to mainland China, describing the indigenous tradition as having paid "attention only to classification and morphology of music," its main aim being "to give service to the composers"; Du Yaxiong, "Recent Issues in Music Research in the People's Republic of China," *Association for Chinese Music Research Newsletter* 5, no. 1 (Winter 1992): 9–12 (9). A more detailed view of the rise of Chinese ethnomusicology during the 1980s is provided by Shen Qia, "Minzu yinyuexue 10 nian," *Zhongguo yinyue nianjian* (Ji'nan: Shandong jiaoyu chubanshe, 1991), 338–55.

18. Ethnomusicological work has paid much attention to the creation of tradition and the ways in which the formation of a musical tradition is as much an ideological construct as a musical one. See Nettl, *Study of Ethnomusicology*, 303–14; Bohlman, *Study of Folk Music*, 134–35; Daniel M. Neuman, *The Life of Music in North India: The Organization of an Artistic Tradition* (Chicago: Chicago University Press, 1990 [first published 1980]); Christopher A. Waterman, *Jùjú: a Social History and Ethnography of an African Popular Music* (Chicago: Chicago University Press, 1990), 12; David B. Coplan, "Ethnomusicology and the Meaning of Tradition," in Blum, Bohlman, and Neuman, *Ethnomusicology*, 35–48 (36–38). This point is further pursued in chapter 6. For a spirited discussion of the question of inheritance and preservation in Chinese music, see Fang Kun's defense of modern-style performances at the 1979 Durham Oriental Music Festival, "A Discussion on Chinese National Musical Traditions," translated by Keith Pratt, *Asian Music* 12, no. 2 (Spring/Summer 1981): 1–16.

19. This general characterization, however, is one that some conservatory musicians would reject, and has also, at times, become politically unacceptable within China itself. For insights into the conflict during the Cultural Revolution over such notions, see Richard Curt Kraus, *Pianos and Politics in China: Middle-Class Ambitions and the Struggle over Western Music* (New York: Oxford University Press, 1989), 100–127.

20. These issues are still set aside by the great majority of scholars; change since 1985 has been very gradual. For overviews of indigenous Chinese music scholarship up to about this date, see Isabel K. F. Wong, "From Reaction to Synthesis: Chinese Musicology in the Twentieth Century," in Nettl and Bohlman, *Comparative Musicology*, 37–55; Thrasher, "China," 311–28.

21. Yang Mu, referring to the indigenous study of Chinese folk song, argues that these scholars were capable of writing about social aspects, but were prevented from doing so by political censorship; "Academic Ignorance or Political Taboo? Some Issues in China's Study of Its Folk Song Culture," *Ethnomusicology* 38 (1994): 303–20. There is certainly merit in Yang's suggestion, but the situation is more complicated than choosing to believe either that the scholars in question were ethnomusicologically incompetent (the view that Yang appears to dispute) or that they were competent but silenced by the heavy hand of political taboo (an interpretation that he favors). While acknowledging the weight of censorship, I would suggest that Chinese folk song collectors were mostly operating under a narrower definition of music than is employed by

the foreign-based ethnomusicologist. To these collectors, "music" meant what the ethnomusicologist might call "musical sound." In my view, research on folk musicians' thoughts and behavior was not so much politically suppressed; rather, it was simply not part of music research.

22. For listings of research see Fredric Lieberman, *Chinese Music: An Annotated Bibliography*, 2nd ed. (New York: Garland, 1979); Thrasher, "China," 332–44. Further Chinese music research is available in the form of Ph.D. dissertations; a useful list is that prepared by Theodore J. Kwok, "Chinese Music Theses and Dissertations, A Preliminary List," *Association for Chinese Music Research Newsletter* 7, no. 1 (Winter 1994): 18–33. Two major studies of Chinese instrumental music have recently been published: Stephen Jones, *Folk Music of China: Living Instrumental Traditions* (Oxford: Clarendon Press, 1995); J. Lawrence Witzleben, *"Silk and Bamboo" Music in Shanghai: The Jiangnan Sizhu Instrumental Ensemble Tradition* (Kent, Ohio: Kent State University Press, 1995). Both are too wide ranging to be classified in any one of the three categories of research outlined above.

23. Feld, *Sound*; Anthony Seeger, *Why Suyá Sing: A Musical Anthropology of an Amazonian People* (Cambridge: Cambridge University Press, 1987).

24. Anthony Seeger, "Ethnography of Music," in Helen Myers, ed., *Ethnomusicology: An Introduction* New Grove Handbooks in Music (London: Macmillan, 1992), 88–109 (89).

25. For example, Chinese libraries typically have a *neibu* "inner area," to which access is strictly controlled. Even its catalogue may be off limits to ordinary researchers. The best material, one tends to imagine, must be held within this inner sanctum. According to unsubstantiated rumors, the *neibu* of a large library may itself have another *neibu* within, rather like a Russian doll. A second example concerns Abing's life as a Daoist. During my fieldwork period, official attitudes in mainland China toward religious activity were generally discouraging, and I found it impossible to locate contacts in Wuxi who wished to explain what this aspect of Abing's life entailed.

26. This period of study, part of a course of graduate research, led to the preparation of a Ph.D. dissertation discussing Chinese fiddle music, "Context and Creativity: The Chinese Two-Stringed Fiddle *Erhu* in Contemporary China," (Queen's University of Belfast, 1991).

27. Seeger, *Why Suyá Sing*, xiii.

28. Jean-Jacques Nattiez, "Simha Arom and the Return of Analysis to Ethnomusicology," translated by Catherine Dale, *Music Analysis* 12 (1993): 241–65 (241–42).

29. For further discussion of the position of music analysis within ethnomusicology, see Jonathan P. J. Stock, "The Application of Schenkerian Analysis to Ethnomusicology: Problems and Possibilities," *Music Analysis* 12 (1993): 215–40 (223–25).

30. Nattiez, "Simha Arom," 262.

31. Seeger, *Why Suyá Sing*, xiii.

32. Purists finding the possibility of music without life difficult to entertain might prefer to read "non-music" for "life" in this sentence.

33. See also Harold S. Powers, review of *The Anthropology of Music* by Alan P.

Merriam, *Perspectives of New Music* 4, no. 2 (Spring/Summer 1966): 161–71 (167–68).

34. See, for example, Rulan Chao Pian, *Sonq Dynasty Musical Sources and Their Interpretation* Cambridge: Harvard University Press, 1967.

35. See, for instance, Laurence E. R. Picken et al., eds., *Music from the Tang Court 1* (Oxford: Oxford University Press, 1981), 19–26; John E. Myers, *The Way of the Pipa: Structure and Imagery in Chinese Lute Music* (Kent, Ohio: Kent State University Press, 1992), 51–58.

36. Those unfamiliar with this form of analysis need not despair; it should be possible to follow the broader musical arguments even without reference to these so-called "graphs."

37. John Blacking, "Tonal Organization in the Music of Two Venda Initiation Schools," *Ethnomusicology* 14 (1970): 1–56; V. Kofi Agawu, "Variation Procedures in Northern Ewe Song," *Ethnomusicology* 34 (1990): 221–43. These examples are further discussed in Stock, "Schenkerian Analysis," where I provide a lengthier consideration of the position, and potential merits, of reductive analysis in ethnomusicological writing.

38. David Loeb, "An Analytic Study of Japanese Koto Music," *Music Forum* 4 (1976): 335–93; Joseph S. C. Lam, "Analyses and Interpretations of Chinese Seven-String Zither Music: The Case of the *Lament of Empress Chen*," *Ethnomusicology* 37 (1993): 353–85.

39. For a detailed discussion of the operation of these value systems in musicological texts, see Janet M. Levy, "Covert and Casual Values in Recent Writings about Music," *Journal of Musicology* 5 (1987): 3–27.

40. In the course of a study of Turkish *arabesk*, Martin Stokes shows how the construction of a sense of rural-urban opposition informs each level of the reception and discussion of this musical tradition; *The Arabesk Debate: Music and Musicians in Modern Turkey* (Oxford: Clarendon Press, 1992). Such a conception is, according to Stokes, a common one in ethnomusicology. Scholars, and others, have insisted "on defining a bounded rural musical culture in opposition to a more volatile and international urban culture" (52).

41. Sun Yat-sen is a regional pronunciation of Sun's alternative name Sun Yixian. Sun Zhongshan, however, is that more commonly used in China today.

*Chapter 1*

# China, and the City of Wuxi, from the 1890s to 1950

Late imperial China is often characterized as a nation seething with social unrest and cowed by foreign aggression. The Manchu court, headed by the empress dowager Cixi (1835–1908), is portrayed as becoming increasingly out of touch with the mood of the Chinese populace. Incapacitated by conservatism, corruption, and factionalism, this ruling clique failed miserably to formulate a coherent modernization policy. Shaken by popular uprisings on a massive scale and the defection of its military wing, the Manchus were then replaced by a coterie of reformists and revolutionaries, pragmatists and ideologues, democrats and warlords. Unable to agree among themselves, to counter foreign territorial ambitions, or to resolve inherited economic and administrative shortcomings, this body quickly fractured into a bevy of short-lived alliance groups, each seizing power wherever it could and using every available political and military means to scheme against rival factions. Even when the Nationalists under Jiang Jieshi (Chiang Kai-shek) (1887–1975) were able to claim around 1930 to have reunited China, their hold on many areas was tenuous at best, real power remaining in the hands of local officials, military governors, bandit chiefs, secret society bosses, and clan heads. Jiang's Nationalist administration also proved unable or unwilling to carry out social or economic reform and soon became an oppressive military regime. Resources raised through punitive taxation and graft were squandered on the suppression of communism rather than devoted to resistance to Japan, which gradually seized ever larger expanses of Chinese territory. Misgovernment exacerbated hyperinflation, corruption, and discontent, and the ensuing civil war with the Communists was handled as incompetently as previous campaigns against the Japanese. The fall of mainland China to the forces of Mao Zedong (1893–1976) in 1949 was inevitable, delayed until then only by the propping up of Jiang's regime by American money and arms.

This narrative has a certain dramatic flair, but hindsight—after-the-event knowledge of imperial and Nationalist collapse—imbues events with an inevitability and interconnectedness they may not have possessed in actuality. Historians are well aware of the dangers of this; Jack Gray, for example, in describing the period from 1911 to 1937 as one of sustained growth, dismisses the dramatic decline scenario as, "largely the reflection of nationalist emotion rationalized in a vulgar Marxism."[1] In seeking to reconstruct the course of significant historical events impinging upon the life of Abing, then, it is perhaps advisable to set aside the impulse to scan past occurrences for their justification of the status quo, and focus instead on the likely immediate impact on Abing of specific happenings.

Subsequent chapters will examine the ways in which Abing's biography and musical products are re-envisaged as socially meaningful symbols in contemporary China. This chapter prepares the way for these analyses by sketching the geographical, social, and historical backgrounds within which Abing lived and worked. A general musical background is provided in chapter 3. As far as is known today, Abing spent the bulk of his life living in or near the city of Wuxi, Jiangsu Province. Before looking chronologically at broader Chinese events, then, I provide an overview of the history and development of this city.

## The City of Wuxi, Origins to 1950

Wuxi is located in what has long been one of China's most densely populated, intensively cultivated, and highly cultured regions, Jiangnan, or the Lower Yangzi region. Wuxi itself has an extensive history, dating back to perhaps the second millennium B.C. Originally a tin-mining settlement whose supplies of the ore were exhausted by A.D. 25, the town was renamed Wuxi, literally "lacking tin." Development into a sizable trading center took place in the seventh and eighth centuries with the construction of the Grand Canal, a waterway linking China's northern capital to its productive southern provinces. Continuity with the past was broken, however, by Mongol destruction of the town in the late thirteenth century. Major reconstruction and repopulation took place only during the ensuing Ming Dynasty (1368–1644).[2]

The Lower Yangzi region was again shattered in the mid-nineteenth century by rebellions against the Qing Dynasty rulers and the ensuing reprisals of Qing armies. Apart from the ruin of towns and razing of cultivated land, the population of the whole area was decimated. Though regional population density was slow to recover, the latter years of the nineteenth century were ones of reconstruction. Fallow agricultural land was claimed by new tenants, and Wuxi became "one of the four main rice markets in China."[3] Simultaneously, industrialization began in major cities across Jiangnan. Steamships followed the principal waterways, bringing raw materials and food to the newly expanding urban centers.[4] A first textile factory opened in Wuxi in 1894, and by the 1930s there were over 200 factories in the city, producing silk and other textiles for sale in Shanghai and abroad.

Crucial to the development of Wuxi's industrial capacity was the opening of the Shanghai to Nanjing railway line, with a station at Wuxi, in 1908. This line ensured access to important markets across the Jiangnan region and, by way of Shanghai, to much of the world. A few years later, further expansion of the rail network linked Wuxi to the cities of Tianjin and Beijing in the north. In a pattern common to many communities, the sector around the railway station quickly became the city's principal commercial district (see map 1). Industrialization affected demographics as well as urban layout. Traditionally, many of those inhabiting Chinese cities were temporary residents: immigrant rural workers, traders, administrators, and garrisons. Urban males considerably outnumbered urban females. Now, the preference of factory bosses for cheaper female and child labor evened out this demographic imbalance, and cities became places of permanent residence for generations of urban families. New urban classes proliferated, and rural and urban societies became polarized to a far greater extent than ever before.[5]

Known sometimes as "Little Shanghai," Wuxi had developed into a significant industrial center by the time of Abing's adulthood, although further growth was retarded by the Sino-Japanese War and the Communist-Nationalist conflict. Estimates of its population during this period differ markedly: Alfred Schinz gives a figure of 270,000 inhabitants, of whom 20 percent were industrial workers,[6] while an anonymous (British?) 1930s account, worth quoting for its colorful imagery, proposes a higher figure:

> Twenty-seven miles West of Soochow [Suzhou], an hour by train, is Wusih [Wuxi], a rapidly growing all-Chinese industrial community of great interest. Smokestacks on the skyline offer a curious contrast to the pagodas further back on the hills, symbols of a vanishing era. Wusih is progressive. From a population of less than 100,000 some twenty years ago it has become a metropolis of more than half a million. Wusih has aptly been termed the "Manchester of China."
> . . . To-day there are ten large cotton mills, eighteen textile weaving plants, forty-five silk filatures, . . . . These plants are all under Chinese ownership and operation. In addition to these are many smaller industries. Electric light and power plants and a modern telephone exchange are further evidences of the advancement of the city.[7]

Wuxi, then, was during the first part of Abing's life an expanding industrial and urban center, connected by both rail and water to major cities along the Yangzi River and beyond. Despite this rapid modernization, Abing's home also retained many traditional features, especially in terms of its cultural and religious life, aspects which must have been significant to a Daoist musician. The friction throughout this period of, on the one hand, modern political and economic aspirations and, on the other, traditional social and cultural values must have been particularly keenly felt by the inhabitants of the newly industrialized cities such as Abing. The remainder of this chapter looks in more detail at these developments, dividing the period in question into three parts: 1890 to 1912, up to the establishment of the Chinese Republic; 1912 to 1937, years of economic growth and political disorder; and

1937 to 1950, from the Sino-Japanese War to the foundation of the People's Republic. Wherever possible, cross-reference will be made to the specific situation of Abing's existence in Wuxi.

## China in Turmoil, 1890–1912

During the closing decade of the nineteenth century, China was in a curious, ambiguous position. Elements of old and new existed side by side. At many levels the pace of change seemed overwhelming and irreversible. Steamboats plied the Yangzi, huge new banks lined the waterfront in Shanghai, military academies were training young officers in Western tactics, scientific textbooks were rolling off the presses, and memorials flashed by telegraph from the provinces to the Grand Council. . . .

Yet much of this apparent change was confined to the treaty port cities and within them to the Western concession areas. . . . For most young Chinese men from well-to-do families, the patterns of education remained unchanged: they memorized the Confucian classics, and laboured to obtain their local *shengyuan* degrees before proceeding to the provincial *juren* and national *jinshi* examinations. In town and country, girls still had little access to formal education, their feet were still bound, and their marriages arranged by their parents. In the fields, sowing and harvesting were done by hand, the produce laboriously carried to market.[8]

Jonathan Spence's sentences evoke the flavor of Chinese urban society in the 1890s, a society caught between the twin poles of old and new. In the eyes of many citizens, old and new had come to equate Chinese and foreign. Increasingly, the foreign dimension became significant, whether in social, cultural, economic, or political vistas. Groups of students departed regularly for studies overseas, Chinese laborers and merchants migrated to nations in the old and new worlds, foreign ideas were translated for publication in China, and western diseases such as scarlet fever ravaged unresistant Chinese victims.[9] Commercial and financial markets within China responded to the fluctuations of global trade, and ever-expanding numbers of foreign missionaries, adventurers, and businessmen flocked to China.

Foreign interest in China was not confined to the saving of souls and the making of fortunes. Japan soundly defeated China on all fronts when both nations clashed militarily on the Korean peninsula in 1894; apart from abandoning its longstanding claim to Korean overlordship, China ceded to Japan territory—most significantly Taiwan—, commercial privileges, and a massive war indemnity. Other foreign powers were swift to seize further land, and, for a time, the partition of the Qing Empire into foreign-run spheres of influence seemed imminent. Yet although Chinese nationalists liked the Japanese presence no more than that of the Western powers, they were encouraged by Japanese victory a decade later in the Russo-Japanese War (1904–5), seeing it in terms of the triumph of a modernized, constitutional Asian power over a despotic European one.

The collapse of the Qing Dynasty, so long sought by reformers and revolutionaries alike, must have seemed surprisingly swift when it eventually occurred. An accidental explosion in October 1911 at a revolutionary bomb factory in the central Chinese city of Wuhan sparked off a series of mutinies. The newly established provincial assemblies turned against the Manchus, backing instead an emerging alliance of revolutionaries and reformers headed by the Nationalist party of Sun Zhongshan (Sun Yat-sen) (1866–1925) and military strongman Yuan Shikai (1859–1916). The Republic of China was proclaimed on 1 January 1912, with provisional president Sun stepping down in favor of Yuan the following day.

Abing was by this time in his teens. While he had been taught to read and write, whether he had studied enough to be able to read a newspaper himself cannot be entirely certain.[10] If so, a profusion of news and commentary on current affairs and the outside world would have been available to him. If not, his primary means of access to topical information would have been through listening to others read the newspaper or discuss national politics; by way of gossip picked up at the Daoist temple or at ceremonies and performances outside; and perhaps from the words of street singers, storytellers, and balladeers. Furthermore, the growing propensity for mass political action and trade boycotts involved the holding of public meetings at which speakers provided up-to-date interpretations of the latest national and international events. We cannot assess how active Abing was in such affairs, or their impact upon him as an apprentice Daoist. Nonetheless, other musicians in the same area did become involved in anti-Qing musical agitation and post-Qing musical celebrations. Examples include the *erhu* player Zhou Shaomei (1885–1938) and the young bandsman Liu Tianhua (1895–1932), later important as a composer of music for *erhu* and one of the first to bring Chinese traditional instruments into the music conservatories.[11]

Although we might imagine his temple environment to have been a conservative one, it is edifying to recall that throughout his youth Abing lived in a thriving economic and industrial center in close touch with other advanced communities across the nation. It is difficult to believe that he remained untouched by, or unaware of, the foreign impact on the Chinese world—whether military, commercial, intellectual, or religious. Similarly, it would be hard to propose that he knew nothing of the growth of anti-Qing sentiment, the rise of Han Chinese nationalism, the manifold and strident calls for reform and revolution, and the uprisings and conflicts which accompanied them.

## China in Development and Disarray, 1912–1937

Chinese society during this twenty-five-year period, the central phase of Abing's life, was at least as fast changing and as externally impinged upon as in the previous two decades. The alliance of reformers and revolutionaries united by the task of overthrowing the Qing quickly fragmented, and by 1916 there were in all effects several semi-autonomous, competing states on Chinese soil. Real power was in many areas held by military governors, regional warlords, bandit chiefs, armed revolutionaries, and Japanese field commanders. Partial reunification of the country under Jiang Jieshi's Nanjing-based Nationalist government during the 1930s was never consolidated, and was completely shattered by the outbreak of the Sino-Japanese war in the summer of 1937. For Abing, the Second World War began in earnest when the Japanese army captured Wuxi later that same year.

The First World War would also have weighed upon Abing's consciousness, not so much because of limited Chinese military involvement in Siberia (1918–20), but due to the "May 4th" political and cultural movements sparked off by Chinese frustrations with the terms of the Treaty of Versailles (1919). Other socio-economic and cultural factors of great significance during this period include the impact of the radio on the dissemination of information and recorded music (increasingly important to Abing as his sight declined), the widespread adoption of the bicycle, and the international depression of the 1930s. These developments and the contexts within which they unfolded are assessed more fully below.

The celebratory mood of early 1912 cannot have endured long. Following elections on 10 August, which left the Nationalists with a majority in the new parliament, Yuan Shikai used his armies to bully the new members of parliament into electing him as president for a five-year term. Duly elected, Yuan then purged Nationalist members from parliament, which, lacking the necessary quorum, he dissolved in January 1914. From then on, Yuan Shikai maintained control over the nation through a combination of force, bribery, murder, and manufactured public opinion. Such measures could prove persuasive: the opium trade was extremely thoroughly suppressed, and Yuan was able to see himself installed as Emperor. But the southern provinces beyond the reach of Yuan's armed forces found such modes of induction less convincing. By 1915, these provinces, led by distant Yunnan, had declared their independence, and shortly thereafter Yuan was compelled to renounce his throne and offices.

Yuan's demise, however, did nothing to aid Chinese reunification. Indeed, further disruption ensued as his lieutenants Duan Qirui (1865–1936) and Feng Guozhang (1859–1919) vied for control of the government and armed forces.[12] Duan shared Yuan Shikai's conviction that the only way to reunite China was by military force financed by Japanese loans. One of Duan's ideas was to lead China into the First World War by declaring war on Germany. Primarily, his intention was to win the return to Chinese sovereignty of German-held territories, such as the port of Qingdao in Shandong Province. However, when precedence was given instead to Japanese claims to German colonial territory, Duan—now dependent on Japanese financial support—found himself compelled to accept, and a protest march in Beijing of several thousand students on 4 May 1919 initiated a series of strikes, marches, political meetings; a boycott of Japanese products; and considerable financial instability.

These currents soon made themselves felt in Wuxi. The local daily newspaper, the *Xi bao*, reported on meetings held on 6–7 June 1919 in the city's parks and temple yards. At these gatherings, audiences of several hundred heard political activists, students, and even school children lecture on the significance of Qingdao, the misery caused by Japanese oppression in Korea, and the necessity of maintaining an embargo upon the sale of Japanese merchandise.[13]

Longer lasting than any of these political activities was a cultural movement of major proportions. Traditional Confucian values were denigrated as impedimentary to progress; the classical written language was officially abandoned in favor of a more contemporary, colloquial style; and the growing urban middle classes began to develop their own forms of cultural self-expression, forms neither rooted in the traditions of the rural hinterlands nor characteristic of Chinese antiquity. As might be expected from a movement born out of frustration with China's position in the world, nationalism was an important element, and encouraged Chinese intellectuals to rationalize the foreign art forms they wished to emulate as "modern" rather than "Western."

This, the May 4th Movement, also created an intellectual atmosphere receptive to the import of Marxist and Socialist theories and writings, though the impact of the Russian Revolution (1917) was only slowly felt in China, and the Chinese Communist Party was formally created only in 1921.[14] These early Communists found their cause advanced when Sun Zhongshan, whose Nationalist Party had retained some influence in southern China, turned to the new Soviet Union for financial aid. Eager to expand the influence of their client party in China, the Soviets insisted upon the involvement of the Chinese Communists in Sun's Nationalist schemes. Initially, however, Communist attempts to organize trades unions and strikes, and to mobilize the peasantry were only sporadically successful. Furthermore, with the rise of the Nationalist military wing, led by Jiang Jieshi, the Communists not only encountered an implacable foe but also lost the opportunity to press for the arming of peasant militias over which they might have had greater influence. At this time, then, it is unlikely that Abing would have known much of the aims of the Chinese Communist Party, although he may have heard something of their attempts to infiltrate the leadership of industrial unions, many of which were run as closed-shop recruiting rackets by secret society gangsters.

In general, industry and communications expanded continuously between 1919 and 1937. Thousands of miles of new roads were built, allowing urban values access to the countryside and peasants access to urban markets.[15] Cheap bicycles proliferated, and the railway network grew steadily. These factors encouraged social mobility and enlarged the personal world views of ordinary Chinese citizens. Electrical supply was extended to smaller cities, as were telephone networks, wirelesses, and new forms of entertainment. The Chinese-owned portion of industrial production rose consistently. Major commercial interests which flourished included cigarette production and banking. Agriculture also did well, with imports of staples falling steadily. Some trades fared less well, however. For example, silk production—important to Wuxi—was badly hit by the invention of rayon in the early 1930s. Simultaneously, American silver purchases drew currency out of China, causing deflation and harming commercial conditions until the introduction of paper currency in 1935. Yet, despite these setbacks, the economic picture for China was generally a positive one throughout this period.

Economic advancement, however, brought in its train a host of social ills. Working conditions in factories were poor: pay was low, especially for women and children; shifts were long; and lodgings execrable. Strikes were ruthlessly suppressed, and their leaders intimidated, arrested, or executed. Opium use reasserted itself, regional warlords cultivating or supplying the crop to finance their military operations.

The depredations of soldiers and bandits—distinction between these was in many cases academic—was the greatest problem acknowledged by peasants in a major agricultural survey of 1929–33.[16] In some regions famine and flooding caused further distress, a situation exacerbated by the diversion of labor away from husbandry and the maintenance of flood defenses and towards soldiering and the construction of military fortifications. Those inhabiting important towns or strategic corridors were increasingly affected by ongoing warfare.

By 1928, Jiang Jieshi's forces had extended Nationalist influence as far north as China's third city, Tianjin, although major expanses of Chinese territory still remained beyond Nationalist control. Given the weakness of his grasp in many areas, Jiang's ability to govern, conduct social reform, and gather taxation was sorely constrained. These limitations may have encouraged Jiang to use contacts among the notorious Shanghai Green Gang, trusted neighbors from his home area in Zhejiang Province, and armed troops as fund-raising, administrative, and disciplinary tools respectively. Significant to Abing among Jiang Jieshi's new measures must have been the mandatory "registration fees" paid by recognized addicts to the new Opium Suppression Bureau, and it is conceivable that his failure to maintain such payments when the Nationalists returned to Jiangsu in 1945 was the factor that led to his incarceration in jail for a period in the later 1940s, rather than his alleged singing of anti-government songs (see also chapter 2).

It is harder to assess what effect the mixed economic fortunes of the period had upon Abing. On the one hand, as discussed above, international advances in manufacturing technology hit certain traditional Chinese export commodities, the global depression caused further hardship, and Jiang Jieshi squeezed prominent Chinese financiers and entrepreneurs for all the capital he could get. On the other, new businesses sprung up in great abundancy, and the widespread adoption of Western-style leisure and fashion products by Chinese urban society suggests that at least part of the population had significant disposable wealth. Cigarette smoking, cycling, visiting the cinema, and listening to radio broadcasts and 78rpm recordings became everyday activities, with the less wealthy hearing the news and the latest music in restaurants and shops if not in their own homes.[17]

The advent of radio and recorded music as means of entertainment may have exerted a very direct influence upon Abing's activities as a street singer and musician. In the first place, the ready availability of both national and local news commentary presented in a medium which even the illiterate could understand may have encouraged Abing to provide the kind of local gossip, rumor, and scandal that were less readily broadcast. Alternatively, his customers may have increasingly come from the lower ranks of society, rural visitors to the urban market places, and others who lived beyond the dialect or reach of public broadcasts. Finally, the availability of news in condensed summaries may have spurred Abing to create accounts which were both dramatically entertaining and artistically polished. Regular listeners might have paid more attention to what Abing did with his story than to the novelty of the information encapsulated within it. But again, these suggestions must remain conjectural for want of hard evidence of what Abing actually did as a street singer. As an instrumentalist, the advent of recorded music would have provided him, and his customary audiences, with greatly increased opportunities to hear music, both in terms of sheer amount and in styles previously unknown, including music from other regions of China and abroad.[18]

It is less probable that Communist ideology exerted a profound influence on him at this time. Throughout the later 1920s the Chinese Communists had attempted to arm the peasantry, to develop militant trades unions, and to seize cities through armed insurrection, but their only significant success was the establishment of a "soviet" revolutionary area by Mao Zedong in a remote mountainous area in Jiangxi Province (1929).

More immediately important to Abing in the early 1930s would have been news of continuing Japanese expansion in north China. In 1931 the northeastern provinces collectively termed Manchuria were occupied by Japanese forces, while by 1933 Japanese-sponsored regimes had been established in Mongolia, further parts of the northeast, and Beijing. Closer to Abing's home, the Japanese had launched a military assault on the city of Shanghai in 1932, though they were held at bay for three weeks by soldiers of the Chinese 19th Route Army. Japanese aerial bombings of civilian residential districts and flood-relief refugee centers, and the widespread killing of Chinese civilians by Japanese foot soldiers were widely reported at the time, not least on the new radio stations. Major anti-Japanese protests flared up again in 1935 when Japanese officers ordered all Chinese troops and officials to quit

Hebei Province, the site of the city of Beijing. According to Chinese student claims, many thousands died in the ensuing protests, although the accuracy of this figure is perhaps less important than the emotive effect its propagation would have had on Chinese such as Abing.

It is certain that Abing would also have known something of the diverse range of anti-Nationalist views then in frequent parlance. While Communist dogma appears to have remained largely unknown in cities such as Wuxi, protests were commonly expressed against administrative corruption and Jiang Jieshi's policy of Japanese appeasement. A high level of public debate focused on China's modernization, its international role, and social policies; and, despite censorship, opinions were in general more freely aired than at any other time in Chinese history. The fact that Abing could operate at all as a street singer would seem to confirm this point. After the Communist victory in 1949, an attempt to earn a livelihood through singing uncensored news stories in public would have been far more dangerous.

## China at War, 1937–1950

This period, the final phase of Abing's life, is bounded by the start of the Japanese invasion of central and southern China in 1937 and the conclusion of the Nationalist-Communist civil war in 1949. Since Abing lived just one more year, until December 1950, it is convenient to include those few months in this section as well.

The outbreak of the Sino-Japanese War in July 1937 may at first have seemed no more than the Japanese seizure of yet another province, though the loss of the old capital Beijing (July 28) and the city of Tianjin (30 July) must have wounded Chinese national pride particularly severely. Extension of the war southwards was, in fact, Jiang Jieshi's doing. Having constructed a defensive cordon of concrete emplacements near Wuxi, Jiang struck at the Japanese forces in Shanghai in August 1937. The battle continued for two months, with the Japanese eventually breaking the Chinese lines. In their rapid advance, a primary Japanese objective would have been the capture of the principal cities in the region, including Wuxi (taken in mid-November 1937), ideally with their industrial plants intact.

By the end of 1937, the Japanese army had sacked Jiang's capital, Nanjing, slaughtering tens of thousands of Chinese prisoners, townsmen, and women in a bloodbath that lasted into February 1938. Some rumor of this atrocity must certainly have reached those such as Abing in Japanese-held Wuxi. Northern Jiangsu withstood Japanese pressure a little longer, until the city of Xuzhou fell in May 1938, a setback to which Jiang Jieshi responded by ordering the Yellow River dikes blown. Massive flooding followed, which impeded the Japanese advance for several months, but at the cost of untold civilian death and suffering. Again, news of this tragedy must have reached those in occupied Wuxi.

As the year progressed, the Japanese extended their control along the southern coastal strip of Fujian and Guangdong while pushing inland to seize important cities. The Nationalist government was forced back to the city of Chongqing in Sichuan Province, southwest China. The war continued for another seven years, but by the end of 1938 the Japanese had captured much of the richest territory in China, and divided it into client states "that would give Japan preferential economic treatment, be staunchly anti-Communist, and provide the puppet troops that would garrison and patrol their own territories in Japan's name."[19] This, of course, allowed the Japanese to commit troops elsewhere during the years which followed.

Fighting between the Communists and Nationalists soon broke out again, with the Nationalists in January 1941 ambushing a Communist army in Jiangxi Province. Though the Nationalists won the short term battle, the Communists quickly regrouped in Jiangsu, not a great distance from Wuxi, and made major propaganda capital out of the incident. The Nationalists subsequently devoted much of their military potential to blockading the Communists in northern China. The Communists, for their part, turned their attention to guerrilla warfare, and to expanding their administrative experience in northern China.

When the Japanese surrendered, both the Nationalists and Communists raced from their strongholds to seize as much territory as possible. The former, aided by American airlifts, occupied most of the main cities, but the Communists, particularly in the north, gained control over extensive sectors of land. The manner in which the Nationalists reasserted themselves in central and eastern China was symptomatic of the moral decline of the party from the time of its successful mobilization of public opinion in 1911 and its optimistic reform plans of the early 1920s. In many cases, war criminals and collaborators were pardoned in return for pledges of support against the Communists. On the other hand, many who had endured the Japanese occupation now found their businesses confiscated by military officials. The Nationalists proved unable to control the crippling hyperinflation which now affected much of China, a problem which forced those on fixed governmental salaries to demand bribes in order to survive.

Gradually the military situation turned against Jiang. His field commanders were defeated, bribed, or won over to the Communist cause, and Nationalist soldiers deserted in droves. By 1948, Communist troops had reached Jiangsu Province, capturing the city of Xuzhou later that year. Refugees crowded into cities further south, including Nanjing, Wuxi, and Shanghai. Yet although there was widespread dissatisfaction with Jiang's government, some were beginning to find little of comfort in the policies of the advancing Communists either. Many liberals had trekked to join Mao's austere encampment at Yan'an. There, in May 1942, they heard Mao deliver a major policy speech on literary and artistic life, espousing the Soviet theme of Socialist Realism: cultural works intended for the masses must project a positive and instructive image of socialist society, art for art's sake was to be outlawed.[20] Others must have recognized the threat to religious expression posed by the Communists' determination to do away with "feudal superstitions." Concern about Communist-led class conflict and enforced land redistribution may also have worried numbers of industrialists, landowners, and members of the middle classes in eastern China.

These must have been particularly hard times for Abing. Economic collapse, civil war, industrial unrest, and agricultural decline flooded the streets with refugees. Competition for alms must have been fierce, and hyperinflation quickly rendered any cash receipts close to useless. For the blind Abing, survival without the help of his adopted family would very likely have been impossible, unless he had regular and well-rewarded engagements at this time, which seems unlikely. Some sources, indeed, suggest that he gave up playing altogether (see chapter 2).

Throughout 1949 the Communists advanced steadily across China. Nanjing was taken on 23 April and Shanghai on 27 May. Wuxi must have changed hands at this time also. By 1 October 1949, although certain areas of the southwest (and Taiwan) still remained in Nationalist hands, Mao Zedong felt confident enough to proclaim the establishment of the People's Republic of China. Land reform was quickly and forcibly introduced to newly captured areas, and possibly as many as a million deaths resulted as peasants settled old scores with former landowners. In the cities, however, the changeover was generally far more calmly handled. Production was maintained and officials re-educated, and massive media campaigns introduced the new rulers' aims to the people at large. Neighborhood committees were established to assist in the administration of new policies and the monitoring of local people.

Of the new programs, that against opium addiction, "with enforced methods of 'cold-turkey' withdrawal,"[21] and a subsequent movement against the members of religious groups must have had the greatest effect upon Abing. As an addict and Daoist, he would certainly have been a target while these campaigns were at their height. It would, however, be pure speculation to connect Abing's death in late 1950 with either political campaign.

## Conclusion

Abing's home, the city of Wuxi, was a thriving city in the early twentieth century. Its communications with China's sometime political capital, Nanjing, and its economic capital, Shanghai, were good, and were extended both nationally and internationally by the new media of newspaper and wireless. Neither new products nor new concepts were in short supply in Wuxi during Abing's youth and early adulthood; it is hard to imagine that even a traditionally trained folk musician would have remained unaware of or uninterested in them.

Civil, international, and world wars; periods of rapid urbanization and industrialization; swings from economic boom to financial chaos; and major switches in governing ideologies: all these bore directly upon Abing's existence as man and musician. Any biography of his life needs to be considered in the context of these factors. As I argue in chapter 2, however, it must also be interpreted in the light of the ideologies of the biographers themselves.

## Notes

1. Jack Gray, *Rebellions and Revolutions: China from the 1800s to the 1980s*, The Short Oxford History of the Modern World, ed. J. M. Roberts (Oxford: Oxford University Press, 1990), 152.
2. Alfred Schinz, *Cities in China*, Urbanization of the Earth 7, ed. Wolf Tietze (Berlin: Gebrüder Borntraeger, 1989), 223.
3. Schinz, *Cities*, 223.
4. S. A. M. Adshead, *China in World History* (London: Macmillan, 1988), 321.
5. Adshead, *China*, 328–29; Schinz, *Cities*, 224.
6. Schinz, *Cities*, 224.
7. Anonymous, *All About Shanghai*, introduced by H. J. Lethbridge (Hong Kong: Oxford University Press, 1983 [Shanghai: University Press, 1934–35]), 140.
8. Jonathan Spence, *The Search for Modern China* (New York: Norton, 1990), 224.
9. Adshead, *China*, 359–60, 363–64.
10. Jiang Xianji and Sun Yunnian, "Minjian yinyuejia Abing," *Taihu*, 1979, nos. 4–5: 7–15 (7). Notably, Abing's father, Hua Qinghe, employed a *hao* (some sources say *zi*) or formal (or literary) name, Hua Xuemei. This, and the fact that Hua Qinghe was a high-ranking Daoist, suggest his level of literacy was high. It is plausible to believe that Hua Qinghe would have striven to instill a similar aptitude into his sole descendent. Cao Anhe, on the other hand, described Abing as "uncultured," though she of course met him only briefly at the end of his life, after many years of blindness and poverty; Cao Anhe, personal communication, 31 January 1992.
11. For a discussion of Zhou Shaomei's activities during 1911–12, see Tian Liu and Zhang Yaozong, "Kaituo chuangxin, hongyang minyue—ji minyue yanzoujia, yinyue jiaoyujia Zhou Shaomei," in Yi Ren, ed., *Youmei de xuanlü piaoxiang de ge—Jiangsu lidai yinyuejia* (Nanjing: Jiangsu wenshi ziliao, 1992), 87–90 (87); for Liu Tianhua, see Cao Anhe, "Xuanlü zouchu shidai de qiangyin—ji zuoqujia, erhu, pipa yanzoujia Liu Tianhua," in Yi, *Youmei de xuanlü*, 115–17 (115). English-language biographies of Zhou and Liu are provided by Terence M. Liu, "The Development of the Chinese Two-Stringed Lute *Erhu* Following the New Culture Movement (c.1915–1985)" (Kent State University: Ph.D. Dissertation, 1988), 106–10, 111–17. An account of the activities of Shanghai actors in the 1911 revolution is given by Colin P. Mackerras, *The Chinese Theatre in Modern Times: From 1849 to the Present Day* (London: Thames and Hudson, 1975), 120–23.
12. According to Jack Gray, Feng Guozhang was "reputed to have earned his living at one stage by playing the fiddle in disreputable theatres"; Gray, *Rebellions*,

172. The fact that Feng's reputation was sullied by report of his fiddle playing illustrates the notoriety with which itinerant professional performing musicians were regarded, an attitude which Abing would very likely have encountered during his own career as a street musician.

13. Yin Yawei, ed., *Wu si yundong zai Jiangsu* (Yangzhou: Jiangsu guji chubanshe, 1992), 140–42.

14. Certain mainland historians have presented this picture in reverse, with the May 4th Movement led by Chinese intellectuals already conversant with the rudiments of Marxist ideology, and inspired by the Russian October Revolution. Again, history is reconstructed to justify the present. Marie-Claire Bergère describes it instead as a bourgeois "bid for liberalism"; Marie-Claire Bergère, *The Golden Age of the Chinese Bourgeoisie 1911–1937*, trans. Janet Lloyd (Cambridge: Cambridge University Press, 1989), 217.

15. Adshead, *China*, 329.

16. This survey of almost 17,000 farms, led by John L. Buck of Nanjing University, is described in Gray, *Rebellions*, 156–61.

17. Chinese public radio broadcasts were initiated in Shanghai in January 1923. Other than by way of privately owned wireless receivers, hotels, coffee shops, and theatres were all potential sites where this new phenomenon could be enjoyed. See Liu Guangqing, ed., *Jiu Zhongguo de Shanghai guangbo shiye* (Beijing: Dang'an & Zhongguo guangbo dianshi chubanshe, 1985), 2, 5–6. Records were produced in Shanghai from the start of the century by branches of foreign companies such as Pathé and Victor as well as local companies. See Ding Guobin, "Huju jiefang qian ge fazhan jieduan de changpian jianjie," *Shanghai xiqu shiliao huicui* 2 (1986): 15–19 (16). Recordings were also imported from the West and Japan. These and locally produced music recordings formed the bulk of the material featured on the quickly proliferating radio stations of the mid–1920s and early 1930s.

18. For instance, Zhang Zhenji mentions local radio broadcasts in Wuxi of the 1930s as including frequent programs of Cantonese instrumental music; Zhang Zhenji, "Abing wubiaoti erhu qu de yinyue neirong, sucai laiyuan ji qi yishu chuangzao," *Nanyi xuebao*, 1980, no. 2:53–64 (55).

19. Spence, *Modern China*, 452.

20. This speech is translated as Mao Zedong, *Talks at the Yenan Forum on Literature and Art* (Beijing: Foreign Languages Press, 1965). For a brief summary of its intent, see A. L. Kagan, "Music and the Hundred Flowers Movement," *Musical Quarterly* 49 (1963): 417–30 (420). For a general discussion of the impact of this doctrine on Chinese musical life, see Arnold Perris, "Music as Propaganda: Art at the Command of Doctrine in the P.R.C.," *Ethnomusicology* 27 (1983): 1–28. A collection of essays placing the policy in the broader context of Chinese performance arts and literature is provided by Bonnie S. McDougall, ed., *Popular Chinese Literature and Performing Arts in the People's Republic of China, 1949–1979* (Berkeley: University of California Press, 1984).

21. Spence, *Modern China*, 518.

# Chapter 2

# Narrative, Ideology,
# and the Life of Abing

I hazard a guess that man will be ultimately known for a mere polity of multifarious, incongruous, and independent denizens.

Robert Louis Stevenson.[1]

In this chapter, I examine aspects of Abing's life and the contrasting ways in which these have been interpreted in Chinese musicology and broader cultural life in general. I do not so much seek to present a new biography of Abing—too little is known with any degree of certainty for such an exercise to transcend hypothesis, however entertaining—as to re-evaluate existing biographical accounts with the purpose of decoding their competing ideological bases. Rather than attempting to uncover the "truth" about Abing then, I look at the ways in which different "truths" have been constructed and negotiated.

I do this by initially examining a typical biography of Abing and its reception by other Chinese scholars. Points which have been fought over are considered in approximate chronological order, beginning with Abing's parentage, his date of birth, and then his alleged progression from Daoist to street musician. I then move away from this biography to evaluate competing accounts and the manner in which they explain subjects such as Abing's loss of sight and the formation of his character. The central portion of this chapter begins with an analysis of the construction for Abing of a patriotic and revolutionary image, and goes on to see what happens when a seemingly innocuous musicological assertion collides with this image. Finally, I introduce the range of music making which Abing would have encountered in Wuxi, with the intention of suggesting how his own musical work meshed with that taking place around him, and discuss his marriage and death. First of all, however, I elaborate on my use of the terms "narrative" and "ideology," explaining why these are important elements in every "life" of Abing.

Jean-Jacques Nattiez has described musical narrative as, "a plot imagined and constructed by [the] listeners."[2] Existing biographical narrative concerning Abing seems to parallel this dictum, forming a series of "plots" imagined and constructed by Chinese musicologists and, in turn, by their readers from a few, often disputed, records of Abing's life. This series of plots may itself be viewed as the ongoing negotiation of musicological metaphor and rhetoric,[3] a process founded on the ideologies of its creators and receivers. By ideology, I refer not so much to some general political or social outlook, as to what Terry Eagleton describes as, "those modes of feeling, valuing, perceiving and believing which have some kind of relation to the maintenance and reproduction of social power."[4] Although the creation of narrative is informed by experience of these ideological modes, the modes, in turn, are themselves partially produced and maintained through the employment of narrative. This ideologization process has also been described by Hayden White as one, "in which individuals are compelled to introject certain 'master-narratives' of imaginary social and life-histories or archetypal plot-structures, on the one side, and taught to think narrativistically, on the other."[5] Narrative "plots," then, are not only imagined and created in light of the disposition of social power but also form a means of discourse through which the ideological basis of that power may be recalled or redefined. Therefore, an analysis of narrative pertaining to Abing not only provides a timely re-evaluation of the significance of this key figure in recent Chinese musical history but also reveals something of the domain of ideology in modern Chinese thought.

Central to this analysis is the biography of Abing produced by the Chinese musicologist Yang Yinliu (1899–1984). This biography, originating during the early 1950s,[6] is the most widely disseminated written account of Abing's life, and has reappeared in several forms.[7] Yang's biography forms an official canon in discussions of Abing; it is the authority on which the arguments of other biographies are based and which rival narratives seek to displace.[8] Therefore, before going on to examine this and other biographies, it is worth presenting a summary translation of Yang's account.

## Yang Yinliu's Official Biography of Abing

Blind Abing's original name was Hua Yanjun, ⁚ . . . He was born in 1893 . . . and died in 1950. . . . His father and mother died very early, . . . he was adopted by the Daoist Hua Qinghe, master of the local Leizundian [temple], and so became a Daoist apprentice. From his childhood onward, Blind Abing learnt music from Hua Qinghe. Later, when Abing came across a tune he liked, whoever it was that was playing it, he did his utmost to learn from them, with the result that he learned to play many of the local instruments quite well.

While a Daoist, since he loved performing, he also joined a *chuigu* [wind and percussion] ensemble, playing in wedding and funeral processions. . . . [T]he Daoists believed this was causing them to lose face, and so they ejected him from their ensemble. Thus, [Abing] became a *chuigu* player. While a *chuigu* player, again because he loved performing, he often went to the market to play, or wandered about the streets until someone called on him to perform. The *chuigu* ensemble believed him to be contravening their customs, and [consequently] excluded him from their group. In this way, he became a pure and simple wandering street musician.

Originally, [Abing] wasn't blind. When he was thirty-five (1927), he didn't get immediate treatment for an eye disease and completely lost the sight of both eyes. From this time onwards, he was known as Blind Abing, and ordinary people gradually forgot his original name. He himself often told people not to use his original name, saying, "I haven't used the name Hua Yanjun for ages, no one knows it. It's better if you call me Blind Abing; that's the name that everyone on the street knows."

There were also those who considered Blind Abing a beggar. But, in fact, he had nothing at all in common with these social parasites. He never freely accepted charity from other people; he simply relied on performance to maintain himself. . . . When people asked him to perform, even without giving him any money, he was still happy to do so. . . .

[N]ot only could he play solos on various instruments, he could also sing, accompanying himself on the *huqin* [two-stringed fiddle] or *pipa*. He could also make up lyrics. Every day he went to small stalls or smoking rooms to [hear] the day's news; what he heard in the morning was on his lips in the afternoon, being sung in a rhythmic, musical form.

When Wuxi was controlled by the [Japanese] puppet regime, information about the anti-Japanese war was naturally not found in the newspapers. But, Blind Abing's singing voice, from start to finish, was never at the service of the puppet regime. He sang numerous songs which discredited them, and although he was often threatened, he paid no regard.

In the summer of 1950, when we went to ask him to perform, he said, "I haven't played for two years, my technique's rusty and, as for my instruments, they're all broken—none of them are any use." When we asked him the reason why he didn't play, he said, "One summer's day, two years ago, I was out playing on the street when a sudden rainstorm soaked me and my instruments through. As I walked in the rain, a rickshaw suddenly tilted over and knocked me down, breaking my *pipa*. The handle of the rickshaw punctured the snakeskin of my *huqin*. That same night, a mouse bit through the horsehair on the *huqin*'s bow. Think of it! It's possible that a mouse might eat the snakeskin, but to bite through rosined horsehair, that's very odd indeed! In one day and night, there were three or four unfortunate events, each of which involved my instruments! These can't have been good omens! From then on, I didn't dare perform again." We talked to him until finally he agreed [to play for us], saying, "I'm too rusty. Let me practice for three days, then I'll perform." We immediately lent him a new *huqin* . . . and a new *pipa*. . . . When the third evening came, he performed for us the six pieces. . . .

Blind Abing was not completely satisfied with his performance. When we asked him to record a few more pieces, he was not very interested. He said: "I've rusted too long, my hands don't obey me, and I play badly. I don't like the sound. I'm happy to record for you, but I need you to be patient. Let me practice for a while, then we'll continue recording." So we decided to record him further during the 1950 winter or 1951 summer holidays.

But the situation changed beyond our expectations! In January 1951, Li Songshou sent a letter saying Abing had died of an illness, spitting blood. . . .

Apart from listening to him perform several times, the author [Yang Yinliu] was able to develop a fairly close connection with him on several occasions. The first was in 1910, when I studied from him the performance of *Three Variations on Plum Blossom* [*Meihua san nong*] on *sanxian* [three-stringed lute] and *pipa*; the second was during Spring 1937, when he wanted me to sort out his fingering, so that he could find a way of playing *Drumming the Retreat* [*Che gu*] from the piece *The General's Orders* [*Jiangjun ling*] on the *pipa*; the last time was in Summer 1950 when, after making the recording, he wanted me to play *Three Variations on Plum Blossom* with him. . . . Truly, our meetings both began and ended with *Three Variations on Plum Blossom*. I never saw him again after that![9]

Yang's biography has since been contradicted, directly or tacitly, by the subsequent publications of other writers and by Yang himself. In the first place, it has commonly been suggested that Abing was the illegitimate son of Hua Qinghe and a widow surnamed Wu, who had earlier married into (or possibly merely worked as a servant for) a prominent Wuxi clan named Qin.[10] In later revisions of his biography of Abing, Yang also mentions the widow Wu, altering (without comment) his earlier account to state that, "Abing was the only son of . . . the Daoist Hua Qinghe." Yang goes on to explain that, due to the opposition of the Qin family, Wu and Hua Qinghe were unable to formally marry, living together until Abing's birth, at which point Wu, accused of blackening the family name, was forced to return to the Qin abode.[11] This theory has been disputed by Yu Siu Wah:

> Yang's version is questionable since rarely will a widow be forced to go back to the family of her deceased husband. Usually, the widow will be ousted by her husband's family once she is found to have an affair with another man, a perfect excuse to deprive her of the share she has in the inheritance of her husband.[12]

If, on the other hand, Wu was a servant, whether married into the Qin clan or not, her labor might have been of some value to them, and her return to the household demanded. Also, had the prominent Qin family permitted a daughter or daughter-in-law to remarry, against clearly articulated Confucian codes, it is possible that they would have lost public status.[13] One of the markers of membership of the Chinese social elite was the ability to afford to retain an unproductive widow, a form of "conspicuous consumption."[14] Wu's death has been variously described as occurring one, three, and eight years after Abing's birth. In each case, no source for this information is given.[15]

In fact, an equally diverse range of birthdates for Abing has also been proposed. Yang discusses the suggestions of 1887, two dates within 1892, and 1898, describing the latter as "absurd," but holds to his earlier statement of the 9th day of the 7th lunar month, [Guangxu reign 19th] Guisi year, (20 August 1893), which, he claims, is based on Abing's personal testimony in 1950.[16] Xu Yihe has recently revived the 1898 theory, advancing the recollections of several of Abing's neighbors and associates, whom Xu interviewed in the 1960s, and the claim that Abing's "memorial tablet" (*paiwei*) bore the following date: 18th day of the 8th lunar month, Guangxu reign 24th Wuxu year (3 November 1898).[17] Apparently, this tablet was destroyed during the Cultural Revolution, although record of its inscription was preserved. Yang, for his part, states that this tablet was (erroneously) marked: "18th day of the 8th lunar month 1892" (8 November 1892).[18] However, he attributes this error to the reliance of Abing's wife Dong Cuidi on the faulty recollection of his uncle, Hua Xiquan, with the inference that Abing had already died and was beyond consultation. Although this may appear reasonable enough, Yang also claims that Dong Cuidi died almost one month before Abing, which would appear to betray a certain lack of critical attention on his part.[19] If Dong Cuidi died before Abing, then she would not have been involved in preparing a tablet for him after his death; if she had, for some reason, prepared the birthdate part of it earlier, she would surely have asked Abing when his birthday was, in which case Abing's personal testament to Yang Yinliu appears of doubtful provenance; and if she died after Abing (as other writers claim) then Yang's unreliability on this detail casts doubt over the soundness of the remainder of his biographical research. More seriously, birthdates were significant not only for annual celebrations and the accurate totalling of age but also for the consultation of fortune-tellers and horoscopes. Since Dong Cuidi lived with Abing for almost twenty years, she surely had ample opportunity to discover his year and day of birth, at least as Abing himself reckoned them.

Such disputes make the point that, despite the seeming authority of Yang's biography, very few verifiable facts about Abing's parentage and early life have survived. According to Arthur Smith's roughly contemporary account, adoption in late imperial China was a "universal practice . . . rooted in ancestral worship."[20] The childless parents took on a son who not only bore their funeral costs but also maintained their graves and assured the continuance of the family name for a further generation. Nonetheless, although the adoption theory is plausible, and is presumably what the unmarried Hua Qinghe might have told Abing, Du Yaxiong claims that as Abing matured his physical resemblance to Hua Qinghe became increasingly apparent,[21] and there seems little doubt that many of Abing's contemporaries believed him to be the bastard son of Hua Qinghe and disparaged him accordingly.

Naming a child, for a Chinese Daoist as for a member of many other societies worldwide, was a decision of some significance. The names selected may also reflect the period in which the child was born. According to Jiang Xianji and Sun Yunnian, the fortune of a child born in 1893 was deficient in the cosmological elements of metal and fire. Thus, Hua Qinghe chose the childhood name (*xiaoming*) "Abing," the "bing" character of which includes the fire radical, and the formal name "Hua Yanjun," "jun" incorporating the metal radical. This latter name also linked Abing to his cousin, Hua Qinghe's elder brother's son, Hua Bingjun.[22] Hua Qinghe, therefore, selected names which gave his son both an increased opportunity of good fortune, and linked him to a senior branch of the family.

If there is little certainty about Abing's parentage and date of birth, there has also been major dispute over subsequent events in his life. In the original version of Yang's biography of Abing, Yang described how Abing's joining of the *chuigu* ensemble caused him to be expelled from the Daoist group, and how his subsequent individual street performances led to his exclusion from the *chuigu* team.[23] Another explanation for Abing's quitting the Daoist music group has also been proposed. According to Yuan Jingfang, a local trouble-maker named Miao Bin charged Abing with defaming Daoism, causing his expulsion from the Daoist ranks.[24] A third suggestion is that internal rivalries, either personal or over property, within the Daoist establishment led to Abing's dismissal.[25]

Shen Qia has published a strong rebuttal of these assertions. Quoting the recollections of various elderly *chuigu* performers from Wuxi, Shen claims that Abing never joined a *chuigu* group. Shen also questions whether a Daoist could be expelled for engaging in wind and percussion ensemble music, pointing out the close connection between the repertories of the two genres, and commenting that the social position of each group was equally low.[26] According to Shen's historical research, Miao Bin (1902–death by firing squad in 1946) spent much of the period in question away from Wuxi, first as a student, then as a recruit at the Nationalist Party's military training school at Huangpu in Guangdong Province, and finally in Japan. Shen was also unable to find surviving evidence of some struggle involving Abing within the Daoist temple.

Concluding his case, Shen Qia lists four pieces of "circumstantial evidence" which support his contention that Abing never stopped being a Daoist. Among these, Abing apparently maintained a Daoist hair bun until his death; his memorial tablet described him as *xian zushi*, "ancestral founder of the faith," a term reserved for deceased Daoists; and he was buried in the local Daoist cemetery. Shen describes the whole expulsion theory as a "historical misunderstanding" and gives its advancement by the prominently placed musicologist Yang Yinliu as reason for its wide dissemination.[27] Incidentally, Yang was quick to alter his account, simply expunging, again without comment, the whole passage concerning Abing's expulsion: his biography of 1977 had restated the 1954 expulsion theory;[28] that of 1980 merely states that as Abing became increasingly blind he had to find work outside the temple.[29]

One pretext for Yang Yinliu and subsequent writers' attraction to the idea of Abing's fall from Daoist grace, is that in "liberated" Communist China, the discussion and performance of the musical compositions of a superstitious Daoist—as opposed to those of a down-trodden street musician—could have been interpreted as unwise by politically correct conservatory musicians, those for whom Yang's biography and transcriptions were prepared. Thus, by describing Abing's expulsion from Daoism, Yang and his ideological confederates distance Abing from the potentially embarrassing taint of an officially outmoded religious system.[30] Sympathy for Abing is elicited by the metaphor of his fall from Daoist to *chuigu* player and again to street musician, and points are scored against the reactionary Daoists and the Nationalist anti-hero, Miao Bin. On the other hand, Yang is careful to insist that Abing was never a beggar. Instead, he promotes the somewhat romantic image of Abing happily performing for anyone, high or low, paid or unpaid.[31]

## Rival Biographies

A certain romanticism is also found in some other accounts, which plug gaps in Yang's biography. Jiang Xianji and Sun Yunnian matter-of-factly describe Abing's early education as including the *Three-Character Classic* (*San zi jing*) and the *Hundred Surnames* (*Bai jia xing*), as well as various types of scripture, calligraphy, and musical performance, which he apparently preferred to reading and writing.[32] Du Yaxiong, on the other hand, in recounting much the same material, adds that Abing often played truant from his studies at an old-style private school, going instead to play or listen to storytellers and musicians, where he would stand silently to one side, motionless in fascination. Only once Hua Qinghe discovered Abing's musical talents did his musical training begin.[33]

Various other segments of Du Yaxiong's biography of Abing are worth examining in more detail, since they reveal quite a different negotiation of the master elements of narrativization than is found in any of Yang Yinliu's accounts. Du begins by summarizing the beginnings of study of Abing and his music in the 1950s. He briefly describes the "Gang of Four" as deeming Abing a "ruffian" (*dipi*) and his music "poisonous weeds overflowing with stench."[34] Du then cites several foreign responses to Abing's *erhu* piece *The Moon Reflected on the Second Springs* (*Er quan ying yue*, hereafter *Second Springs*), including its comparison with the evocative power of Pablo Casals' cello playing. Before completing his introductory section with a periodization of Abing's life, Du states that false material and "audacious fabrications" have led to the portrayal of Abing as a revolutionary musician akin to the composers Nie Er (1912–35) and Xian Xinghai (1905–45). To allow a true assessment of Abing and a better understanding of his compositions, Du continues, he has carried out on-the-spot investigation at Abing's birthplace.[35]

Having established Abing as a musician of international stature, Du's agenda is to rehabilitate Abing as a folk musician, and as a creation of his time and social context.[36] He begins by portraying the baby Abing crying out in hunger while Hua Qinghe lulls him to sleep by playing the *pipa*. After describing Abing's early childhood among Hua Qinghe's relatives at Dongting Xiaosifang village outside Wuxi, his return at the age of 7 or 8 to his father's keeping, and his musical training in the many instruments and styles of Daoist and local folk musics, Du introduces Abing's discovery of his illegitimacy:

Abing grew up at Hua Qinghe's side. From the two men's physical similarity, the Daoists at Leizundian and their neighbors gradually worked out that Abing was Hua Qinghe's illegitimate son. Whenever Abing heard people call him "bastard" [*tianluozi*], he would start a fight. His discovery, later, that he really was illegitimate became a great wound in his heart. People's cold-shouldering of him from childhood onwards formed in him a stubborn, uncommunicative character. Musical instruments, only musical instruments were his dear friends. He often played the *erhu* or *pipa* on his own, pouring out his unhappiness in music.[37]

Du then mentions that after Hua Qinghe's death, Abing began to frequent brothels and smoke opium.[38] Since the income from temple offerings wasn't enough to support these habits, Abing gradually sold off the temple's ritual objects and also two of the three houses Hua Qinghe had bequeathed to him (see photo 1). Du continues:

Abing contracted syphilis from a prostitute, and his eyes began to trouble him. . . . The decline in his sight prevented him from taking part in Daoist ceremonies, thus severing the source of his livelihood. Many times, his remorse and pain made him want to kill himself, but music was the only thing on this world that made him reluctant to do so. He couldn't bear to be parted by death from his *erhu* and *pipa*. . . . He began to play *erhu* on the street. From then on, he was part of the lowest echelon of society, living among the miserable, suffering laboring classes. If he hadn't had this existence, then there couldn't be the kind of composition like

Photo 1. Three Houses Inherited by Abing (Tushuguan Rd., Wuxi).

*Second Springs*, which represents the innermost aspirations of countless multitudes of laboring peoples, or the musician Abing.[39]

Labelling a well-liked folk musician as a brothel-visiting drug addict is powerfully direct writing for a Chinese musicologist. Some musicians whom I interviewed in Wuxi and Shanghai in Spring 1992, unaware of Du's article, said that no editor would allow the publication of such material. There are mitigating circumstances, however. Effectively, Du Yaxiong asserts that it was only through Abing's fall to the most abject level of human existence that he was able to become—through music, his one true companion—the voice of the downtrodden masses. Just as music proved Abing's consolation as a hungry baby deprived of his mother's love, it was his resort when taunted with his illegitimacy, and his preservation when blindness and disease robbed him of his livelihood. Rhetorically speaking, Du argues that without this ordeal by insult, blindness, and degradation, Abing would never have understood the masses, and his music would never have achieved its internationally recognized and lasting transcendence. The subsequent version of Yang Yinliu's biography, however, makes no reference to Abing's visits to brothels or illicit smoking habits.[40]

Abing's introduction to prostitution and opium has, in fact, been presented in another way in mainland China, both by Jiang Xianji and Sun Yunnian in their article of 1979 and in the 1992 television series dramatizing Abing's life. According to the first of these narratives, after the death of Hua Qinghe, Abing was led astray by a grocer known as Lu Xiaokai. Lu not only took Abing into the red-light districts but also introduced him to drugs. Abing contracted gonorrhoea and, when it became more acute, found he lacked the money to pay for medical attention, hence his blindness.[41] In the television series, the story is similar, although not quite so explicitly handled. As an extra feature, Abing, distraught at the disappearance of his love interest, the ballad singer Cui Mengzhu, is taken to get drunk by the dissolute Lu. Thoroughly intoxicated, Abing is taken to a brothel where one of the girls, whom he mistakes for his sweetheart, convinces him that it is their wedding night. When Abing learns that his beloved has been forced to marry an old man in another city, his friend again makes him imbibe large quantities of alcohol, this time giving him opium before returning him to the brothel.[42]

Abing's blindness has also been accounted for in other ways. Yu Siu Wah, for example, quotes a 1977 program note by *erhu* pedagogue Zhang Shao in which Abing's blindness is attributed to "his grief at the death of his father."[43] In the 1979 film dramatization of Abing's life, his blindness resulted instead from wounds suffered in a beating Abing received at the hands of Nationalist thugs.[44] In such ways, the image of Abing, the filial or downtrodden and abused folk musician, has been invoked to serve what Eagleton describes as, "the maintenance and reproduction of social power."[45] And lest it be thought that I am overemphasizing the consciousness of such in-vocations, the title of one of Shen Qia's citations speaks for itself: "On the Question of the Portrayal of the Folk Musician Abing's Artistic Image."[46]

The activities of the blind Abing are similarly open to varying interpre-tations. Existing biographies discuss two principal subjects, his deeds as a street musician and the source and naming of his recorded instrumental works, both of which themes I now examine in turn. First, I focus on the manner in which the image of Abing as street singer and instrumentalist has been employed to project the values of nationalism and revolution. Second, concentrating on Abing's music for *erhu*, I examine ideological conflict un-derpinning rival explanations of the source and names of these compositions. This leads in turn to a reconsideration of Yang Yinliu's role in the collection and presentation of Abing's music and life.

## A Patriotic and Revolutionary Street-Singer: The Construction of a Text

Although Yang Yinliu notes that, "It is a pity that at that time [the decades before the Communist victory in 1949] nobody wrote down the militant kind of songs that Abing himself arranged and sang, which were more than a few in number," he does mention Abing's creation and performance of var-ious songs.[47] Among these were those directed against a "despotic landlord" who allegedly raped a young servant girl; also, enraged by the Nationalist Miao Bin's seizure of Leizundian as a stable for his horses, Abing's public sung reportage apparently shamed Miao's mother into ordering the removal of the offending beasts; further songs were directed at the Japanese invaders and still others at the Nationalist Government.[48]

Jiang Xianji and Sun Yunnian discuss these songs more fully, quoting (or, if Yang Yinliu is correct about the non-survival of records of Abing's songs, recalling from four decades earlier) samples of his lyrics. The tone of such texts is illustrated by a section of one of these, which refers to Chinese-Japanese military clashes in Shanghai during January–February 1932 (see chapter 1):

> [I'll] call out some news, [I'll] speak out some news,
> [But] where did this news take place?
> On the banks of the Huangpu River, the 19th Route Army,
> Ranks of warriors, heroically fought the enemy.
> The Japanese ghosts, had nowhere to flee,
> Their heads toppled to the ground, like severed melon vines. . . .[49]

Patriotism, as exemplified in lyrics such as these, is an attribute many commentators have credited to Abing,[50] and is, of course, a powerful redress in the crafting of a biographical narrative to his potentially embarrassing association with prostitution and opium abuse. The ascription of patriotism to Abing, however, is based on more than his apparent selection of song texts. For example, the title of the *erhu* solo *Listening to the Pines* (*Ting song*) is understood to refer to an (apocryphal) episode during the Song Dynasty general Yue Fei's campaign against the forces of the invading Jin tribesmen. According to this tale, the barbarian leader Jin Wushu pursued Yue Fei and his defeated troops to Huiquan mountain, near Wuxi. Prior to ordering the final attack, Jin Wushu lay down to rest on a large, flat rock set amidst pine trees and named the "Listening to the Pines Stone." Lying on the rock, Jin Wushu was terrified to feel the vibrations of the hooves of an approaching relief force of Song cavalry, and thus Yue Fei was able to escape.[51] Zeng Xun introduces this composition as follows:

> The eight-year-long War of Resistance Against Japan [1937–45] was Abing's most difficult period. Under the rule of the enemy and their puppet regime, his intense feelings of patriotism naturally found sustenance in the story of Yue Fei. Normally, he set his own words to folk tunes to denounce wicked traitors. But his 1939 piece *Listening to the Pines* more profoundly embodies the lofty aspirations of resistance and national salvation. We can experience this mood from its vigorous melody, its particular musical figures, and its well-knit structure of musical imagery.[52]

Closely connected to the presentation of Abing's patriotism is that of his revolutionary character. But, returning to his performance of news stories disparaging the rich and powerful, we can interpret this activity in another way. What a communist writer presents as the selfless exposé of the evils of Nationalist society the market-forces capitalist may see as Abing's provision of lurid gossip to titilate his paying audiences. Although Chinese musicologists (must) write as if the rise of Communism in China was an inevitable stage of historical evolution, and embrace every prerevolutionary antiestablishment voice as part of this common cause, the possibility remains that raising class consciousness was of no more significance to Abing than it is to the *paparazzo* journalist: when he encountered a promising story, its popular appeal, whether patriotic, salacious, or whatever, is exploited to the full. As Henry Kingsbury states:

> The interpretation of texts is rarely simple interpretation. It frequently entails elements of enactment or rendition, but equally frequently consists more of textual invocation in the context of ongoing social negotiation. In all of these cases what is crucial is the link connecting textual interpretation to social organization, the rhetorical links connecting the fictions of the text with the social facts—and perhaps the factions—of the interpreting institutions.[53]

In this case, the "text" is the narrative of Abing's life and its invocation takes place in the context of government-controlled scholarly publication.

Abing the active revolutionary is, then, a rhetorical device created and wielded by the dominant Communist faction of contemporary Chinese society. His activities, as interpreted by them, are presented in narrative to serve, justify, and maintain the academic sociopolitical status quo.

However, it should be emphasized that the construction of such historical narratives is hardly the preserve of Chinese Communist music theorists alone, rather these narratives are likely to be a feature of all human discourse.[54] Derek Scott, in the course of a discussion of music and sociology, identifies a further example:

> Music history has been interpreted since the nineteenth century according to distinctively romantic and modernist tenets, with the emphasis being on formal and technical values, on novelty and compositional "coups," on the composition in itself and its place in an autonomous musical process, and on internationalism— or, more precisely, on internationalism defined by the idea of a *single* culture with *universal* values. This method of interpreting music history, though nineteenth-century in origin, affects the way we understand the music and composers of earlier periods.[55]

Another aspect of this musicological ideology, according to Scott, is its foundation on "an abstracted linear account of music history."[56] Romantic and modernist musical narratives, then, rest on the often unspoken acceptance of the validity of a chronologically ordered series of autonomous, universally acclaimed musical masterworks. Clearly, this is a different ideology from that which guides musicological discourse concerned with Abing, although, as mentioned above, romantic tenets have informed the interpretation of such factors as Abing's discovery of his illegitimacy and his drug taking. Before discussing in more detail the ideology which underpins narrative about Abing, however, it is pertinent to return to the second aspect of his life as a blind street musician normally privileged by Chinese authors, the source and identification of the musical works he performed for Yang Yinliu in 1950.

## Issues of Source and Identity: The Case of *The Moon Reflected on the Second Springs*

The most controversial introduction to the issues of source and naming is furnished by Abing's best known piece, the *erhu* solo *Second Springs*. In his original account, Yang Yinliu gave this composition the following, seemingly innocuous, description:

> Looking at the piece's name: Second Springs is a spring, the "Second Springs Under Heaven" of Wuxi's famous scenic point Huiquan mountain. The meaning of the whole name is heavenly moonlight reflected in the Second Springs. According to Abing himself, this was originally a Daoist *suona* [oboe] piece. But this name, with its local color, was probably added later through blind Abing's

acceptance of local tastes, and is unlikely to have been the piece's original name. When Abing was asked [about this], he wasn't sure at all. He said, "Right, originally it had another name, maybe it was *When Spring Comes* [*Dao chun lai*]." But this can't be true either.[57]

Yang then goes on to report on his inability to find musical correspondences between *When Spring Comes* (as well as various other traditional pieces) and *Second Springs*. He concludes that *Second Springs* is most likely Abing's own composition, "formed from a long period of performance and development," proposing that Abing lacked self-confidence and thus preferred to ascribe his own music to some earlier source.[58] Antoinet Schimmelpenninck's comments on the problems of eliciting ingenuous responses from folk musicians in the Wuxi area in recent years may have been as true for Yang Yinliu in 1950.[59] The polite informant may agree with (almost) any suggestion made by the outsider, whether foreign ethnomusicologist or high-ranking, city-based academic, and may attempt to second-guess the responses he or she believes are expected. The ability to recognize, negotiate, and overcome such difficulties is critical to the success of short field trips and of tours by mobile ethnomusicologists through large swathes of territory.

Yang's account of the naming of this piece was, in fact, one of the first parts of his biography of Abing to be questioned. It was pointed out that the Second Springs fountain and pool is actually covered by a very substantial stone roof and the whole enclosure ringed by fairly high walls (see photo 2).

Photo 2. The Second Springs Under Heaven, Wuxi.

The penetration of moonlight to the small pool, let alone its reflection in an aesthetically consequential way, was therefore considered unlikely by many Chinese musicologists.[60] In later publications Yang moved the site of the moon's reflection to a small lake just south of the Second Springs pavilion.[61]

Even if we set aside the exact theater of reflection, the image conjured up by the title *The Moon Reflected on the Second Springs* has resonated through subsequent Abing narratives. A typical example is Zhou Chang's description:

> [Abing] employs lovely musical language of the most expressive qualities to depict the beauty of this famous scenic spot of the motherland and to voice his own boundless, heartfelt love for it. Second Springs is just so calm, exquisite, and beautiful; [so, too,] the [music's] rhythm is smooth and steady, its speed leisurely, and its melody indirectly flowing . . . . This is music in complete harmony with its setting, and this kind of music could only have been produced if its author profoundly loved the scenery of his motherland.[62]

Noting again the rhetorical appeal to patriotism, it is striking that when Zhou returns to *Second Springs* in his analysis of Abing's music he added the words: "In *Second Springs* it is very hard to point out which section depicts the spring water and which section depicts the moonlight. . . ."[63] The latent significance of this remark exploded into bitter dispute when, in 1979, Yang Yinliu's ex-student and companion at the 1950 recording session, Zhu Shikuang, published a quite different account of the way in which *Second Springs* was named:

> After making the recording, when Yang asked Abing what the name of this piece was, Abing said: "This piece doesn't have a name, it became the way it is now just from me playing around with the material for a long time." Yang then asked: "Where do you usually play it?" Abing replied: "Usually on the streets, and also at the courtyard by the spring on Hui Mountain." Yang blurted out: "Then why not call it *Second Springs* [*Er quan*]." I said: "*Second Springs* doesn't seem like a complete name on its own. In Cantonese music there's a piece called *The Moon Engraved on Three Pools* [*San tan yin yue*]. Couldn't we call it *The Moon Engraved on Second Springs* [*Er quan yin yue*]?" Yang said: "It's not good enough to borrow that '*yin*' character. Here in Wuxi there's a Yingshan River, so let's call it *Er quan ying yue*!" Abing nodded his assent at once, and that's how the name *The Moon Reflected on the Second Springs* got chosen and handed down.[64]

This provided just the ammunition needed by those who had found the pastoral title and nocturnal, scenic theme of Abing's highly expressive piece ill fitting. Writers such as Shen Qia and Zhang Zhenji were quick to capitalize on Zhu's disclosure, promoting the rival conception of *Second Springs* as a kind of "non-program music."[65] Nevertheless, in distinction to the instances detailed above where Yang Yinliu either revised his account or simply ignored rival suggestions, he speedily refuted the heart of Zhu's argument, stating: "The title *Second Springs* was given by Abing himself. [Thus] it can be conceived that it accurately represents his compositional intentions and performance inclinations."[66]

In 1992, I interviewed both Cao Anhe (b.1905) and Zhu Shikuang (b.1915), the two survivors of the 1950 recording session.[67] Cao, whose understanding of and association with Yang Yinliu was profound, maintained Yang's story with some passion: the title was Abing's; we should respect his wishes by using it. Zhu was just talking big. Zhu Shikuang, on the other hand, stood by his statement of 1979 (quoted above). In attempting to gain further perspective on this matter, I then asked Zhu Shikuang about the naming of Abing's other compositions, and in talking about *Listening to the Pines*, we had the following discussion:

> Zhu:  . . . originally, this piece didn't have a name, but because of where it was played [at the "Listening to the Pines" stone on Hui Mountain], it took that name.
> Stock: So, the names were all chosen [at the recording session] in 1950?
> Zhu: That's right.

If this is true, then reference to the Song Dynasty patriot Yue Fei (see above) in the proposed program to *Listening to the Pines* may be as questionable as that to the moonlight in *Second Springs*. Similarly, the name of the third *erhu* piece recorded in 1950, *Cold Spring Wind* (*Han chun feng qu*), may be equally arbitrary. And if that is so, support is given to the contention that this piece is a second improvisation on the same themes and basic structural procedures as *Second Springs* (see chapter 4). On this same subject, Yang Yinliu was unable to find a source for *Cold Spring Wind*, although he does comment on its resemblance to *Second Springs*.[68] Intriguingly, Zhu Shikuang informed me that at the recording session Abing had not been told to play three solos, merely to play, recording continuing until time ran out. By all accounts, Abing had not performed for some considerable time prior to a few days before the recording session. Is it conceivable that he decided to rework his favorite and most familiar melodic material, leaving the business of naming the recorded results to the academics who seemed to find it so important?

Such conjecture aside, several sources for the individual melodic elements of *Second Springs* (and, by implication, *Cold Spring Wind* and major sections of *Listening to the Pines* as well, see chapter 4) have been put forward. Zhang Zhenji summarizes several of these in his paper of 1980, mentioning music from Daoist music, folk song, Cantonese instrumental music like *The Moon Engraved on Three Pools* (a popular genre in Wuxi during the early twentieth century), and the local dramatic form *tanhuang* and its operatic descendant *xiju* (Wuxi opera), which was taking shape during Abing's lifetime.

Other authors have found correspondences between Abing's music and Jiangnan *sizhu*, the instrumental ensemble genre hailing from central east China where Wuxi is situated. These proposals are not examined here, since at present it is merely necessary to suggest that they could only be asserted with confidence once the definite "moonlight on the springs" program had been rejected, and that they mark a shift in ideological paradigm from Abing the inspired, revolutionary creator to Abing the assimilative craftsman.

This new narrative archetype has not, however, entirely displaced the older one. A new perception of the source of Abing's music calls in turn for a reinterpretation of his life and a re-evaluation of the significance and function of his compositions in contemporary China, and not all musicians are ready to countenance this. A single instance of the interpretative dilemmas raised for the socialist musician by such seemingly "autonomously" musicological propositions will illustrate this point. That chosen is the melodic similarity noted by a number of musicians between one theme of *Second Springs* and the song *Intimate Companion* (*Zhixin ke*):

> Heaven has predestined this opportunity to find an intimate companion.
> This slave promises to be his the whole of her life.
> Darling, come in and you won't feel tired.
> Darling, come in and you won't feel tired (padding syllables omitted).[69]

Although Yang Yinliu quotes a version of this song, he strongly refutes its connection with *Second Springs*. As the text of this song makes clear, and as informants in Wuxi confirmed, *Intimate Companion* was a brothel song, addressed in an enticing manner by courtesans to potential customers among those passing by. Zhang Zhenji provides versions of this tune which he argues are similar to the *Second Springs* theme. He then charges Yang with "from among the numerous versions of the *Intimate Companion* tune, choosing the most 'dissimilar' one" (see fig. 2.1).[70]

But why should Yang Yinliu have dismissed this apparently plausible connection? Was Yang musically incompetent, hasty in his selection of an example, or did he wish to denigrate the discovery of a rival scholar? Perhaps none of these, because by discrediting any melodic connection between *Second Springs* and *Intimate Companion*, Yang appears again to have been attempting to distance his Abing narrative from the taint of prostitution. The admission that Abing might have known such a song well enough to use it in his own composition would not only raise awkward questions about Abing's private life but also threaten the programmatic and nationalist content of his *erhu* piece (and contaminate the reputations of those who had promoted the music, including Yang Yinliu). If music is linked to its context, adoption of a prostitute's pandering ditty might express not so much the beauty of the motherland or the struggles of the laboring masses but attractions and grapples of quite another order. Zhang Zhenji, for his part, seeks

Stave A: excerpt from Yang's version of *Intimate Companion*, text omitted, transposed down a fourth

System B: Zhang's comparative alignment of part of *Intimate Companion* with a theme from *Second Springs*

Fig. 2.1. Themes from **Intimate Companion** and **Second Springs**

to evade this contention through his insistence on the non-programmatic nature of the piece. Although Abing, Zhang claims, adopted such material, he developed it to create, "a musical image of such vigor, grief, and indignation."[71] In Zhang's ideology, then, source of material does not precondition its use; interpretation is to be based on the final result alone. Nattiez might refer to such an interpretation as an *esthesic* construct arising from the *material trace* created through a largely inaccessible *poietic* process.[72] Zhang Zhenji, incidentally, deems himself primarily a composer, not a musicologist or semiologist;[73] he may, therefore, have a personal interest in privileging the composer's autonomy of control over raw melodic material above any implications already invested in the crude sonic stuff itself.

Yang Yinliu's rejection of the *Intimate Companion* connection is as striking as his disavowal of Zhu Shikuang's attribution of the naming of *Second*

*Springs* to Yang and Zhu rather than Abing. Although Yang claims to be unimpressed by the suggestion of melodic resemblance between the Cantonese piece *The Moon Engraved on Three Pools* and *Second Springs*,[74] he never addresses the suggestion of melodic adaptation from operatic, instrumental music, or Daoist music in any detail. In fact, it is possible to get the impression that Yang Yinliu was neither greatly interested in Abing nor his music. When revising the biography and associated material, Yang typically made few alterations, preferring to omit discredited passages without further comment. Only the controversy over the naming of *Second Springs* elicited a direct rebuttal, and the *Intimate Companion* connection was economically fended off through the provision of what Yang's rivals saw as a deliberately obscuritanist musical example. Yang Yinliu was more than capable of advanced musical research, yet neither he nor the other members of his team appear to have published detailed analyses of Abing's music. Instead, Yang contented himself by reporting that he had checked similarly named compositions, and by reproducing a comparative chart listing resemblances in *Second Springs* and *Cold Spring Wind* sent to him by Li Songshou.[75]

Supporting this view is Cao Anhe's recollection that the recording of Abing was "accidental." Apparently, Cao, Yang, and a few others had gone to Wuxi with the intention of recording local *chuida* and *shifan luogu* (wind- and percussion-centered) ensemble music (see chapter 3). Li Songshou, who had mentioned Abing to them before, insisted on taking them to see the blind musician. Abing was then ill and needed to be loaned instruments on which to practice, including Cao's own *pipa*. After three days he was brought very late one evening to a local primary school where it was noisy and unlit. There, he performed the three *erhu* pieces. On the following evening he played *pipa* pieces at Cao's family home, apparently experiencing some difficulty with unfamiliar fretwork on Cao's instrument.[76] Since the recording of Abing's music was no more than an incidental aside to Yang's serious research of traditional instrumental ensemble music in Wuxi, it may be wondered whether he felt it necessary at that time to interview Abing with great care. Indeed, some of the inconsistencies which other writers gradually challenged may have arisen from Yang's fleshing out of sparse interview notes or memories once both Abing had died and the publication of his music was confirmed. Although vague intentions for a further recording session were expressed, no mention of how Abing would find instruments to practice on during the intervening period is found in Yang's published accounts.

Nonetheless, this is not to claim that Yang Yinliu was unable to recognize the value of the material he had acquired, however serendipitously. After all, its publication and dissemination quickly took place, and if Yang imbued his official narrative with elements which appear overtly romantic and uncritically revolutionary, this may simply stem from his deference to and internalization of the ideology of the period. Without the "introjection" of appropriate "archetypal plot-structures,"[77] Yang would have been unable to encourage musicians in the new conservatory system to embrace and perform the transcriptions of Abing's six recorded performances or to convince the cultural authorities that this was music fit for performance in Communist China. And when, in recent times, Chinese musicologists began to revise details of Abing's life, Yang was in most cases content to silently acquiesce.

## Further Biographical Details: Music, Marriage, and Death

Returning to Abing's life, a few further details require brief deliberation. As already noted in the discussion of the source of *Second Springs'* melodic material, a wide range of musical genres and styles were performed and heard in early-twentieth-century Wuxi. These included Daoist music, *chuigu* and other instrumental ensemble styles, folk song, various forms of ballad singing, regional opera performances at temples and fairs, literary *kunqu* opera, fashionable Cantonese music, Western-style military band music, and radio and gramophone musics.[78] Philip Bohlman has pointed to the opportunities that the urban marketplace brings for musical crossfertilization,[79] and it would appear that Abing was well aware of these too, adapting, for example, a few phrases of military band music during *Listening to the Pines* and quoting a number of folk songs in his *pipa* piece *Dragon Boats* (*Long chuan*). According to a number of accounts, Abing was also an expert at imitating speech and animal sounds on his fiddle, a technique more usually associated with northern *zhuihu* fiddle players but also a peripheral part of the conservatory tradition of *erhu* performance in pieces such as Liu Tianhua's *Birds Singing in the Deserted Mountains* (*Kong shan niao yu*) of 1928. This diversity of musical activity should not be surprising, since by the early 1930s Wuxi was already a major industrial and residential center (see chapter 1). Chapter 3 examines in more detail the musical environment within which Abing lived.

One major alteration in Abing's personal situation was his marriage in 1932 to the widow Dong Cuidi, an association that was to last until his death in 1950.[80] Abing and Dong Cuidi may have met at an opium den, since she shared his taste for the drug,[81] and, since the death of her first husband, had been employed as a servant in a smoking establishment. According to Yang Yinliu, Dong was Abing's second wife; the former was another man's ex-concubine, A Zhu.[82] No other account mentions A Zhu's existence, although the 1979 film introduced a singer named Qin Mei. Dong Cuidi, who was born in 1889, had four children by her previous marriage,[83] but all biographies agree that Abing himself left no children, although his name was carried on for another generation by one of Dong Cuidi's granddaughters, Hua Qiudi, who was born on 15 January 1944.[84]

According to Jiang Xianji and Sun Yunnian, Abing and Dong Cuidi spent at least part of the period of the Japanese occupation of Wuxi outside the city, either at his childhood home in Dongting or at Dong's home village of

Beiguo, northeast of Wuxi in Jiangyin County.[85] At some point during the 1940s they returned to Abing's remaining house in central Wuxi, and Abing continued his street-singing activities, although these began to diminish during 1947 once ill health became a significant problem. Apparently, his health was further harmed, and career as a street musician ended, by a two-month incarceration in an anti-opium institution in 1948. Jiang and Sun describe this period of internment as, "yet another example of the oppression Abing received from the Nationalist reactionaries."[86] Yang Yinliu's account does not include this episode, the equivalent event halting Abing's performing life being the inauspicious trio of rainstorm, rickshaw, and rodent.

Abing's death may have occurred on 4 December 1950, although a delay in its registration has led several biographers to cite 12 December instead.[87] All biographies give worsening illness and coughing fits as the cause of his death, although one musician from Wuxi said to me that there was a rumor that an opium overdose may have been a contributing factor. When I raised this possibility with other scholars, however, it was generally discounted, the reason advanced being that after the Communist "liberation" in 1949 opium was no longer available. Nonetheless, the anonymous oral history of a former Shanghai prostitute and heroin addict suggests that she was able to maintain her drug habit until sent to labor reform school in September 1952, considerably after Abing's death.[88] Whatever the truth of this matter, some distrust of Abing's reputation has lingered on in the Wuxi area. A stone memorial to him was vandalized during the Cultural Revolution, and post–Cultural Revolution plans to erect a statue in his honor were, in 1992, still deadlocked.[89] Holistic readers will perhaps find it satisfying that there remains a slight hint of controversy around the cause of Abing's death, just as there is around his lineage; birthdate; Daoist status; blindness; street singing; and compositional techniques, names, and sources.

## Conclusion

As mentioned above, despite the scepticism now accorded by many Chinese musicologists to so much of Yang Yinliu's account, segments of it have yet to be displaced from the affections of many performers and members of the public. The composition *Second Springs*, however, does now seem to be more commonly interpreted as an autobiographical comment on the sorrows of Abing's life than a piece of nocturnal scene painting. The 1979 film, mentioned above, may have accelerated this kind of re-evaluation in post–Cultural Revolution China. On the one hand, Abing was officially rehabilitated after his damning during the previous decade, and a wide public was reminded of the beauty of his compositions. On the other, a number of scholars, motivated by what they saw as the overromanticism of his portrayal and the manipulation of historical fact to further dramatize the story, began to look more deeply into the substance of Abing's life and music. The

1992 television series, which contains some of the results of these investigations, has the power to stimulate further such reinterpretations of Abing, although it still depicts him as a heroically romantic figure, desperately struggling to bring to the world the music that was within him. However, it takes more than an influential film or television series to establish a new interpretation of Abing or his music. For a key to understanding the processes which underlie such interpretational shifts I turn again to Derek Scott:

> I would claim that, contrary to Stravinsky's opinion that expressive devices are established by convention within an autonomous musical practice, they are established as conventions through social practice and may be related to social changes. Musical meanings are not labels arbitrarily thrust upon abstract sounds; these sounds and their meanings originate in a social process and achieve their significance within a particular social context.[90]

Thus, as the "particular social context" within which Abing is invoked continues to change, we can expect new narratives to arise from his life, from his music, and from the modes of ideology needed to perceive and explain them. Although Abing the Daoist, Abing the revolutionary, Abing the romantic, and Abing the drug addict appear, to borrow Stevenson's phrase, "a mere polity of multifarious, incongruous, and independent denizens," there was but one Abing, one from whom all these stories, and possibly many more, can be spun. The task for the reader of a musical biography, as with any other form of personal or historical narrative, is then to recognize those "plots imagined and created" by the author, those "introjected" during the construction of meaning by the reader, and those present in the life of the subject him- or herself. The telling of narrative, whether or not biographical in intent, is never a passive process of construction, dissemination, and reception; in making sense of stories, we actively *make* sense.

In chapter 6, I examine a musical parallel to the construction of biographical identities for Abing in modern China, focusing there on the ways in which his music is taught, performed, and rearranged by contemporary musicians. That analysis, however, would be premature if it preceded a consideration of Abing's music as he created and performed it himself (chapters 4 and 5). And a discussion of his solo compositions necessarily benefits from the prior review of the broader musical environment within which these solos were created, the subject of chapter 3.

## Notes

1. Robert Louis Stevenson, *Dr. Jekyll and Mr. Hyde* (London: Penguin, 1994 [1886]), 70. See also Marshall Brown, "Origins of Modernism: Musical Structures and Narrative Forms," in Steven P. Scher, ed., *Music and Text: Critical Enquiries* (Cambridge: Cambridge University Press, 1992), 75–92 (85).

2. Jean-Jacques Nattiez, "Can One Speak of Narrativity in Music?" trans. Katharine Ellis, *Journal of the Royal Musical Association* 115/2 (1990): 240–57 (249).

3. See also Henry Kingsbury, "Sociological Factors in Musicological Poetics," *Ethnomusicology* 35 (1991): 195–219.

4. Terry Eagleton, *Literary Theory* (Oxford: Blackwell, 1983), 15. This differs in an important respect from the picture of ideology outlined by Clifford Geertz, wherein ideology and scientific knowledge or analysis are deemed as different, though not unrelated enterprises in that both "make empirical claims about the condition and direction of society"; Clifford Geertz, "Ideology as a Cultural System," in David E. Apter, ed., *Ideology and Discontent* (New York: Free Press of Glencoe, 1964), 47–76 (72).

5. Hayden White, "Form, Reference, and Ideology in Musical Discourse," in Steven P. Scher, ed., *Music and Text: Critical Enquiries* (Cambridge: Cambridge University Press, 1992), 288–319 (297).

6. This biography was first published in 1952 as introductory material to transcriptions of six pieces performed by Abing; Zhao Weiqing, ed., *Yang Yinliu yinyue lunwen xuanji* (Shanghai: Shanghai wenyi chubanshe 1986), 406. My summary is based on the version issued in 1954: Zhongyang yinyue xueyuan minzu yinyue yanjiusuo, ed., *Xiazi Abing qu ji* (Shanghai: Yinyue chubanshe, 1954).

7. For example, Yang Yinliu and Cao Anhe, "Er quan ying yue de zuozhe—Abing," *Renmin yinyue*, 1977, no. 6:32–33; Yang Yinliu, "Abing qi ren qi qu," *Renmin yinyue*, 1980, no. 3:31–34; Zhongguo yishu yanjiuyuan yinyue yanjiusuo, ed., *Abing qu ji* (Beijing: Renmin yinyue chubanshe, 1983).

8. With reference to the life of Mozart, Maynard Solomon describes biography as "a contest for possession"; Maynard Solomon, "The Rochlitz Anecdotes: Issues of Authenticity in Early Mozart Biography," in Cliff Eisen, ed., *Mozart Studies* (Oxford: Clarendon Press, 1991), 1–59 (55). As exemplified in the discussion below of the source of Abing's *erhu* solos, this contest can embrace extensive and surprising facets of a musician's life and career.

9. Zhongyang, *Xiazi Abing*, 5–7.

10. See, for instance, Jiang Xianji and Sun Yunnian, "Minjian yinyuejia Abing," *Taihu*, 1979, nos. 4–5:7–15 (7); Du Yaxiong, "Abing zhuanlüe," *Nanyi xuebao*, 1981, no. 1:78–83 (78); Yu Siu Wah, "Three Er-hu Pieces from Jiangnan," (Queen's University of Belfast: M.A. Dissertation, 1985), 49.

11. Yang, "Abing qi ren," 31.

12. Yu, "Er-hu Pieces," 49.

13. According to Xu Yihe, the name of Abing's mother was actually Qin Wumei. If so, she was more likely a direct member of the Qin family, not a daughter-in-law. Xu Yihe, interview, 7 March 1992.

14. James P. McGough, "Deviant Marriage Patterns in Chinese Society," in Arthur Kleinman and Tsung-Yi Lin, eds., *Normal and Abnormal Behaviour in Chinese Culture* (Dordrecht, Holland: D. Reidel, 1981), 171–201 (194).

15. Jiang and Sun, "Minjian yinyuejia," 7; Zhongguo, *Abing qu ji*, 1; Zhongyang dianshi tai, *Xiazi Abing* (eight-part TV series, first broadcast March 1992).

16. Yang, "Abing qi ren," 31.

17. Xu Yihe, "Abing shengnian kao," *Yinyue yanjiu*, 1989, no. 3:98–99. For

description of soul tablets in the late imperial period see James Watson, "The Structure of Chinese Funerary Rites: Elementary Forms, Ritual Sequence, and the Primacy of Performance," in James L. Watson and Evelyn S. Rawski, eds., *Death Ritual in Late Imperial and Modern China* (Berkeley: University of California Press, 1988), 3–19 (13–14). Different customs appear to have prevailed in disparate parts of China: see Susan Naquin, "Funerals in North China: Uniformity and Variation," in Watson and Rawski, *Death Ritual*, 37–70; Rubie Watson, "Remembering the Dead: Graves and Politics in Southeastern China," in Watson and Rawski, *Death Ritual*, 203–27. See also Paul Chao, *Chinese Kinship* (London: Kegan Paul International, 1983), 121–22.

18. Yang, "Abing qi ren," 31.
19. Yang, "Abing qi ren," 33.
20. Arthur H. Smith, *Village Life in China* (Edinburgh: Oliphant, Anderson, and Ferrier, 1900), 251.
21. Du, "Abing zhuanlüe," 79.
22. Jiang and Sun, "Minjian yinyuejia," 7. Hua Bingjun is more commonly referred to as Hua Baiyang. According to Du Yaxiong, among other sources (many of which quote verbatim from one another without acknowledgement), this name was formally given at Hua Qinghe's request to the three-year old Abing by a sixty-fourth generation Daoist master surnamed Zhang: Du, "Abing zhuanlüe," 78. In fact, it is fairly common for children born into the same Chinese family to share a common character in their personal names; the "jun" segment of Abing and his cousin's formal names may have been no more than a generational name.
23. Zhongyang, *Xiazi Abing*, 5.
24. Cited in Shen Qia, "Abing shikao yi er ji qita," *Nanyi xuebao*, 1980, no. 2:41–47 (41).
25. Jiang and Sun, "Minjian yinyuejia," 9; Shen, "Abing shikao," 41, 42–43.
26. Shen, "Abing shikao," 41–42. But Stephen Jones, on the topic of wind bands, writes: "These shawm bands, most common of all Chinese ensembles, have little prestige . . . the musicians are often illiterate, and some are blind. They have sometimes even been called a pariah group, both before and since 1949, despite official slogans of esteem for folk artists: in practice, both the CCP and village society tend to degrade them. The traditional litany of social outcasts, 'bastards, actors, and blowing-and-drumming musicians' (*wangba, xizi, chuigu shou*) may still apply in some areas"; Stephen Jones, *Folk Music of China: Living Instrumental Traditions*, (Oxford: Clarendon Press, 1995), 82. Xu Yihe mentioned that the Daoists despised (*kanbuqi*) Abing in his later life: interview, 7 March 1992, Wuxi.
27. Shen, "Abing shikao," 43.
28. Yang and Cao, "Er quan," 32.
29. Yang, "Abing qi ren," 31.
30. See also Shen, "Abing shikao," 46.
31. Zhongyang, *Xiazi Abing*, 5. David Schak provides a description of the musical activities of Chinese beggars, including fiddle players: David C. Schak, *A Chinese Beggars' Den: Poverty and Mobility in an Underclass Community* (Pittsburgh: University of Pittsburgh Press, 1988), 51–55. Abing certainly undertook several of the beggarly activities described by Schak.

32. Jiang and Sun, "Minjian yinyuejia," 7. For a contemporary view of late-nineteenth-century Chinese educational practices, see Smith, *Village Life*, 82–84.
33. Du, "Abing zhuanlüe," 79.
34. It is possible that the attack on Abing during the Cultural Revolution was actually part of a larger campaign against Yang Yinliu. As a highly placed, middle-class music expert with a history of foreign contacts and pre-Communist government service, Yang would have been a clear target for mass aggression during this decade. For information on Yang's career, see Han Kuo-Huang, "Three Chinese Musicologists: Yang Yinliu, Yin Falu, Li Chunyi," *Ethnomusicology* 24 (1980): 483–529. A parallel is offered by contemporaneous attacks on Beethoven's symphonies, these a pretext for criticism of Deng Xiaoping, apparently very fond of Beethoven's orchestral pieces. See also Chao Hua, "Has Absolute Music No Class Character?" *Peking Review* 17, no. 9 (1974): 15–17; Mao Yu Run, "Music under Mao: Its Background and Aftermath," *Asian Music* 22, no. 2 (Spring/Summer 1991): 97–125 (117, 122).
35. Du, "Abing zhuanlüe," 78.
36. Du sees himself as one of the first Chinese ethnomusicologists, as opposed to the historians and musicologists of Yang Yinliu's generation; see Du Yaxiong, "Recent Issues in Music Research in the People's Republic of China," *Association for Chinese Music Research Newsletter* 5, no. 1 (Winter 1992): 9–12. This may explain his desire to draw attention to both his fieldwork in Wuxi and his consideration of social context. Nonetheless, Du gives no sources for the information he provides on Abing's early childhood, and the reader may wish to remain sceptical about the sources of his romantic descriptions of such events as Hua Qinghe's lulling the hungry baby to sleep, almost ninety years after the event.
37. Du, "Abing zhuanlüe," 78.
38. The association of brothels with opium smoking and, indeed, music making is not a new one in a Chinese context. For instance, scenes from a mid-nineteenth-century series of watercolors entitled *The Decline of the Opium-Smoker*, portray a scene of musical performance and female companionship; see Jonathan Spence, *The Search for Modern China* (New York: Norton, 1990), illustration p. 9 between text pp. 132–33. Notably perhaps, the instrumentalists include a fiddle player. Several Chinese musicians commented that Abing, having exhausted his inheritance, may then have earned pipes of opium by performing at brothels and smoking dens.
39. Du, "Abing zhuanlüe," 79.
40. Zhongguo, *Abing qu ji*.
41. Jiang and Sun, "Minjian yinyuejia," 9.
42. Zhongyang dianshi tai, *Xiazi Abing*.
43. Yu, "Er-hu Pieces," 50.
44. Colin P. Mackerras, *The Performing Arts in Contemporary China* (London: Routledge and Kegan Paul, 1981), 141.
45. Eagleton, *Literary Theory*, 15.
46. Shen, "Abing shikao," 41, 47. This article by E Yunwen and Liu Baoyi appears in *Trends in Propaganda*, 1979, no. 33. I have translated both the title of the article and the journal in which it appears. Unfortunately, attempts to locate a copy of this Chinese Ministry of Propaganda internal publication have proven unsuccessful.

47. Yang, "Abing qi ren," 31–32.
48. Cheng Ruxin provides a transcription of the melody to which Abing apparently sung his news items; Cheng Ruxin, "*Er quan ying yue* yindiao yuanyuan tansuo," *Nanyi xuebao*, 1980, no. 2:48–52 (51). See also fig. 3.7.
49. Jiang and Sun, "Minjian yinyuejia," 11.
50. See, for instance, Du Yaxiong, "Abing de san shou erhu qu," *Yuefu xinsheng*, 1985, no. 4:32–33 (32).
51. Zeng Xun, "*Ting song* yu 'Ting song'," in Zhang Rui et al., eds., *Mingqu xinshang yu yanzou* (Beijing: Jiefangjun wenyi chubanshe, 1987), 12–13 (12).
52. Zeng Xun, "*Ting song*," 13.
53. Kingsbury, "Sociological Factors," 217.
54. For further examination of the roles of narrative, fiction, and approaches to music history, see Leo Treitler, *Music and the Historical Imagination* (Cambridge, Mass.: Harvard University Press, 1989), 39; Leo Treitler, "The Politics of Reception: Tailoring the Present as Fulfilment of a Desired Past," *Journal of the Royal Musical Association* 116 (1991): 280–98. Cross-reference may be made to biographical work on Franz Schubert. Commenting that "Schubert is remarkable in the way in which he manages to elude his biographers," Ernst Hilmar decries creation of an overly sentimental, *Biedermeier* image for this composer and his music. Ernst Hilmar, *Franz Schubert in His Time*, trans. Reinhard G. Pauly (Portland: Amadeus Press, 1988), 8. For discussion of the flexible employment of the image of the Chinese mass-song and art-music composer Xian Xinghai in Communist China, see Richard Curt Kraus, *Pianos and Politics in China: Middle-Class Ambitions and the Struggle over Western Music* (New York: Oxford University Press, 1989), 65–69. For an exposition of the role of mythic models in the construction of biographical reality in Turkish popular music and film, see Martin Stokes, *The Arabesk Debate: Music and Musicians in Modern Turkey* (Oxford: Clarendon Press, 1992), 114–24. A musicological ideology can also be constructed to lend credence to a religious or political position; see, for instance, Peter Jeffery, *Re-Envisioning Past Musical Cultures: Ethnomusicology in the Study of Gregorian Chant* (Chicago: University of Chicago Press, 1992), 78–84.
55. Derek Scott, "Music and Sociology for the 1990s: A Changing Critical Perspective," *Musical Quarterly* 74 (1990): 385–410 (391).
56. Scott, "Sociology," 392.
57. Zhongyang, *Xiazi Abing*, 8.
58. Zhongyang, *Xiazi Abing*, 8.
59. Antoinet Schimmelpenninck, "Jiangsu Folk Song," *Chime*, no. 1 (1990): 16–29 (27–28).
60. During trips to Wuxi in December 1989 and March 1992 I visited the Second Springs, now part of a public park. As the park closes at dusk I was unable to test for myself just how implausible the reflection theory really is. It is certainly true that the pool is largely shaded during daylight hours.
61. See, for example, Yang and Cao, "Er quan," 33.
62. Zhou Chang, "Lun Hua Yanjun chuangzuo," *Renmin yinyue*, 1963, no. 12:34–35 (34).
63. Zhou, "Hua Yanjun," 35.
64. Zhu Shikuang, as quoted in Shen, "Abing shikao," 44.

65. Zhang Zhenji, "Abing wubiaoti erhu qu de yinyue neirong, sucai laiyuan ji qi yishu chuangzao," *Nanyi xuebao*, 1980, no. 2:53–64 (53).

66. Yang, "Abing qi ren," 34.

67. Cao Anhe, interview, 31 January 1992, Beijing. Zhu Shikuang, interview, 7 March 1992, Wuxi. Discussion with Zhu, at the Wuxi Cultural Bureau, was held in the presence of one of the Bureau's officials, Bao Ronggang, and also Xu Yihe, another Abing expert.

68. Zhongyang, *Xiazi Abing*, 8–9.

69. Yang, "Abing qi ren," 34.

70. Zhang, "Erhu qu," 56–57. Fig. 2.1 combines melodies from Zhongguo, *Abing qu ji*, 7 (stave A) and Zhang, "Erhu qu," 56.

71. Zhang, "Erhu qu," 57.

72. Jean-Jacques Nattiez, *Music and Discourse: Toward a Semiology of Music*, trans. Carolyn Abbate (Princeton: Princeton University Press, 1990), 10–16.

73. Zhang Zhenji, interview, 4 March 1992, Nanjing.

74. Zhongyang, *Xiazi Abing*, 8.

75. Zhongyang, *Xiazi Abing*, 9.

76. Cao Anhe, letter, 6 May 1990.

77. White, "Form," 297.

78. See Xu Yihe, "Abing de shenghuo daolu yu yishu chengjiu," *Zhongguo yinyue*, 1983, no. 4:32–34 (33).

79. Philip V. Bohlman, *The Study of Folk Music in the Modern World* (Bloomington: Indiana University Press, 1988), 121–24.

80. Jiang and Sun, "Minjian yinyuejia," 10.

81. Xu Yihe, interview, 7 March 1992, Wuxi.

82. Zhongguo, *Abing qu ji*, 4.

83. Jiang and Sun, "Minjian yinyuejia," 10.

84. Zhongguo, *Abing qu ji*, 4.

85. Jiang and Sun, "Minjian yinyuejia," 11.

86. Jiang and Sun, "Minjian yinyuejia," 12. Some Chinese sources infer that it was his activities as a fearless, outspoken revolutionary singer that singled him out for Nationalist oppression. In chapter 1, I suggested that the reason for Abing's arrest may rather have been his failure to maintain "registration" payments to the governmental Opium Suppression Bureau.

87. Xu, "Abing shengnian," 99.

88. Zhang Xinxin and Sang Ye, "Her Past," trans. Delia Davin and Cheng Lingfang, in W. J. F. Jenner and Delia Davin, eds., *Chinese Lives: An Oral History of Contemporary China* (Harmonsworth, Middlesex: Penguin, 1989), 31–38 (34). On two occasions during fieldwork in Shanghai, even though the Chinese Government's attitude toward drug taking remains one of strict disapproval, I was offered "hashish" by street salesmen in Shanghai. The suggestion that the Communist Party was immediately or lastingly able to suppress all drug trafficking may be simplistic, though this does not, of course, substantiate the rumor of Abing's overdose mentioned above. See also S. A. M. Adshead, *China in World History* (London: Macmillan, 1988), 367–68.

89. Bao Ronggang, personal communication, 6 March 1992. According to Bao, the stone was hidden by a museum attendant and replaced in the early 1980s.

90. Scott, "Sociology," 402.

*Chapter 3*

# Musical Life
# in Early-Twentieth-Century Wuxi

This chapter places Abing's personal activities as a singer and instrumentalist within the context of music making in Wuxi during the first half of the twentieth century. It begins with a discussion of the traditional Chinese musical instruments on which Abing's performance skills were especially renowned, with particular weight given to the two-stringed fiddle *erhu* and the four-stringed lute *pipa*—instruments which form the performance medium of the music studied in the following two chapters. The place of notation in traditional Chinese music making is briefly introduced, since several genres rely in part on written scores for their transmission. Following this, musical genres and styles which Abing would have known in Wuxi, ranging from Daoist music for percussion ensemble to local balladry and early popular Chinese songs, are introduced.

Naturally, Chinese music experts will already be familiar with the instruments and many of the genres described below. Some have also been documented in Western-langauge publications as well. Nonetheless, for the nonspecialist reader, an overview of Abing's musical environment is necessary at this point. Whatever the extent of the reader's experience of Chinese music, the establishment of a picture of common musical practices within early-twentieth-century China forms a useful prelude for subsequent discussion of the potential sources of Abing's recorded works, the individuality or conventionality they demonstrate, and the re-creation of these pieces in contemporary China.

## Musical Instruments

Abing is particularly celebrated in China today as an exponent of the traditional fiddle *erhu*. In fact, he was at least as well known during his own lifetime as a performer of the pear-shaped lute *pipa*, and some sources hint that he may have been a more proficient musician on this latter instrument. Accounts of his singing mention his employment of a wooden clapper *ban* as a provider of rhythmic for his voice. Additionally, Abing is known to have learnt the Daoist wind and percussion ensemble repertory, mastering both the bamboo flute *di* and various forms of drum. According to Yang Yinliu, he was also adept on the three-stringed, long-necked lute *sanxian*,[1] and it is believed that he learnt a number of other Chinese folk instruments as well. In many instances, performance techniques are semi-transferable from one instrument to another: a tolerable performer of the transverse flute *di* would know how to finger the vertical, notched flute *xiao*, even if his style of ornamentation and articulation remained unidiomatic. The principal instruments known to have been played by Abing are examined in turn below.

### Erhu

Abing is most closely identified with the fiddle for two reasons. First, this was the instrument on which he performed his most widely known composition, *Second Springs*, and for which the transcription of this piece was subsequently published. Second, and embedded at a deeper level in the Chinese consciousness, the *erhu* is in many respects the typical blindman's and beggar's instrument in China.[2] The fiddle functions for many Chinese as an emblem and reminder of Abing's blindness, his lowly social position, and his presumed miserable life, thus reinforcing the image of Abing as the archetypal, downtrodden street musician. Wei Ren and Wei Minghua describe the most elementary form of traditional *qingqu* ballad singing from the city of Yangzhou, Jiangsu Province, as follows: "When destitute *qingqu* artists sold their performances alone, they generally used only an *erhu*."[3] Several Western writers have also noted these associations, Louis Laloy commenting that, "This instrument is reserved for street singers and mendicants who scrape it mercilessly," while Georges Soulié mentions that the fiddle was used in many provinces by the blind to signal their approach.[4] Robert Marks, writing two decades later, similarly linked the affliction of blindness with the profession of music making in Beijing.[5]

Up until the 1950s, the term more normally employed for the traditional Chinese two-stringed spike fiddle was *huqin*, literally "barbarian stringed instrument," a reference to its putative introduction to China from the lands to China's north and west. This instrumental form has an extensive history in China, where friction-sounded lutes may have been played for more than 1200 years.[6] Originally, such instruments may have consisted of a board-faced tubular resonator transfixed by a bamboo neck. Silk strings were attached to the stub of neck, stretched over a bridge on the face of the resonator, and wound onto frontally inserted tuning pegs set in the upper section of the neck. The strings were excited by pressure from a strip of bamboo. Later, perhaps in the eleventh century, the horsehair bow began to replace the bamboo strip as the principal means of sounding Chinese fiddle-type instruments. Very probably, a cord loop was bound around the strings below the pegs to regulate their height from the neck and provide an even vibrating length on each string. Often, the head of the instrument was carved to resemble a dragon's head, a propitious symbol in imperial China. Many regional forms of *huqin* developed over the centuries. Local materials were used, for instance coconut shells as resonators in southern China or wood in place of bamboo neck in the north, and snakeskin became common as belly material for the instrument's soundbox. Abing's *erhu* was most likely a wooden instrument with a hexagonal resonator faced with snakeskin. These regional varieties of fiddle were widely employed in many contrasting musical genres, ranging from opera accompaniment to folk ensemble music, fortune telling, and begging.

Unlike those of Europe and most other regions of Asia, Chinese fiddles are distinguished by the practice of the permanent insertion of the bow hair between the instrument's two strings. As such, the fiddle player is obliged, through right-hand finger pressure, to direct the bow hair to press on either one string or the other.[7] In general, the two strings are tuned a perfect fifth apart, though there was until recently no convention of absolute tuning from one musician or fiddle form to another. Abing is believed to have used fairly thick strings on his fiddle,[8] giving an absolute tuning approximately equivalent to g and d', a perfect fifth below that considered standard by conservatory-trained musicians today.

In performance, the absolute pitches of the strings are redefined in relative terms depending on the mode (*diao*) of the piece in question. Thus, without retuning, the two strings may be treated as do (*shang*) and sol (*liu*) in one mode, sol (*he*) and re (*che*) in a second, and in a third la (*si*) and mi (*gong*). Fiddle players learn contrasting patterns of left-hand fingering and hand positioning for each mode. Since certain common ornamentations are associated with shifts of hand position or with the use of specific fingers, the surface style of fiddle music in different modes can differ markedly.[9] Fig. 3.1 presents schematically the standard fingerings and hand positions associated with the "do-sol" mode of *erhu* performance, assuming an absolute string tuning of g and d' (see fig. 3.1).

The two pairs of parallel vertical lines in fig. 3.1 represent the *erhu* strings. Markings show traditional patterns of left-hand fingerings and the nearest equivalent Western pitches produced thereby.[10] Folk musicians generally stopped the strings with the inside pads of their fingers, rather than the fingertips. The strings are so close that the left hand fingers stop both simultaneously, touching them lightly rather than pushing them back to the neck. Sometimes one finger is responsible for the production of two notes—connected in fig. 3.1 with a short square bracket—and, generally, positions overlap by one note or finger. Hand positions are traditionally referred to as "upper," "middle," and "lower," the term following the relative height of the left hand above the soundbox rather than the relative "height," in the Western sense, of the notes produced in each position.

Right-hand techniques in Chinese fiddle performance are primarily concerned with use of the bow. The structure of the instrument militates against the production of clearly audible pizzicato notes, although pizzicato passages are found as a kind of special effect in *erhu* music of the conservatory tradition.[11] The bow is drawn horizontally across one or other of the strings, passing closely over the top of the soundbox to ensure maximum resonance.

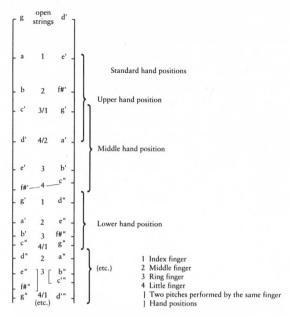

Fig. 3.1. "Do-Sol" Mode Fingerings on the *Erhu*.

The principal bowing techniques are *lagong* and *tuigong*, "pulling bow" and "pushing bow" respectively. The former describes the bowing action in which the performer's right hand moves away from the strings, the latter its approach movement. These bowing actions are generally employed alternately, with *lagong* used on stronger beats, since it is considered more forceful than the *tuigong* movement. Other bowing techniques used in traditional *erhu* music such as Abing's pieces include *changong* (tremolo) and *diangong*, a rapid shake of the bow back and forth, in effect a very short tremolo giving rise to two swift articulations.

Traditional performance posture involves sitting with the instrument resting on the left thigh, its neck supported by the palm of the left hand. However, in the past, standing and walking performances also took place, in which case the soundbox might be attached by a loop to the player's clothing. At such times, changes of left-hand position are inconvenient, and may be avoided by the expedience of transposing higher notes into the range covered by the upper position.

## Pipa

The second instrument with which Abing is particularly associated today is the four-stringed, pear-shaped lute *pipa*. This instrument has both a longer and a more elevated history in China than the spike fiddle, having been introduced from Central Asia during or before the seventh century.[12] Its name is onomatopoeic, combining early terms for hand movements across the strings and back.[13] If the fiddle was the archetypal beggar's instrument, the *pipa* was that of the professional court entertainer. Nonetheless, by the time of Abing's birth, the *pipa* had acquired a long history of use in entertainment and ritual genres outside the court.

A *pipa* is constructed from attaching a soundboard of *wutong* wood (*firmiana platanifolia*) to a hollowed-out, pear-shaped shell of varnished teak. Relative to the Western lute, its body is shallow. Four tuning pegs are inserted, two on each side of the head, which, in the past, like that of the fiddle, was often shaped to resemble an auspicious creature: a dragon head, phoenix tail, or bat.[14] Each of the four silk strings is stretched from a combined string-attachment and bridge located towards the base of the belly upwards to its own tuning peg. Lying under the strings are a series of frets (horizontal bamboo lengths glued onto the tapering upper body) and triangular blocks (projecting from the neck). The number of frets varied from one *pipa* to another, even during Abing's lifetime. A traditional instrument at the time of Abing's death had four blocks and either ten (see photo 3), twelve, or thirteen frets.[15] According to Cao Anhe, whose thirteen-fret *pipa* was borrowed by Abing for the recording session in 1950, he had some problems coping with its additional fret, and may have been more familiar with the twelve-fret variety.[16]

Given a standard tuning of A, d, e, and a, an expert player of the old-form instrument, had access to a three octave range (see fig. 3.2).[17] In addition to these notes, the skilled traditional *pipa* player produced others through the use of harmonics and by pressing a stopped string sideways, a

|        | Open Strings |       |       |       |
|--------|:---:|:---:|:---:|:---:|
|        | A | d | e | a |
| Blocks |   |   |   |   |
| 1      | B | e | f# | b |
| 2      | c | f | g | c' |
| 3      | c# | f# | g# | c#' |
| 4      | d | g | a | d' |
| Frets  |   |   |   |   |
| 1      | e | a | b | e' |
| 2      | f | a# | c' | f' |
| 3      | f# | b | c#' | f#' |
| 4      | g | c' | d' | g' |
| 5      | a | d' | e' | a' |
| 6      | b | e' | f#' | b' |
| 7      | c' | f' | g' | c" |
| 8      | c#' | f#' | g#' | c#" |
| 9      | d' | g' | a' | d" |
| 10     | e' | a' | b' | e" |
| 11     | f#' | b' | c#" | f#" |
| 12     |   |   | d" | g" |
| 13     |   |   | e" | a" |

Figure 3.2. Position of Standard Notes on a Thirteen-Fret *Pipa*.

Photo 3. A Traditional Ten-Fret *Pipa* (Horniman Museum 15.10.48/284).

technique which increases its tension, resulting in a rise in pitch. Multiple pitches are commonly plucked together, a melody played on the highest-pitched string perhaps being accompanied by open-string strums across the lower three.

Plucking techniques involve every finger of the right hand, but most frequently the thumb and index finger. Standard strokes include *tan*, a rightwards pluck with the index finger, and *tiao*, a stroke in the opposite direction with the thumb. When these strokes are repeated in quick succession the resulting tremolo is termed *gun*, literally a "roll." A second mode of producing a sustained tone is called *lun*, or "wheel." This technique involves plucking the string alternately and continuously with all the fingers in rapid and smooth succession.

Rather like the *erhu*, the *pipa* is set on the left part of the player's lap during seated performance. Most contemporary performers hold it in an almost perpendicular position, the instrument's neck and head close to the performer's left ear, though some traditional genres retain what appears to be a more ancient practice, that of holding the *pipa* at a more horizontal angle.

### Sanxian

The *sanxian*, literally "three strings," is a three-stringed lute, much used in the accompaniment of ballad singing and regional instrumental ensemble music. Details of its origin or provenance are unrecorded, definite references to instruments of this kind appearing for the first time only in fourteenth-century Chinese historical records and poems, though precursors of the instrument are believed by Chinese scholars to have been in use long before then.[18]

Similarly to the *erhu*, the *sanxian* consists of a snakeskin-faced soundbox pierced by a long, wooden neck. Again, the strings are stretched from a stub at the base of the instrument to tuning pegs inserted at the top of the neck. However, in the case of the *sanxian*, the tuning pegs are laterally inserted, and the flat neck functions as an unfretted fingerboard. The performer sounds the strings with false fingernails or, more rarely, a small plectrum above the a small bamboo bridge placed towards the base of the instrument's snakeskin belly.[19] As on the *pipa*, the right hand is used for plucking while the left hand stops the strings. Similarly to both the *erhu* and *pipa*, when the instrument is rested on the (right) thigh in playing position, the "nearest" string, that leftmost to the viewer (as in figs. 3.1 and 3.2), is the thickest and lowest pitched. The *sanxian* is tuned in various ways, but generally the outer strings are tuned an octave apart (as on the *pipa*) with the middle string a fourth or fifth above the lowest, often to the pitches G, d, and g. An experienced player can, when required, produce a range of over three octaves on the *sanxian*,[20] though two octaves is adequate for most traditional genres. Principal performance techniques include plucking both ways across the strings, strumming all three strings at once, tremolo, vibrato, and glissando.

## *Di* and *Xiao*

The primary aerophones which Abing is known to have played were the transverse bamboo flute *di*, or *dizi*, and the vertical notched flute *xiao*, also made of bamboo.[21] Both of these are ancient instruments in Chinese terms, with various different forms of side-blown flute proving popular in court ritual music, military musical ensembles, and folk genres. Due to its softer tone, the *xiao* has tended to be found more in indoor leisure and entertainment musics than in exuberant, outdoor styles.

The *di* consists of a length of bamboo perforated by a breath-hole, membrane-hole, six finger-holes, and a number of sound-holes. The membrane-hole, situated between the breath- and the uppermost finger-holes, is covered by an extremely thin but carefully creased membrane of bamboo or some other vegetable substance. The membrane adds a "buzzing" edge to the timbre of the *di*, and has been a feature of Chinese flutes since the Song Dynasty.[22] The six finger-holes were traditionally equidistantly spaced and equally sized. The index, middle, and ring fingers of both hands are used to cover the finger-holes; either hand may be placed uppermost. Generally, each end of the *di* is capped with a ring of polished cow bone, which protects the bamboo tube from accidental knocks. The tube itself is often bound at various points with thread, the thread then being coated with a thick, red varnish. Again, this is primarily a protective measure, bamboo being prone to split when major changes of humidity occur. Inside the tube, above the breath-hole, there is a cork plug; the other end of the tube is left open.

There is no fixed absolute tuning for the *di*, musicians often owning several different-sized instruments, each differently pitched, though a flute on which the lowest available note corresponds to the pitch a' is commonly employed. By lifting the fingers, broadly speaking in sequence, and overblowing, the *di* player can produce a heptatonic scale over a range of two octaves, although some music employs a narrower range. Assuming an instrument with equidistantly spaced and equal sized holes, and a bottom note of a', the primary pitches available and their usual fingerings are those shown in fig. 3.3.[23] As in the case of the other instruments so far described, the flute player rationalizes these pitches as relative modal degrees (see p. 68).

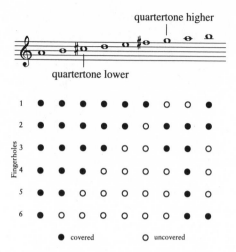

Fig. 3.3. Basic Notes and Fingerings on the Traditional *Di*.

While the *xiao* also has six finger-holes, the uppermost of these is placed on the rear of the tube and is closed by the performer's left or right thumb, depending on which hand is positioned highest. The five remaining finger-holes are covered by the fingers; possibly, if the *xiao* is a relatively long, low-pitched one, by the index and ring fingers of the upper hand and index, middle, and little fingers of the lower. Instead of blowing across a breath-hole, as on the *di*, the musician must learn to direct his breath to strike the edge of the small notch cut through the upper tip of the *xiao*.

### *Luogu* and *Ban*

*Luogu* is a collective term meaning either "gongs and drums," ensembles consisting principally of these instruments, or the music performed by these ensembles. In this instance, I use the term to refer to the various percussion instruments Abing may have learnt as a Daoist musician or observed in use at local *shifan* ("mixed") *luogu* and *shifan gu* instrumental ensemble performances. Other than a variety of gongs, cymbals, and drums, these ensembles often included wooden clappers (*ban*), and the *muyu* or struck "wooden fish." Later in the chapter I look at the structure of these ensembles and their music. At present, I deal only with the introduction of the above-listed percussion instruments.

Numerous different types of gong are used in Daoist and local music ensembles in the Jiangsu area. Several types of gong are struck individually with wooden beaters, either with the tip of a knobbed stick or the edge of a light, flat wooden strip (as also occurs in many traditional opera forms). More unusual to the Western reader is the set of tuned gongs called *yunluo*, or "cloud gongs." Ten gongs are suspended from a wooden frame approximately half a metre in height and beaten with a pair of long-handled mallets. Yang Yinliu gives their tuning and arrangement as shown in fig. 3.4.[24] As can be seen, the gongs are ordered in an ascending scale, beginning in the lower right corner. Once again, these actual pitches are referred to as relative modal degrees by traditionally trained musicians (see fig. 3.4).

The players of the other gongs do not simply strike their instruments. They learn performance techniques which specify whether the rim, midpoint, or center of the gong is to be struck, together with a special rhythmic terminology that exists in both spoken and written forms (see Notation below).

Cymbals, of which several different specifications are employed, are much like their Western counterparts, and need no further introduction here. More important are the drums used in these ensembles, which are given periodic solo sections. The two principal drums found are the medium-sized *tonggu* barrel drum and the smaller *bangu*, literally "clapper drum." The *tonggu* is a double-headed wooden drum, the top face of which is played with a pair of wooden drum sticks. Its performance requires considerable skill, in terms of not only developing an impressive speed of performance for rolls and other complex and fast rhythmic patterns but also maintaining an even attack overall. The *bangu* will be familiar to aficionadi of traditional Chinese opera styles such as Beijing opera *jingju*. The body of the drum is a squat wooden cylinder, the underside of which has been hollowed out in the shape of a truncated cone, such that beneath the center of the drum-head there is a circular opening while beneath the rim there is solid wood. The head and sides of the drum are covered by a tightly stretched piece of skin. The whole drum is suspended from a special frame. *Bangu* technique is similar to that of the *tonggu*, two short drumsticks being used to strike the drum. As on

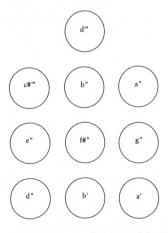

Fig. 3.4. Arrangement and Tuning of the *Yunluo*.

the *tonggu*, the drummer must be able to perform complex and demanding rhythmic patterns, exploiting the different sonorities of the drum's center, rim, and intermediate areas.[25]

The final category of percussion instruments with which Abing would have been familiar were the clappers *ban* and the wooden fish *muyu*. Clappers are employed in many genres of Chinese traditional music and consist of three shaped lengths of wood, the first two lashed together tightly and the third allowed a hand's width of play on a strong lace or cord. In performance, the instrument is gripped by the fingers of the left hand and swung such that the third segment strikes the face of the central piece. In general, one such strike announces the main beat of the music's current metrical unit. Apart from its use in the accompaniment of traditional opera and instrumental ensembles, *ban* were also adopted by street singers. *Muyu* occur in assorted sizes and are struck with a knobbed beater. Originally a Buddhist ritual instrument, the *muyu* is a rounded hollowed-out wooden block with a slot cut into it.

## Notation

At first sight it might appear perverse to include a discussion of notation in a book about a blind musician. However, as mentioned in chapter 2, Abing lost his sight only gradually, and it is not unlikely that he would have learnt to read one or more forms of traditional Chinese notation during his musical education.

The employment and importance of scores vary quite widely from one form of music making to another in the Chinese context. At the literate end of the spectrum we find the elite *qin* seven-stringed zither tradition, with its complex system of *jianzipu*, or "abbreviated character notation"; thousands of printed scores and handwritten manuscripts; and the *dapu* process, through which tabulated techniques are interpretively re-created as musical sound.[26] Towards the oral end are numerous styles in which musicians learnt to extemporize on the basis of set tunes or melodic outlines but only rarely if ever made recourse to written notation. This appears generally to have been the case in the transmission of folk songs and Cantonese *yueju* opera, for instance.[27] Somewhere between the oral and literate poles were certain styles in which notated scores were preserved by ensemble leaders and used in the training of new members but not referred to during eventual performances. Discussing such a form, Wu Ben describes the preparation of young musicians for a village music ensemble in northern China. Apprentice performers repeatedly sang back *en masse* the ensemble's repertory phrase by phrase while looking at notated melodic outlines. Although they followed these outlines, they immediately sang elaborated forms of each phrase in imitation of their master. When able to recite a whole piece, the novices began to re-create the tunes on specific wind instruments, learning the instrument

合 四 一 上 尺 工 凡 六 五 乙 仕 伬 仜

Pronunciation

*he   si   yi   shang   che   gong   fan   liu   wu   yi   shang   che   gong*

Sol-fa equivalents

sol   la   si   do   re   mi   fa   sol   la   si   do   re   mi

Fig. 3.5. *Gongche* Notation Symbols.

at the same time. Interlocking percussion parts were prepared for similarly. Each apprentice was required to attend every one of the village ensemble's performances, allowing them to absorb in more general terms the ensemble's repertory and playing techniques.[28]

It is quite plausible to imagine Abing's musical education following a similar pattern, especially as far as performing in the Daoist temple ensemble was concerned. It is also probable that he encountered music notation while learning the *pipa*, surviving solo and ensemble scores dating back to the early nineteenth century.[29] The primary form of notation, whether for Daoist music or *pipa*, was called *gongche*, or *gongchepu*, a relative pitch system which may have developed from early forms of tablature.[30] In *gongche* notation, a simple Chinese character represents each scale degree. Absolute performance pitch was fixed by some external means, or perhaps by convention. *Gongche* notation is typically written in columns, arrayed right to left across the page, following the conventions of traditional Chinese writing. Metrical and rhythmic annotations are, by Western standards, sparse: occasional dot, dash, circle, cross, or triangle marks beside note-symbols indicating the metrical beat on which the requisite pitch should be performed. Rhythmic subdivision of beats and the insertion of ornamentation were left to oral transmission or to the performer's interpretation, although the relative spacing of symbols was sometimes suggestive of a particular subdivision. In some scores, phrase endings are shown by the allocation of extra space, and the start of a new section by the beginning of a new column. The main pitch symbols used in *gongche* notation are listed in fig. 3.5, with their pronunciations and sol-fa equivalents in vertical alignment underneath.[31]

The exact conventions of *gongche* notation vary distinctly from one genre or instrumental tradition to another. *Pipa* scores, for instance, can contain technical symbols pertaining to strumming technique, while an extensive set of shorthand symbols for individual and combined percussion strokes was designed for use in *luogu* scores.

## Musical Genres

In the remainder of this chapter I provide overviews and examples of the kinds of music Abing would regularly have heard in the courtyards, tea shops, streets, and homes of Wuxi. Since to describe these musical forms in full would take far more space than is available, only a few comments are offered on salient characteristics of each form and the contexts within which its reception occurred; reference to fuller accounts, where such exist, is given as appropriate. For convenience, related musical genres are described in combination, as in the first category below, which includes regional opera, local ballad styles, and street singing music. Instrumental ensemble genres are considered next, beginning with Daoist music, then mixed wind or string and percussion styles, then Jiangnan *sizhu* and Cantonese music. Solo music for *erhu* and *pipa* is then featured, and the focus finally moves to the other new musical forms that proliferated in early-twentieth-century Chinese cities. These include radio broadcast popular songs, revolutionary and other forms of mass songs, and both live and broadcast Western music.

### Dramatic and Narrative Genres

Western research into Chinese dramatic and narrative genres has embraced a range of topics including: the history and musical structure of Beijing opera; the history of the literary opera style *kunqu*; historical, social and musical issues concerned with Cantonese opera in Hong Kong and abroad; the creation and reception of drama scripts as literature; Communist drama reform; and the description of several styles of musical storytelling, most notably Suzhou *tanci*.[32] Despite this and other work, hundreds of regional opera and narrative forms, past and present, remain entirely or almost entirely undocumented in Western languages. Regrettably, those created and performed around Wuxi during the first half of this century are, almost without exception, part of the still-submerged portion of this ethnomusicological iceberg. Fortunately, a number of general Chinese writings exist, and from these and discussion with Wuxi-based musicians it is possible to put together a sketch of opera and ballad-singing performance in early modern Wuxi.

During the nineteenth century, teahouse-theaters were the primary places in Chinese cities for seeing dramatic performances. Performances at these locations took place all year round, as did those on stages both temporary and permanent erected in or near temples and dedicated to one or another of imperial China's many deities. Town-dwellers also had the chance to enjoy the performance skills of singsong girls in brothels and drinking establishments. A few upper-class families maintained private troupes, although the hiring of a troupe for a private performance at home was by now more usual.

The whole area along the Yangzi River from Nanjing to the coast had been an important center of operatic innovation during the eighteenth century, with the elegant styles of the cities of Suzhou and Yangzhou, such as *kunqu*, acquiring national preeminence. However, during the nineteenth century, a musically simpler, more colloquial, and small-scale style known as *tanhuang* appears to have gradually superseded the older, more refined opera styles.[33] Early *tanhuang* performances required modest resources: a few actors, a handful of instrumentalists, and no staging or costuming, being delivered in temple, tea-shop, or domestic performances with a minimum of acting or movement.

Using local folk melodies and dialect, the early *tanhuang* players performed romantic, historical, and mythical tales derived from other opera
and ballad styles, in a format known as *duizixi*, or "pair drama." Two male
singers, one impersonating a woman, fleshed out the story using a mixture
of speech and song, with a simple accompaniment played perhaps on the
two-stringed fiddle. Fixed scripts and scores were generally not used, the
performers creating their own words and tunes as they progressed.

At around the start of the twentieth century, *tanhuang* began to be
brought into larger towns and cities, a development spurred both by the economic migration of peasants into the rapidly industrializing urban centers
of the Jiangsu-Shanghai area and the speedier communications permitted
by the railways. Open-air performances were already taking place in central Wuxi and the city of Changzhou in the 1900s. The best performers,
such as Yuan Renyi (d. 1943), were popular in Wuxi and also visited Shanghai, where they shared the stages of entertainment complexes such as the
Great World with the leading singers from a diverse range of other operatic
and ballad-singing styles. There too, they made gramophone recordings for
companies such as Victor (*Shengli*) and Pathé (*Baidai*).[34] The most popular themes at this time appear to have been romances, and thus, at first in
Shanghai and then elsewhere, this style of staged and costumed performance became identified as *changxi wenxi*, or Changzhou-Wuxi "civilian
drama."[35] Performance style still included a large degree of extemporiza-
tion, although gradually increasing troupe sizes meant that the leading actor
would normally talk the troupe through a synopsis of the story prior to its
performance.

Proximity to other dramatic styles gradually led to the expansion of the
musical ingredients of Wuxi *tanhuang*, with new melodies adopted from a
diverse variety of sources, including *jingju*, Suzhou *tanci* balladry, and
Hangzhou *wulinban* balladry. Additional accompaniment instruments were
added, including a percussion ensemble modeled on that found in *jingju*.
Early-twentieth-century Wuxi *tanhuang* vocal sections are understood to
have consisted, at their most basic level, of a two-part phrase structure
matching each textual couplet. Longer arias were constructed by repeating
the unit, possibly inserting a brief instrumental link passage between each
couplet. A further option was the use of *qingban* phrases, in which case the
singer's first and last phrases were heterophonically accompanied but those
between sung to the accompaniment of the clapper alone. Contrasting role-
types were distinguished through the use of different modes and vocal reg-
isters, even when all roles were sung by male performers.

The melody, or rather "aria type," considered fundamental to Wuxi *tanhuang* is known as *huang diao*. This, the equivalent of the *xipi* and *erhuang*
structures in *jingju*, is effectively a family of tunes sharing certain melodic,
modal, and structural characteristics but differing in terms of meter, rhythmic style, and melodic details.[36] The role-type acted by a singer prompts the

use of a specific vocal range, cadence patterns, and styles of ornamentation. The dramatic situation proposes selection of an appropriate metrical format within which the aria and its accompanying heterophonic instrumental parts are realized. This, in turn, provides a standard template for the insertion of syllables of song text. Textual tone level and emotional content suggest small-scale manipulations of melodic contour. In Abing's lifetime, learning to perform opera meant learning, in effect, to master such creative processes. Nonetheless, the musicians in question may very likely have seen the learning process more as one of the memorization of specific roles than structured improvisation.[37]

Fig. 3.6 gives some idea of how the opening line of the same female role *huang diao* aria might differ from one performance to another. The examples are arranged in comparative alignment to stress basic melodic affinity over specific rhythmic variance. Other than the immediately apparent difference of the opening instrumental introduction, more fully realized in the second example, both arias follow the same melodic skeleton, and the syllables of text are inserted in the same positions in each. After an instrumental introduction which establishes the mode and highlights its fifth degree (F), the vocal line begins with a decorated fall of a ninth to the fundamental of the mode (B flat) over syllables 1 and 2. A second fall takes place over syllables 3 and 4, this time terminating back on the fifth modal degree (F). Syllables 5 and 6 echo the contour of syllables 1 and 2, and syllable 7, likewise, imitates that of syllables 3 and 4. The instrumental interlude (*guomen*) leading to the second line is also included. In this case, both versions are more similar, the tremolo pattern used at the start of the first excerpt being one reserved for the opening of an aria. The interlude not only allows for stage movement but also returns to emphasis of the fundamental pitch. The line is thus structured around an alternate weighting of fundamental and fifth modal degrees, do and sol in modern Chinese musical terminology.[38]

Apart from watching the emergence of this opera style from local ballad singing, Abing was also well placed in Wuxi to hear several styles of narrative drama, such as the local style Wuxi *shuo yinguo* and Suzhou *tanci*. The former, literally "explaining karma," was performed by one or two entertainers, one of whom sang while striking a bamboo or wooden *ban*. The other played a drum, joined in some of the singing, and explained the song lyrics. In its early days, these apparently consisted principally of Buddhist material sung in street-corner, wine-shop, or tea-shop performances to lead the ignorant toward virtue. Later, popular stories, including many of those dramatized in *tanhuang,* were performed also. *Shuo yinguo* also used many of the same melodies as *tanhuang*.[39]

Suzhou *tanci*, literally "performed poetry," is better known than *shuo yinguo* both within and outside China, several major studies of it having been completed.[40] Certain schools of performance, still recognized today, have been in existence for two centuries. Like *shuo yinguo*, Suzhou *tanci*

On Spring nights every moment is precious

Heterophonic instrumental sections enclosed by square brackets
Song text identical in each example, padding syllable (*ya*, stave A only) bracketed

**Fig. 3.6.** *Changxi Tanhuang,* Two Female-Role *Huang Diao*:
**Excerpts in Comparative Alignment.**

was most often performed by one or two balladeers, but unlike *shuo yin-guo*, the *tanci* singer was normally expected to provide himself with an accompaniment on a plucked instrument, most often *pipa* or *sanxian*. Typical performance context was that of a tea shop or amateur club. The entertainer sat at a small table, speaking, singing, and playing while customers enjoyed tea, talked among themselves, and listened to the performance. Since the texts chosen were those generally shared by Chinese fiction and drama, audience members were expected to be familiar with the details and to appreciate the nuances that individual singers brought to the realization in performance of a story. Skills at improvisation, the insertion of apposite comic episodes, and the development of an individual performance style were the hallmarks of a good *tanci* performer.[41] As in most other narrative forms, a few basic tunes, perhaps specific to each school of performance, were used for many different texts, the singer learning to fit new couplets of text to a previously memorized melodic structure. *Tanci* singers also used local folk songs, similar to those used by *tanhuang* musicians, and melodies borrowed from *kunqu* opera.[42]

Many other styles of narrative music were heard in the streets and shops of Wuxi during the early twentieth century. Among these were *xiao re hun*, a style of popular farce, and *chang chun*, "singing of Spring," a spontaneous style of folk singing in which new texts were extemporized during performance over the same musical stanza to the accompaniment of drum and gong.[43] Low-brow styles such as these are less well documented in contemporary, written source-orientated Chinese research, as are the musical street calls of vendors or the songs of itinerant performing-animal trainers. More important for present purposes is an examination of the type of street singing practiced by Abing himself, the content and interpretation of which was addressed in chapter 2.

Cheng Ruxin, in the midst of an article assessing the extent of the influence of *huang diao* and other local themes on the composition of Abing's *Second Springs*, includes an example of a *qupai*, or "labelled tune" called *Ballad-Singing Tune (Wenshu diao)* apparently now found in Wuxi opera. This tune, Cheng states, "was arranged by Abing. This *qupai* has four characters per phrase, each phrase lasts five beats, and each section has four measures, which can be repeated in performance" (see fig. 3.7).[44]

An early publication of Wuxi opera music includes a transcription of another melody entitled *Ballad-Singing Tune*.[45] However, this and Cheng's example, cited above, appear so different as to be incomparable. Nonetheless, the Suzhou *tanci* scholar Peng Benle has shown me the transcription of a *xiao re hun* tune named *Singing the News (Chang xinwen)*, which is very similar in terms of textual and metrical organization, though not in melodic detail, to the tune produced by Cheng Ruxin.[46] It may be that each street singer in this area developed his own, personal form of news singing, based on the common structure of regular patterning of four-character textual lines punctuated by an additional beat marked by the clapper *ban*.[47]

### Instrumental Ensemble Genres

The streets, squares, tea shops, and gardens of early-twentieth-century Wuxi were also popular venues for the performance of a wide range of instrumental forms. Ensemble genres are examined in this section, with solo music for Abing's favored instruments, *pipa* and *erhu*, discussed separately below.

Speaking out the news, sing out the news.
News, news, from the West Gate.
News, news, everyone listen well.

*(ge)* – padding syllable

**Fig. 3.7. *Ballad-Singing Tune,* Street Music Attributed to Abing.**

Such a division is expedient for the purposes of this study, allowing the style of pieces such as Abing's recorded solo *pipa* and *erhu* performances to be more fully introduced, but, if interpreted as a general characteristic about instrumental music, would be as musicologically misleading as the drawing of a strict dividing line between ballad singing and operatic styles. Many instrumentalists playing alone simply performed solo versions of music more normally executed by a larger group in heterophonic style. The ensemble styles discussed below are Daoist ensemble music, then mixed wind or string and percussion styles, Jiangnan *sizhu* and Cantonese music.

Daoist music includes singing and chanting as well as instrumental ensemble performance; only the latter is examined here. The congregation does not take an active musical role in Daoist religious observances; instead, highly trained specialist musicians provide the music. During the period of Abing's life, many of the tunes in which Daoist groups specialized were also performed by lay musicians, if less well, and it is generally believed that Daoist repertories, instrumentation, and performance style were closely related to those of secular ensembles.[48] The ensemble in which Abing played as a Daoist would have performed principally at calendrical rituals (both religious and agricultural), funerals, and perhaps weddings. Exact instrumentation appears to have depended on the function and performance context of the music, some situations calling for an ensemble consisting primarily of wind and percussion instruments, others for a more mixed group including singers, strings, winds, and percussion. This last combination was that used in seated performances within the temple. Stephen Jones documents a contemporary Daoist wind and percussion ensemble from northern China as including the following instruments: two *sheng* or mouth organs, two *guan* or double-reed pipes, *di* as an optional replacement for the *guan*, *yunluo*, *gu*, small cymbals, and other percussion. The musicians also play ritual percussion music on sets of paired large and small cymbals, drum, frame gong, bowl, bell, and conch.[49] Chen Dacan has recorded a present-day ensemble of the seated kind from Shanghai which includes one drummer, three singers, one cymbal player, two gong players, three flute players (two *di*, one *xiao*), one *suona* (oboe) executant, one *pipa* performer, and one *erhu* player.[50] I was unable to gather information on the present situation of Daoist ensembles in Wuxi, being informed by cultural officials that there are no longer any Daoists in Wuxi.[51]

Mixed wind or string and percussion styles, whether Daoist or not, are known to have been popular in pre-modern Wuxi, and have been documented by Yang Yinliu and Cao Anhe in two books.[52] Indeed, it was due to his ongoing research into such material that Yang Yinliu and his team went to Wuxi in 1950, where they also happened to record Abing's solo pieces. In Southern Jiangsu Province, around the cities of Wuxi and Suzhou, these styles were known as *shifan gu* "mixed drum" and *shifan luogu* "mixed gong and drum" music.[53] Both styles, which appear to differ primarily in terms of most fundamental instrumentation—as their names suggest—and repertory, were frequently performed by Buddhist and Daoist musicians, who renamed the style *fanyin*, literally "Buddhist music." According to historical records, since at least the early sixteenth century, bands purveying this music were hired for weddings, funerals, and similar festive occasions.[54]

Within each style, instrumentation was considerably flexible, certain pieces being played by an ensemble of percussion instruments (those described on pp. 68–70 alone, others with additional wind and string instruments, including *erhu*, *sanxian*, *pipa*, *xiao*, *sheng*, and possibly *di* and *suona* as well.[55] During Abing's lifetime, the typical musical structure for a piece involving the whole ensemble was sectional, passages of percussion music interspersing melodic segments, each of which was a fresh *qupai*. An overall plan of moderate start, then slow tempo, moderate, and fast gave direction to the suite.

An excerpt which offers a microcosm of the suite structure as a whole is given in fig. 3.8. Heterophonic melodic passages are linked by phases of percussive activity within a gradually accelerating metric structure. Once full speed is achieved, at points of climax, both melodic and percussive instruments play together. Tonally, the excerpt is fairly stable, emphasizing principally the pitches B and F# (la and mi in contemporary Chinese theoretical parlance). The first phrase begins on B, maintaining this pitch from the cadence of the previous section, and moves up to close on F#, using a pattern of repeated offbeat notes a (pentatonic) step above F# as a cadential figure. Such a pattern underlies the second phrase also, although the melody is now repeated an octave higher and is ushered in by the insertion of an extra few notes. The third phrase opens by adopting the same falling pattern that began phrase 2, but then moves towards a cadence on B, adapting the cadential offbeat figuration to reiterate C# before falling a (heptatonic) step to B. Phrase 4 returns to the F# cadence, now heard an octave lower than in

[Section 4: Melody entitled *Waves Washing the Sand (Lang tao sha)* ]

Fig. 3.8. Two Sections from a Suite for *Shifan Gu* Ensemble.
The → symbol used in this and subsequent figures means "with gradual acceleration."

[Section 5: fast *(kuaiban),* performed without a break from the previous section]

[Section 6 follows: percussion only]

1st stave: composite melodic outline (played on *di, erhu, sanxian, pipa,* etc.)
2nd stave: combined drum patterns (played on *bangu,* etc.)

Fig. 3.8 *Concluded.*

phrase 2. The fifth phrase again employs the falling melodic incipit and is closed by a return to low B, the opening register. Section 5 is effectively a prolonged, decorated version of the cadential, repeated-note figure, extended temporarily a step higher to E before the eventual fall from C# to B takes place. As in the *tanhuang* excerpt above (fig. 3.6) there are alternate cadence points a fifth apart, although in this case they would be rationalized as la-mi rather than do-sol. This organizational principle was clearly well known to Abing, as will be seen in chapters 4 and 5, as were the ideas of juxtaposing sections of contrasting material together and of performing with a gradual acceleration.[56]

These principles are also operative in music performed by the Jiangnan *sizhu* ensemble, a style of recreational music most usually performed as a leisure activity in tea shops and at festive occasions by an assemblage of amateur musicians.[57] Effectively, this music employs the same instrumentation as the *shifan gu* and *luogu* ensembles described above, but omits the percussion, although a single player of the woodblock may keep time. Scholars such as Jin Zuli have suggested that *sizhu* developed from wind and percussion music styles indigenous to southern Jiangsu Province during the late nineteenth and early twentieth centuries. Other than at informal and domestic meetings, enthusiasts also formed clubs which met regularly at tea shops, including several in Wuxi.[58] As such, the heterophonic performance style of *sizhu* music is similar to that of the melodic sections of *luogu* music.

Variation in performance, *bianzou*, is held to be a primary characteristic of the *sizhu* aesthetic, with no two performances of any one of the so-called *ba daqu*, the core repertory of "eight great pieces," intended to be quite alike.[59] Although each instrumentalist realizes the same melodic outline simultaneously with his fellows, a different style of elaboration is used for each instrument, and performers traditionally put considerable effort into establishing a personal performance style.[60] A second noteworthy feature of the musical style of Jiangnan *sizhu* is its encouragement of spontaneous interaction, whether in terms of brief imitative passages, or of temporary manipulations of texture, dynamics, and register intended to highlight an individual musician. Abing would certainly have been familiar both with the core repertory of Jiangnan *sizhu* and with its fostering of interactive, flexible variation skills on the part of the performer.

Thirdly, *sizhu* music, together with much operatic music, provides some of the clearest demonstration of the traditional Chinese custom of reusing a single melodic outline in different metrical formats. A theme may thus be performed in a slow, metrically expanded version, in a moderate form, or in a fast, metrically condensed style. The process of expansion may be likened to the accretion of different layers of ornamental notes between metrically significant pitches. Contraction suggests the stripping away of such decorative insertions. Although Chinese musicians memorize each version of these tunes as separate melodies, they may combine several versions of each theme as a suite, proceeding from slow, through moderate, to fast varieties of the same outline. Broadly speaking, melodic elaboration decreases as tempo increases, so cumulative metrical contraction is, in a way, negated by a corresponding reduction of melodic density. The flow of each version of a tune remains audibly similar; structural strong beats, possibly known as *ban* from their marking by the clapper, simply seem closer together in metrically contracted forms. To illustrate this point, fig. 3.9 arranges two versions of the opening of the *sizhu* melody *Liuban* in parallel alignment.[61] The upper stave shows a fast, condensed version normally entitled *Old Six-Beat* (*Lao liuban*), while the lower contains a more moderately paced interpretation known as *Decorated Six-Beat* (*Hua liuban*). Other than a deviation from the standard pattern of this tune in measure 6 of *Decorated Six-Beat*, these two themes are closely alike. Almost every note of *Old Six-Beat* is preserved in *Decorated Six-Beat*, but a layer of decorative pitches has been added, one beat in *Old Six-Beat* equating two in the second tune (see fig. 3.9).[62]

A final style of traditional instrumental ensemble music known to have been popular in Wuxi during the first part of the twentieth century was *Guangdong yinyue*, Cantonese music.[63] As mentioned in chapter 1, this popularity was encouraged by the frequent programming of Cantonese pieces on local radio broadcasts, but also through live performances of Cantonese music given by local musicians.[64] Paralleling the emergence of Jiangnan *sizhu* from older, percussion-oriented rural styles, Cantonese music was developed during the first decades of the twentieth century from the instrumental music of Cantonese *yueju* opera. An early, professional use of this ensemble was in the accompaniment of silent films, but it was also performed in urban dance halls and by touring ensembles.

Early Cantonese music ensembles comprised *erxian* (two-stringed fiddle with bamboo, tubular resonator), *tiqin* (two-stringed fiddle with a

Upper stave: *Old Six-Beat*
Lower stave: *Decorated Six-Beat*

**Fig. 3.9. Fast and Moderate Forms of the *Sizhu* Melody *Six-Beat*, Opening.**

wooden-faced bamboo resonator), *sanxian*, *yueqin* (short-necked, four-stringed lute with a large, rounded wooden body), and *hengxiao* (literally "transverse flute," a form of *di*). By the mid-1920s the musician Lü Wencheng (1898–1981), until then resident in Shanghai, had introduced the Jiangnan style *erhu* to the group. He adapted the instrument by replacing its silk strings with tighter ones made of steel, resulting in a clear, high-pitched sonority. Renamed the *gaohu* "high fiddle" or *yuehu* "Cantonese fiddle," the instrument was rested on the lap in such a way that its tone was partially damped by the performer's leg, hence its tone quality was quite distinct from that of the *erhu* employed in Jiangnan *sizhu*. In further distinction to the *sizhu erhu*, but in common with Abing's *erhu* solos, early-twentieth-century *gaohu* performance made use of frequent shifts of left-hand position, covering a melodic range of more than an octave. Gradually, further instruments such as *yangqin* (hammered dulcimer), *yehu* (two-stringed fiddle with coconut shell resonator), and *xiao* were added, and the *gaohu* displaced the *erxian* and *tiqin* as leading bowed instrument. Commonly, Western instruments, such as saxophone and violin, were added as well. The usual performance style of the Cantonese music ensemble during this period was, again, heterophonic, but certain performances featured one musician as a soloist above a specially arranged ensemble accompaniment.[65]

## Solo Music for *Erhu* and *Pipa*

As mentioned above, much solo music for these traditional Chinese instruments during this period was basically ensemble music performed alone. Necessarily, this removed the interactive characteristic from styles such as Jiangnan *sizhu*, and may have encouraged the creation of more uniformly ornamented, soloistic versions of this repertory. Players of the *pipa* also had access to a firmly established solo tradition of classical pieces, many of which were notated and distributed in *gongche* notation. Finally, during the period of Abing's life, a new category of solo (and ensemble) repertory was being created, the *guoyue* "national music" style. The rise of this style is discussed in more detail in chapter 6, but it is salient to mention here the ascendancy within *guoyue* of prescriptive notation (scores carefully arranged by a specialist "composer" as instructions for musically literate performers) and the increasing importance of contemporary means of dissemination (the recital, radio broadcast, gramophone recording, Western-style instruction at schools and music conservatories). Musically, early solos written by *guoyue* composers were in fact often very similar to those performed by traditionally trained musicians, indeed many of the first national music pieces were written-out arrangements of existing traditional pieces. A vital difference in performance practice, however, is that as these pieces became fixed in notation, they became more and more identified with the authoritative figure of a single composer or arranger. While the traditional musician was expected to re-create, within well-established stylistic boundaries, a relatively novel version of an internalized musical outline each time he performed, the *guoyue* musician sought to reproduce to a high degree of fidelity the same, carefully constructed composition. Solos for each instrument are briefly examined below, beginning with classical music for *pipa*.

John Myers has provided a book-length study of a collection of *pipa* solos from nineteenth-century Wuxi, the three-volume *Pipa pu* of 1819, "the first mass-produced edition of solo music for the *pipa*."[66] Intriguingly, this collection was produced by brothers surnamed Hua, principally Hua Qiuping (1784–1859). It is not known whether one of these brothers was an ancestor of Abing (Hua Yanjun) or his *pipa*-playing father Hua Qinghe, but whether there is any family connection or not, it would not be unreasonable to imagine that Abing was familiar with this local style of *pipa* performance and its favored repertory.

Classical *pipa* music included both short, free-standing pieces and compilations of several of these into sectional suites.[67] Myers notes that many of the short pieces in the Hua collection are exactly sixty-eight *ban* (metrical strong beats) in length, but that their employment as sections within suites may be less strict. In suites, each section was commonly given a programmatic, or at least evocative, title, although these were not necessarily employed with any consistency.[68] "It is also possible that individual [short pieces] were used to generate larger pieces through repetition with variations,"[69] a technique certainly used by Abing (see chapter 5). Pieces were also generally considered either *wen*, civil, or *wu*, military, in terms of performance style, the latter category including dramatic special effects simulative of battlefield noises. As an illustration of the classical *pipa* music Abing may have studied, fig. 3.10 shows part of a civil repertory suite *Song of the Green Lotus* (*Qing lian yuefu*, hereafter *Green Lotus*).[70]

Even a cursory examination of this section, which incidentally lasts exactly sixty-eight *ban* (here transcribed as one measure each), reveals its use and variation of short themes and phrases. Compare, for example, measures 1–4 with 42–46 or, more simply, 13–14 with 15–16. In terms of cadential emphasis, the piece reveals a slightly broader tonal palette than some of those studied above, cadencing most often to D and A but also to F# (measure 21) and E (measure 33). Nonetheless, the majority of phrases end with either A (sol) or D (do). After the section shown in fig. 3.10, the suite continues with three more sections of similar length. While each section is given a contrasting, descriptive title, they share major portions of their musical material (most notably, the first twenty-eight measures of each) and are stylistically and tonally uniform, cadencing to the same pitch degree (usually do or sol) at the end of nearly every commensurate four- or eight-measure segment.

As we turn now to fiddle music, it is possible to provide an example of the kind of solo that a traditional musician might have made from a traditional ensemble piece. The piece in question is better known today as a *di* solo, *Partridges Flying* (*Zhegu fei*), originally a folk piece from Hunan

[1. Offering a Toast to the Moon *(Ju bei yao yue)* ]

Fig. 3.10. Section 1 of *Pipa* Piece *Green Lotus*.

Ornamentation omitted

**Fig. 3.10.** *Concluded.*

Province but popular also in Jiangnan.[71] Fig. 3.11 is a transcription of the opening section of an (undated but early) recording issued by Pathé (Shanghai) of *Partridges Flying* by *erhu* player Zhang Lisheng and an unnamed *ban* performer.[72] One *ban* strike is heard at the beginning of each measure. There is a moderate tempo acceleration throughout, as in some of the *sizhu* and *pipa* pieces discussed above. The note F is the equivalent of the Western tonic

**Fig. 3.11.** Opening Section of *Partridges Flying* for *Erhu.*

Original (recorded) pitch one semitone higher

Arrows show fingered glissandi

**Fig. 3.11. *Concluded.***

in this piece, with the fiddle's open strings tuned to d' and a' (la-mi mode). This provides the *erhu* player with an established set of left-hand fingering patterns and associated decorative possibilities, such as the slides between the open-string notes and the standard index-finger position for this mode (F on the lower string and C on the higher). Other than these ornamental slides, there are no changes of hand position (the high f" in measure 2 can be reached with the little finger). There are occasional adjustments of melodic contour when a note is required which is not available in this absolute tuning, for instance, c" stands in for c' (see measures 10–11 and elsewhere). Similarly, material that would necessitate change to a lower hand position may be moved down an octave (see measure 38). Transposition of material into a single, convenient hand position on the *erhu* has already been mentioned as a traditional performance technique, although it is one that Abing used relatively little in his three recorded solos (see fig. 3.11; CD track 5).

Classical pieces and solo versions of traditional instrumental music aside, Abing would have become increasing exposed to the *guoyue* repertory as the 1930s progressed. Liu Tianhua has already been mentioned as a fiddle-playing musician who took part as a youth in anti-Qing musical activities in the Jiangsu area. He was also active as a composer and instructor of both *erhu* and *pipa* at universities in Northern China during the late 1920s and early 1930s. The solos that Liu composed for these instruments were performed by him and his pupils. By the early 1930s they had been published, recorded by gramophone companies, and broadcast on the radio.[73] Liu's pieces are small in scale and, despite his interest in Western music, are in many respects traditional—they have descriptive titles and sectional structure, and rely primarily on established modes and fingering patterns.[74] Although we cannot know whether Abing heard any of Liu's pieces, Liu Tianhua was merely the best known of a group of performer-composers who were creating new music for instruments such as the *erhu*. His pupils Jiang Fengzhi (1908–86), Chen Zhenduo, and Lu Xiutang (1911–66) were all influential during the 1930s and 1940s, and it is not improbable that Abing would have encountered at least some of their arrangements and compositions, either through music-loving friends who were able to read and perform from the newly printed scores or by way of radio broadcasts.

### New Musical Forms

Some of the new musical forms Abing would have encountered in Wuxi during the first half of the twentieth century have already been discussed or referred to: Wuxi opera, Cantonese instrumental music, and the rise of the conservatory tradition, for example. Other new forms which remain to be examined include the mass song movement, early Chinese popular songs and cinema music, and the increasing presence of Western musical instruments and forms in Chinese cities. Liang Mingyue evokes something of the flavor of the early decades of the twentieth century as follows:

> The introduction of democratic ideals leading to the establishment of the Republic of China initiated the first stage of Westernization in China. With it came brass buttoned uniforms, ties and hats, ballroom dancing, wide-scale public education, Western-style music conservatories and universities, all new and fresh to the Chinese scene. Talented musicians were going abroad to Japan, Europe and the United States for Western music education.[75]

The establishment of Western-style music education and the adoption of new modes of social and political organization functioned together to promote a new genre of mass songs, although initial moves in this direction can be traced to the activities of nineteenth-century missionaries.[76] Mass songs were used in several contexts. On the one hand, there were those composed for use in schools, which "reflected the times, and were full of revolutionary fervor, propaganda for democracy, freedom and even women's liberation."[77] Outside the classroom, there were also songs designed for use at political mass meetings and protest marches, as well as others used for training soldiers. Musically, many of these songs combined aspects of Chinese and nineteenth-century Western musical styles, with predominantly pentatonic themes (some of which were adapted from folk song tunes) set to simple, functional harmonies. Other songs were adopted from abroad, the Communists translating a number of Russian revolutionary songs for reuse in China.[78] Strophic structures were preferred, and marchlike meter favored.[79] In performance, voices sang in unison or octaves, with accompaniment, if any, provided by instruments such as the accordion, harmonium, or piano.

Many of the composers of mass songs were also active in the fields of Chinese popular and film music. According to Andrew Jones, film and popular music are not to be separated, cinema serving "as the principal medium for the dissemination of popular music" from the 1920s until the impact of television and the audiocassette player during the 1980s.[80] 1920s popular songs, many of which were intended for use in Shanghai's dynamic movie industry, were quickly issued on record by the city's gramophone companies. A principal composer was Li Jinhui (1891–1967), whose "music was essentially a kind of sinified jazz which fused Western instrumentation and harmony with largely pentatonic Chinese folk melodies."[81] In general, lyrics were romantic in content, and vocal styles lyrical, but among these songs a proportion presented a pronounced socialist ideological content, by means of which leftwing composers such as Nie Er sought to mobilize and heighten social consciousness.[82] A typical song of the lyrical kind is *Full Moon and Blooming Flowers* (*Yueyuan huahao*), a composition by Yan Hua performed by actress-singer Zhou Xuan (1918?–57), a member of Li Jinhui's troupe (see fig. 3.12).[83]

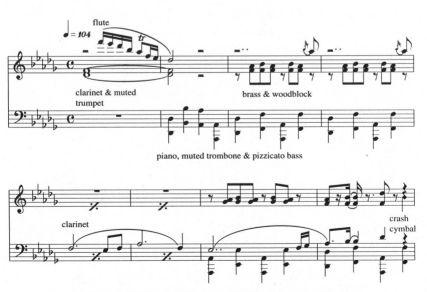

Fig. 3.12. *Full Moon and Blooming Flowers,* 1930s Popular Song by Yan Hua (excerpt, melodic highlights).

Translation:

> Floating clouds disperse,
> And the bright moon shines down on folk arriving,
> United in happiness, this day more than any other.

### Fig. 3.12. *Concluded.*

During the years of war between Japan and the various Chinese factions (warlord troops, Nationalists, and Communists), each side used song to further their own image building and assail their foes. There can be little doubt that Abing became familiar with a great deal of this music: strains warbled by school pupils (such as Abing's adopted children and grandchildren), protest songs sung at public meetings, politically aware anthems performed by rival social groups, and love songs broadcast over the radio or played on the gramophone.

Such vocal styles are all redolent of Western influence, and Abing is also likely to have encountered certain Western forms of instrumental music, most notably, in this violent period, music for military and brass bands. Jiang

Tianyi's contemporaneous collection of *huqin* music contains several pieces, described as "foreign drills" (*yang cao*), which appear to be bugle-type tonic-mediant-dominant fanfares.[84] Pieces for other ensembles, both popular and classical, were broadcast on the radio and it is probable that some live Western music performance also took place in Wuxi in the latter part of Abing's life, although his access to or interest in such events cannot be ascertained.[85] Judging from his recorded performances, with the exception of the apparent quotation from military band music in *Listening to the Pines* mentioned in chapter 2 and returned to in chapter 4, Abing was little affected by whatever Western music he may have heard.

## Conclusion

Abing lived within a diverse and vibrant musical environment. Old and new forms competed for the hearts, minds, and cash of musical listeners. Traditional modes of musical organization and transmission overlapped with newer ones. Conventional Chinese instruments, instrumental performance techniques, and musical expectations came into increasing contact with those of the West, whether through the medium of Western inspired *guoyue* reformers and the commercially motivated composers of new popular musical styles or more directly in the shape of Western musical instruments, ensembles, and recordings. The rise of the Jiangnan *sizhu* leisure style, the impact of Cantonese and Western instrumental musics, the creation of a professional *guoyue* national style, the expansion of local balladry into regional opera, the introduction of recorded and broadcast sound, and the adoption of mass song as a means of exerting social pressure provide a musical parallel to the turbulent but also innovative social and political history through which Abing lived.

Abing's personal musical activities took place within the plethora of musical creation, transmission, and reception characteristic of a rapidly growing and well-connected modern city. Nonetheless, with certain notable exceptions, Abing retained a conservative style in his own music making. Reasons why this should have been so are incorporated into the discussion of Abing's six recorded solos, which occupies the following two chapters.

## Notes

1. Zhongyang yinyue xueyuan minzu yinyue, ed., *Xiazi Abing qu ji* (Shanghai: Yinyue chubanshe, 1954), 7.

2. Charles Hamm reports on his own interest in a blind street singer cum *erhu* player whom he encountered in the city of Xi'an during 1988; Charles Hamm, "Music and Radio in the People's Republic of China," *Asian Music* 22, no. 2 (Spring/Summer 1991): 1–42 (38). Hamm's translator's comment, "You've come all the way from America to hear that?," is suggestive of the low regard in which musical beggars are held.

3. Wei Ren and Wei Minghua, *Yangzhou qingqu* (Shanghai: Shanghai wenyi chubanshe, 1985), 27.

4. Louis Laloy, *La Musique chinoise* (Paris: Laurens, 1909), 78; Georges Soulié de Morant, *La Musique en Chine* (Paris: Ernest Leroux, 1911), 28.

5. Robert W. Marks, "The Music and Musical Instruments of Ancient China," *Musical Quarterly* 18 (1932): 593–607 (606).

6. The earliest reference to such an instrument appears to be that in a poem by Meng Haoren (689–740); see Terence M. Liu, "The Development of the Chinese Two-Stringed Lute *Erhu* Following the New Culture Movement (c.1915–1985)," (Kent State University: Ph.D. Dissertation, 1988), 29, 226. For an account of the history, construction, and proliferation of the fiddle form in China, see Jonathan P. J. Stock, "A Historical Account of the Chinese Two-Stringed Fiddle *Erhu*," *Galpin Society Journal* 46 (1993): 83–113.

7. The impact of this and other constructional givens on fiddle performance technique, and hence musical style, is analyzed more fully in Jonathan P. J. Stock, "An Ethnomusicological Perspective on Musical Style, With Reference to Music for Chinese Two-Stringed Fiddles," *Journal of the Royal Musical Association* 118/2 (1993): 276–99.

8. Zhongyang, *Xiazi Abing*, 7–8.

9. The most commonly employed surface decorations include short slides *huayin*, trills *chanyin*, and grace notes (variously named). Decorative additions to pieces for *erhu* in different modes are analyzed in Stock, "Ethnomusicological Perspective," 285–89. The point is not pursued here, since all three of Abing's surviving fiddle solos share the same mode.

10. As in the case of the other instruments discussed below, intonation did not entirely accord to Western equal temperament.

11. A general introduction to this repertory, and analysis of representative pieces, is provided in Jonathan P. J. Stock, "Contemporary Recital Solos for the Chinese Two-Stringed Fiddle *Erhu*," *British Journal of Ethnomusicology* 1 (1992): 55–88.

12. On the origin of this instrument, see Laurence E. R. Picken, "The Origin of the Short Lute," *Galpin Society Journal* 8 (1955): 32–42. For an introduction to *pipa* notation and performance techniques, see Don Addison, "Elements of Style in Performing the Chinese P'i-P'a," *Selected Reports in Ethnomusicology* 2, no. 1 (1974): 119–39. Wu Ben provides a comparative analysis of the social context of the *pipa*, both at different stages during its history and in the hands of differing social groups; Wu Ben, "Pipa yinyue yu qi shehui beijing," *Zhongguo yinyuexue*, 1992, no. 2:57–67. A detailed study of an early-nineteenth-century printed collection of *pipa* music, and a more detailed historical account of the *pipa*, may be found in John E. Myers, *The Way of the Pipa: Structure and Imagery in Chinese Lute Music* (Kent, Ohio: Kent State University Press, 1992).

13. Early illustrations of the Chinese *pipa* show it sounded by a large, hand-held plectrum. Gradually, the plectrum was replaced by false fingernails of bone, horn, or tortoiseshell, tied or taped on by the performer prior to performance.

14. Lui Tsun-Yuen, "Pipa," in Stanley Sadie, ed., *New Grove Dictionary of Musical Instruments* (London: Macmillan, 1984), 3:115.

15. Liu Dongsheng et al., eds., *Zhongguo yueqi tu zhi* (Beijing: Qinggongye chubanshe, 1987), 219.

16. Cao Anhe, letter, 6 May 1990. This additional fret resulted from the desire of conservatory musicians to construct an equal-tempered instrument. On a twelve-fret *pipa* the seventh fret was set three-quarters of a tone between (on the lowest string) those for the pitches b and d'. In the same sector on a thirteen-fret instrument, however, there were two frets (nos. 7 and 8 in fig. 3.2), each a semitone apart. The penultimate fret of the twelve-fret *pipa* was similarly adjusted in position, its equivalent on the thirteen-fret instrument (fret 12 in fig. 3.2) producing pitches a quarter tone lower than before. See also Wu, "Pipa yinyue," 61. For a photograph of a twelve-fret *pipa* in playing position, see Myers, *Pipa*, 27. A ten-fret instrument is akin to the twelve-fret model, lacking its upper two frets.

17. Fig. 3.2 is derived, with modifications, from Zhongguo yishu yanjiuyuan yinyue yanjiusuo, ed., *Abing qu ji* (Beijing: Renmin yinyue chubanshe, 1983), 16.

18. Yang Yinliu, *Zhongguo gudai yinyue shi gao* (Beijing: Renmin yinyue chubanshe, 1981), 725–26. A photograph of a tomb carving believed to date from the late twelfth century showing instruments of this shape is reproduced in Liu, *Zhongguo yueqi*, 213.

19. An excellent photograph of a street singer with *sanxian* appears in Liang Mingyue, *Music of the Billion: An Introduction to Chinese Musical Culture* (New York: Heinrichshofen, 1985), Photo 7, between 154–55.

20. Tan Longjian, *Sanxian yanzou yishu* (Beijing: Renmin yinyue chubanshe, 1989), 2–3.

21. For further detail on the *di*, see Alan R. Thrasher, "The Transverse Flute in Chinese Traditional Music," *Asian Music* 10, no. 1 (Winter 1978): 92–114.

22. Thrasher, "Transverse Flute," 93.

23. Fig. 3.3 is adapted from Yang Yinliu and Cao Anhe, *Sunan shifan gu qu: datao qiyue hezouqu* (Beijing: Renmin yinyue chubanshe, 1982), 11.

24. Yang and Cao, *Sunan*, 10.

25. Yang and Cao, *Sunan*, 7–9.

26. See Bell Yung, "*Da Pu*: The Recreative Process for the Music of the Seven-String Zither," in Anne Dhu Shapiro, ed., *Music and Context: Essays in Honor of John Ward* (Cambridge: Harvard University Press, 1985), 370–84.

27. In each of these styles, texts were sometimes written down. Cantonese (and other traditional) opera scores could also include the titles of the preexistent tunes and percussion patterns to which each segment of text or stage movement was to be performed; see Bell Yung, *Cantonese Opera: Performance as Creative Process* (Cambridge: Cambridge University Press, 1989), 14.

28. Wu Ben, "How Music Is Transmitted in a Typical Chinese Folk Musical Group," *I.T.C.M. UK Chapter Bulletin* 21 (1988): 5–12 (9–11). For further information on northern village ensembles, see Stephen Jones and Xue Yibing, "The Music Associations of Hebei Province, China: A Preliminary Report," *Ethnomusicology* 35 (1991): 1–29; Stephen Jones, *Folk Music of China: Living Instrumental Traditions* (Oxford: Clarendon Press, 1995), 157–245.

29. Liu, *Zhongguo yueqi*, 173, 176.

30. *Gong* and *che* are the pronunciations of two of the characters used in this form of notation. *Pu* is translated in this context as "notation," but in other instances can mean "chart," "score," or "manual."

31. For more on *gongche* notation, see Walter Kaufmann, *Musical Notations of the*

*Orient: Notational Systems of East, South, and Central Asia* (Bloomington: Indiana University Press, 1967), 69–106.

32. A bibliography of representative publications in Chinese and Western languages is given by Alan R. Thrasher, "China," in Helen Myers, ed., *Ethnomusicology: Historical and Regional Studies* (London: Macmillan, 1993), 311–44 (341–43). Recent studies on operatic music include, on Beijing opera, Elizabeth Wichmann, *Listening to Theatre: The Aural Dimension of Beijing Opera*, (Honolulu: University of Hawaii Press, 1991), and, on Cantonese opera, Yung, *Cantonese Opera*. An overview of narrative music is provided by Tsao Pen-yeh, "Structural Elements in the Music of Chinese Story-Telling," *Asian Music* 20, no. 2 (Spring/Summer 1989): 129–51; see also Helen Rees, "An Annotated Bibliography on Shuochang (Narrative Singing)," *Chime*, no. 3 (Spring 1991): 88–96. Chinese music scholars habitually separate ballad-singing forms from acted and sung drama, but it may be more rewarding in future large-scale research projects to imagine each form of Chinese musical narrative as variously positioned on the following continua: speech-song, unaccompanied-instrumentally supported, static-fully staged, solo-group, rural-urban, regional-national, sacred-secular, traditional-contemporary (stories, costumes, musical style), etc. Such an approach would emphasize similarities between these forms, and quite possibly reveal more about the underlying characteristics of Chinese musical culture than the compartmentalized study of individual genres.

33. Chinese authorities differ in their explanation of the adoption of the term *tanhuang*, the etymology of which is complicated by the possibility of its having arisen from a regional pronunciation. For detailed discussions of this point, see Zhu Jianming, "Tanhuang kao lun," *Xiqu yinyue ziliao huibian* 4 (1987): 13–16; Chen Yibing, "Xiju de xingcheng he fazhan," in Jin Yi et al., eds., *Xiju chuantong jumu kao lüe* (Shanghai: Shanghai wenyi chubanshe, 1989), 9–20 (9–13). This historical overview is largely derived from interviews in Wuxi with Qian Huirong, Bao Ronggang (6 March 1992), and in Shanghai with Zhou Liangcai and Peng Benle (3 June 1993). See also Colin P. Mackerras, *The Chinese Theatre in Modern Times: From 1840 to the Present Day*, (London: Thames and Hudson, 1975), 100–111; Zhou Liangcai, "Tanhuangxi yu shidai de guanxi," *Shanghai xiqu shiliao huicui* 2 (1986): 9–15; Wang Can, "Xiju ji 'Shuang tui mo'," in Dongfang yinyuehui, ed., *Zhongguo minzu yinyue da xi—xiqu yinyue juan* (Shanghai: Shanghai yinyue chubanshe, 1989), 301–4; Zheng Hua, "Xiju," in Zhang Geng et al., eds., *Zhongguo dabaikequanshu: xiqu, quyi* (Beijing: Zhongguo dabaikequanshu chubanshe, 1983), 425.

34. Useful contextual flavor on the life of a successful ballad singer in the first half of the twentieth century is provided by Rulan Chao Pian, translator, "My Life as a Drum Singer: The Autobiography of Jang Tsueyfenq (As Told to Liou Fang)," *Chinoperl Papers*, no. 13 (1984–85): 7–106. More details of Yuan Renyi and the development of Wuxi *tanhuang* in Shanghai are given by Qian Huirong, "Shanghai—xiju de faxiang di," *Shanghai xiqu shiliao huicui* 3 (1987): 43–44.

35. Traditionally, Chinese theater recognizes two principal categories of drama, civil (*wen*) and military (*wu*), a duality also found in the role-types important in these dramas and in the repertory of such instruments as the *pipa*. For further information on role-types (young scholar, military male, etc.), see Mackerras, *Chinese Theatre*, 23–25. Changzhou *tanhuang* and Wuxi *tanhuang* were technically

separate, though closely related, until their combination in Shanghai. In 1952, the name *changxi wenxi* was further abbreviated to *xiju*, Wuxi opera, the term in common use today.

36. Yung, *Cantonese Opera*, 67. For further on use of the term "aria type," see also Rulan Chao Pian, "Text Setting with the *Shipyi* Animated Aria," in Laurence Berman, ed., *Words and Music: The Scholar's View* (Cambridge: Harvard University Press, 1972), 237–70.

37. I have not been able to interview any old Wuxi opera singers, but discussion with Shao Binsun (11 April 1992), Zhao Chunfang, and Yang Feifei (both 10 June 1993)—performers of the closely related style (now known as) *huju*, or Shanghai opera, in the 1930s and 1940s—suggests that singers of this generation tend to understand the term "improvisation" (*jixing*) in terms of relatively major experimentation with and refinement of pre-memorized melodic ideas.

38. Stave A of fig. 3.6 is derived from Zheng Hua and Cheng Ruxin, *Xiju qudiao jieshao* (Nanjing: Jiangsu wenyi chubanshe, 1954), 54. Stave B is transposed down a tone from Huadong wenhua bu yishu shiye guanli, ed., *Huadong difang xiqu jieshao* (Shanghai: Xin wenyi chubanshe, 1952), 113. Unfortunately, neither of these cipher notation sources name the singer whose performance they show. However, a transcription identical to stave A and attributed to the singer Wang Cuifeng is published in Zhongguo yinyuejia xiehui, ed., *Jiangsu minjian yinyue xuanji* (Nanjing: Jiangsu wenyi chubanshe, 1959), 323.

39. After 1949, the name of this narrative genre was altered to the less "superstitious" Wuxi *pingqu*. *Ping*, to comment or narrate, refers in this context to the spoken ingredient of the genre, while *qu*, or "piece," indicates its musical element. Instrumental accompaniment (commonly *erhu* and *pipa*) has since been added, and percussion interludes replaced with instrumental ones; see Shanghai yishu yanjiusuo and Zhongguo xijujia xiehui Shanghai fenhui, eds., *Zhongguo xiqu quyi cidian* ( Shanghai: Shanghai cishu chubanshe, 1981), 694; Shen Yuan, "Wuxi pingqu," in Zhang et al., *Zhongguo dabaikequanshu*, 416.

40. See, for example, Tsao Pen-yeh, *The Music of Su-chou T'an-tz'u: A Study of the Structural Elements of the Chinese Southern Singing-Narrative* (Hong Kong: Chinese University Press, 1988).

41. Tsao, "Structural Elements," 132.

42. Tsao, "Structural Elements," 140–41.

43. Peng Benle, personal communication, 10 June 1993, Shanghai.

44. Cheng Ruxin, "*Er quan ying yue* yindiao yuanyuan tansuo," *Nanyi xuebao*, 1980, no. 2: 48–52 (51, adapted).

45. Huadong, *Huadong difang xiqu*, 111.

46. Another version, related to that of Cheng Ruxin, is given by Qian Tiemin, who compares it to a Daoist song. Qian Tiemin, "Abing yu daojiao," *Zhongguo yinyuexue*, 1994, no. 4: 51–62 (56).

47. Circumstantial support for this suggestion may come from the case of three retired fishermen recorded and interviewed on 6 June 1990 at Xijiagang, Chongming Island, Shanghai. Each man performed "his own version" of the *dian shui* depth-measuring work song. Their sung calls shared several characteristics: general rhythmic organization, basic textual content, a falling melodic contour for almost every phrase, and a slide down at phrase ends. Details of text, melodic ornamentation, and extent and style of glissando were more individually interpreted.

I am grateful to Frank Kouwenhoven and Antoinet Schimmelpenninck for invit-
ing me to join them on their field trip to Chongming.

48. Chen Dacan, "Daojiao yinyue," in Lü Ji et al., eds., *Zhongguo dabaikequanshu: yinyue, wudao* (Beijing: Zhongguo dabaikequanshu chubanshe, 1989),
113; Jones and Xue, "Associations," 6.

49. Stephen Jones et al., "Field Notes, 1991: Funeral Music in Shanxi," *Chime*, no.
5 (Spring 1992): 4–28 (8, 11–13).

50. Chen Dacan, *Chinese Taoist Music* (Shanghai: China Record Co., 1986),
16–18. [Booklet accompanying music cassette HL–508.]

51. These same officials were in all other respects extremely helpful and open, particularly as concerned Wuxi opera and Abing biography. The subject of Daoism
was clearly a sensitive one at that time (Spring 1992), and I did not wish to press
the point. Several sources on Daoist music have already been mentioned. Further
publications include Stephen Jones, "Daoism and Instrumental Music of Jiangsu," *Chime*, no. 8 (Spring 1995): 117–46; Stephen Jones, *Music of China*. See
also the overview and listing of Daoist ritual music research by Tsao Pen-yeh
and Shi Xinmin, "Current Research of Taoist Ritual Music in Mainland China
and Hong Kong," *Yearbook for Traditional Music* 24 (1992): 118–25.

52. Yang Yinliu, *Shifan luogu* (Beijing: Renmin yinyue chubanshe, 1980); Yang and
Cao, *Sunan*.

53. A brief English-language introduction to this subject is given by Peng Xiuwen,
"Chuida Music of Sunan," trans. and introduced by Phoebe Hsu, *Asian Music*
13, no. 2 (Spring/Summer 1985): 31–38. Discussion and illustration of a sub-
category, *shifan qingluogu*, is provided by Liang, *Music of the Billion*, 223–29.

54. Zhongguo yishu yanjiuyuan yinyue yanjiusuo, ed., *Zhongguo yinyue cidian*
(Beijing: Renmin yinyue chubanshe, 1985), 354–55.

55. Yang, *Shifan luogu*, 3.

56. Fig. 3.8 is adapted from Yang and Cao, *Sunan*, 43–44.

57. Important articles in the English language include Alan R. Thrasher, "The
Melodic Structure of Jiangnan Sizhu," *Ethnomusicology* 29 (1985): 237–63; J.
Lawrence Witzleben, "*Jiangnan Sizhu* Music Clubs in Shanghai: Context, Concept and Identity," *Ethnomusicology* 31 (1987): 240–60; Alan R. Thrasher,
"Structural Continuity in Chinese Sizhu: The Baban Model," *Asian Music* 20,
no. 2 (Spring/Summer 1989): 67–106; Alan R. Thrasher, "Bianzou—Performance Variation Techniques in Jiangnan Sizhu," *Chime*, no. 6 (Spring 1993):
4–20. A valuable (Chinese-language) historical survey is that of Jin Zuli and
Xu Ziren, "Shanghai minjian sizhu yinyue shi," *Zhongguo yinyue*, 1983, no.3:
28–31. Witzleben has also contributed a book on this tradition: *"Silk and Bamboo" Music in Shanghai: The Jiangnan Sizhu Instrumental Ensemble Tradition*
(Kent, Ohio: Kent State University Press, 1995).

58. Jin and Xu, "Minjian sizhu," 28, 30.

59. On the subject of the "eight great pieces," the Chinese have a love for numer-
ical classifications—one thinks perhaps of the "Five Dynasties" or the "Four
Modernizations." However, according to Gao Houyong, although the notion
of "eight great pieces" is widely accepted, *sizhu* musicians are not entirely in
agreement on exactly which pieces form the central set of eight; Gao Houyong,
"The Unique Chinese Stringed and Woodwind Ensemble of the South of the
Changjiang River," (Unpublished paper distributed at the International Seminar

on Chinese Music, Kingston-on-Thames, UK, April 1988), 6–7. Alan Thrasher has further demonstrated that seven of the eight pieces most commonly selected are actually derived from three basic pieces, and that two of these three are themselves related. Thrasher, "Melodic Structure," 256–58.

60. Melodic decoration in Jiangnan *sizhu* fiddle music is closely related to modal fingerings patterns and changes of hand position. See Jonathan P. J. Stock, "Ethnomusicological Perspective."

61. Fig. 3.9 is assembled from *gongche* notations contained in Jiang Tianyi, *Xiaodiao gongchepu* (Shanghai: Shanghai shijie shuju, 1922), 5.

62. Both versions are transnotations of *gongchepu* scores in which exact rhythmic subdivision of beats is unspecified. In performance, both would be fleshed out with further melodic decorations. For a comparison of three versions of this theme, see Stock, "Ethnomusicological Perspective," 289–92. See also Thrasher, "Melodic Structure," "Structural Continuity"; Huang Jinpei, "Concerning the Variants of '*Lao lioban*'," translated by Alan R. Thrasher, *Asian Music* 13, no. 2 (Spring/Summer 1982): 19–31; Marnix St. J. Wells, "Rhythm and Phrasing in Chinese Tune-Title Lyrics; Old Eight-Beat and Its 3–2–3 Meter," *Asian Music* 23, no. 1 (Winter 1991): 119–83.

63. A useful account of Cantonese music is included in Jones, *Music of China*, 344–61.

64. Wang Yi, an *erhu* player born in 1919 in Anhui Province, mentioned that among the first music he learnt on the fiddle in the late 1920s and early 1930s were tunes from the Cantonese music repertory which he heard in Shanghai (Wang Yi, personal communication, 4 May 1990). Zhang Zhenji states that Abing studied Cantonese pieces from the musician Li Songshou; Zhang Zhenji, "Abing wubiaoti erhu qu de yinyue neirong, sucai laiyuan ji qi yishu chuangzao," *Nanyi xuebao*, 1980, no. 2:53–64 (55).

65. Jones, *Music of China*, 354.

66. Myers, *Pipa*, 1.

67. Yang Yinliu and Cao Anhe, *Qing lian yuefu* (Beijing: Yinyue chubanshe, 1956), 5.

68. Han Kuo-Huang, "The Chinese Concept of Program Music," *Asian Music* 10, no. 1 (Winter 1978): 17–38 (21–24).

69. Myers, *Pipa*, 40.

70. This composition is found both in the Hua collection and also in a set edited by the *pipa* player Li Fangyuan and issued towards the start of Abing's lifetime (1895). The latter edition is the source (by way of Yang and Cao, *Qing lian*, 9–10) of fig. 3.10. See also Han, "Progam Music," 22–23; Myers, *Pipa*, 21.

71. Zhongguo, *Zhongguo yinyue cidian*, 499.

72. Pathé (*Baidai*) 33937: undated 78rpm recording held in the Shanghai Library Recording Archive, the curators of which kindly made available a cassette copy from which transcription has been made. Recordings with the serial numbers 34498, 34667, 34672, and 34848 (all songs by Nie Er) were issued between 1933 and May 1935, so Zhang's recording likely predates these.

73. Zhongguo, *Zhongguo yinyue cidian*, 26; Yu Siu Wah, "Three Er-hu Pieces from Jiangnan" (Queen's University of Belfast: M.A. Dissertation, 1985), 30.

74. Stock, "Recital Solos," 61. Liu Tianhua's *erhu* composition *Groaning in Sickness* (*Bing zhong yin*) is examined in Yu, "Er-hu Pieces," 33–44, and also in

Liu, "Two-Stringed Lute," 196–201; the piece *Reciting During Leisure (Xian ju yin)* is partially analyzed in Stock, "Recital Solos," 61–64; and *Festival Night Canzonetta (Chu ye xiaochang)* is studied in Stock, "Ethnomusicological Perspective," 285–87.

75. Liang, *Music of the Billion,* 136.
76. Peter Manuel, *Popular Musics of the Non-Western World: An Introductory Survey* (New York: Oxford University Press, 1988), 222.
77. Liang, *Music of the Billion,* 139. Examples of mass songs are also given by Arnold Perris, "Music as Propaganda: Art at the Command of Doctrine in the P.R.C.," *Ethnomusicology* 27 (1983): 1–28 (10), and, most plentifully, in the key source on this subject, Isabel K. F. Wong, "*Geming Gequ*: Songs for the Education of the Masses," in Bonnie S. McDougall, ed., *Popular Chinese Literature and Performing Arts in the People's Republic of China 1949–1979* (Berkeley: University of California Press, 1984), 112–43. See also Richard Curt Kraus, *Pianos and Politics in China: Middle-Class Ambitions and the Struggle over Western Music* (New York: Oxford University Press, 1989), 48–59.
78. Wong. "*Geming Gequ*," 122.
79. Hamm, "Music and Radio," 9.
80. Andrew F. Jones, *Like a Knife: Ideology and Genre in Contemporary Chinese Popular Music,* Cornell East Asia Series 57 (New York: Cornell University, 1992), 8.
81. Jones, *Like a Knife,* 11. Peter Manuel quotes from a 1934 critique of Li Jinhui, in which Li is described as "vulgar and depraved beyond the hope of redemption . . . . [but] as popular as ever"; Manuel, *Popular Musics,* 224.
82. Jones, *Like a Knife,* 10–12.
83. The song title *Yueyuan huahao* is an inverted form of a traditional Chinese adage, *huahao-yueyuan,* meaning perfect conjugal bliss. Transcription has been made from China Record Co. & Hong Kong Pathé Record Co. cassette CL–51 (Shanghai, 1993), a remastered reissue of Pathé's 1930s original. Yi Ren, in her biographical sketch of Zhou Xuan, gives Zhou's date of birth as 1920: Yi Ren, "Zhongguo getan yi ke shanliang de mingxing—ji 'jin sangzi' Zhou Xuan," in Yi Ren, ed., *Youmei de xuanlü piaoxiang de ge—Jiangsu lidai yinyuejia* (Nanjing: Jiangsu wenshi ziliao, 1992) 277–80 (277). For further on the reintroduction of this repertory to present day China, see Jonathan P. J. Stock, "Reconsidering the Past: Zhou Xuan and the Rehabilitation of Early Twentieth-Century Popular Music," *Asian Music* 26, no. 1 (Winter 1995): 119–35.
84. Jiang , *Xiaodiao,* 20.
85. For a history of the Shanghai Music Conservatory which contains general contextual information on the rise of Western music studies in East China from the 1920s onwards, see Antoinet Schimmelpenninck and Frank Kouwenhoven, "The Shanghai Conservatory of Music—History and Foreign Students' Experiences," *Chime,* no. 6 (Spring 1993): 56–91.

# Chapter 4

# Music for *Erhu*

A great deal of writing in musicology and ethnomusicology has been about products: Beethoven's Ninth, Plains Indian song, and fiddle tunes, for example. These studies usually begin with the question "What is it?" and use musical transcriptions and other analytic methods to arrive at a description of the structure and performance of a certain genre or period. Detailed musical analysis can produce highly competent descriptions of musical forms from around the world, but rarely relate their musical analysis to other aspects of the social and cultural environment of which music is always a part. Very few studies ask "Why is the music performed in that way rather than another?" and "Why perform music at all in a given situation in a society?"     Anthony Seeger.[1]

In discussing the topic of music analysis during the introduction to this book, I twice cited segments of Seeger's charge that scholarly descriptions of musical products are too rarely related to the social and cultural contexts of music making. In this chapter, however, there remains a concern with sound products, even with fiddle tunes, as musical structures in themselves. There are two reasons why such a concern may still be worthwhile. First, as I suggested during the Introduction, the problem is not music analysis *per se* but relating that analysis to the concepts and behavior of the individuals and groups concerned. Second, and perhaps this is devious, it may sometimes be possible to answer Seeger's question "Why is the music performed in that way rather than another?" through a technical analysis of the music itself. A close investigation of musical organization and the creative processes brought to bear on a particular set of musical resources may in itself be quite suggestive of musical thought.

In this particular case, there is an extra dimension. We know that the way in which Abing's music is performed by conservatory-trained musicians is quite distinct from the manner and context in which Abing performed it himself. It is possible to study the ways in which contemporary players perform this music, but we are no longer able to observe Abing's own musical performances or talk to him about his particular performance decisions. However, there is surviving evidence of his musical practices in the shape of the recordings and transcriptions of his solos. Through analysis of this evidence, we may be able to reconstruct Abing's own creative and performative processes. Having done so, we can use this description as a benchmark against which to evaluate more recent re-creations. Any changes in style, structure, or aesthetic which emerge can then be related to changes in context and perspective. As such, music analysis has an important contribution to make in explaining how it is that Chinese musicians perform Abing's pieces today, and how they and their listeners go about making sense of this music.

This chapter concentrates on the three *erhu* solos performed by Abing in 1950, and subsequently published in transcription; music for *pipa* is discussed in the following chapter. I argue below that the three *erhu* solos are closely related in melodic terms, drawing in evidence already mentioned in chapters 2 and 3 to support the view that Abing may have produced three improvisations on similar thematic material rather than performed three disparate, memorized, fixed compositions. The latter view is that implicitly accepted by almost all scholarly views of this music which I have been able to locate in print or elicit in discussion.[2] Typical might be Liang Mingyue's casual judgement that Abing's music is "composed in fixed form rather than improvisatory."[3] In chapter 6, I will contend that this vision of the nature of musical creativity has been shaped by Western, romantic conceptions of the musical work espoused by modern Chinese musicians during the training they now receive;[4] a musicological parallel to the manner in which those impelled by new social movements pieced the scattered facts of Abing's life into new narratives. For the time being, then, I discuss Chinese analytical accounts of Abing's music only in so far as these shed light on, or obfuscate, particular structural and procedural features of Abing's recorded performances. More general discussion of their ideological content is postponed until the final chapter, which should be read as the completion of the music analysis begun here.

## Analysis

In order to demonstrate the close melodic and structural affinities between Abing's three surviving *erhu* performances, it is not necessary to analyze each in detail. Instead, it is practicable to focus, in the main, on that most frequently performed and discussed, *Second Springs*. However, additional evidence from *Cold Spring Wind* and *Listening to the Pines* is incorporated when the contrasting employment of shared material from one solo to another allows the analyst to draw attention to processes of melodic development and construction which Abing may have employed.

*Second Springs* has been analyzed a large number of times, both within China and without.[5] However, as I have already claimed, existing analyses have not considered *Second Springs* as one of several preserved performances by a traditional Chinese musician with recognized improvisatory skills; rather, the score (transcription) of the solo has been analyzed as a self-contained, written composition. In other words, previous analyses have accepted the performance transcription as an exact and prescriptive representation of Abing's compositional intentions. The analysis below begins from the observation that similar material is used in each of Abing's *erhu* solos, and proceeds to compare and contrast this material and its employment within each solo. Such comparison allows the drawing of certain conclusions about the function of this common melodic material in each solo, which lead, in turn, to a consideration of the processes through which Abing structured his musical performances.

*Second Springs* has a basic structure of six sections (CD track 1). Each section incorporates largely the same musical material, four basic thematic elements (identified as A to D) plus possibly some additional contents (repetition of themes C and D, and/or other themes identified here as E, B', and F). The piece is also begun by a very short introductory passage, I. The division of *Second Springs* into these elements would be disputed by certain Chinese analysts. Although I justify my sectioning of the music more fully below, the fundamental principle followed in the process of selecting where each melodic element (or theme) starts and ends is that of thematic independence. For instance, although in *Second Springs* the material I call theme B occurs only in direct tandem with that I label theme A, its more independent reuse as theme B' suggests a breaking point at which it and theme A may be divided into two disparate thematic elements.

### Introductory Passages

In fig. 4.1 introductory passages from all three *erhu* pieces are aligned as in paradigmatic analysis to show similarities on a vertical plane.[6] It is immediately apparent that the phrase with which Abing initiated his performance of *Listening to the Pines* is closely akin to those opening the main sections of *Cold Spring Wind*. This phrase is an elaborated fall from the sixth modal degree (E) to the fifth (D—hereafter, sol-fa pitch names are more generally employed), as shown in the melodic reduction at the base of fig. 4.1. On the other hand, the introduction of *Second Springs* can be at best only very tenuously connected with the others by the sustaining of the second degree re, and may indeed be little more than a check that the left-hand fingers are positioned correctly.

Annotations such as "insertion" and "extension" have been added to fig. 4.1 and also to certain subsequent figures. These draw attention to the contrasting use of material from one appearance of a common theme to another, and are discussed in more detail later. If, as I argue, each performance of Abing's was improvisatory in nature and each theme within each performance a more or less conscious variation of an internalized melodic pattern, material marked as inserted in one appearance of a theme could equally be described as omitted in other appearances. Only when Abing very commonly followed one course of melodic presentation and very rarely another would it be useful to consider these terms absolute rather than relative.[7]

Fig. 4.1. Introductory Material in Abing's *Erhu* Solos.

## Low-Register Melodies

Following on in the order of occurrence of themes in *Second Springs*, the next melodic element to appear is a low-register theme which Abing used consistently to start each of the piece's six sections. This melodic element is characterized by its rise from do through mi to sol, and subsequent return to do.

Fig. 4.2. Low-Register Themes in *Second Springs*.

Fig. 4.3. Low-Register Themes in *Cold Spring Wind.*

Although each performance of the theme differs in some respects from the others, three basic versions of this theme occur in *Second Springs* (see fig. 4.2).

The same thematic component is also found in *Cold Spring Wind*, where one of the two primary versions substitutes a cadence to la (see fig. 4.3). *Listening to the Pines* does not include a related low-register theme.

### Middle-Register Melodies

In *Second Springs*, the short, middle-register theme (theme B) is always preceded by the low-register melody and followed by a high-register one. A related melody occurs once in *Listening to the Pines*, where it is also used between low- and high-register themes. The theme has two alternative forms in *Second Springs* (examples from measures 6 and 53 are given in fig. 4.4), and appears in another form an octave higher (theme B'). In each case, the structural outline consists of alternation of do and re followed by descent to a cadence on sol. Fig 4.4 provides examples of each version of this theme, together with a reduction emphasizing the common melodic skeleton.

Fig. 4.4. Related Middle-Register Themes
in Abing's *Erhu* Solos and a High-Register Variant.

**High-Register Melodies**

The same high-register melody appears in all three of Abing's *erhu* solos but its employment differs in each composition. In *Second Springs*, it occurs regularly after each middle-register theme, and is almost invariably followed by a relatively fixed codetta theme. In *Listening to the Pines*, on the other hand, it is initially approached by way of the shared middle-register theme already shown in fig. 4.4 but then twice replayed immediately, without recourse to any other melodic element. In his performance of *Cold Spring Wind*, Abing juxtaposed the theme freely with his introductory, low-register, and codetta material. Whatever its positioning within the solo, the theme reverses the melodic emphasis of the middle-register melody, consisting of descent from sol through mi and re to do. A selection of the realizations of this thematic idea is shown in fig. 4.5.

**Codettas**

The codetta is the final, standard constituent of each section of *Second Springs*. Shared by *Cold Spring Wind*, where it also occurs an octave lower (a point returned to below), it is normally a one-measure phrase moving from the high-register theme's tonic cadence to rest on the fifth modal degree. This theme demonstrates especially well Abing's use of the techniques of substitution and extension (see fig. 4.6).

Fig. 4.5. High-Register Themes in Abing's *Erhu* Music.

Fig. 4.6. Selected Codetta Phrases from Abing's *Erhu* Music.

## Other Material

All three solos contain an amount of other melodic material. That in *Second Springs* (identified as themes E and F) is of minor structural significance, comprising link passages to theme B' and an additional codetta after the second performance of B'. The situation is similar in *Cold Spring Wind*, where an even smaller amount of unrelated melodic material occurs. In *Listening to the Pines* there are more substantial unrelated passages, including those commonly understood to be imitative of Western-style bugle calls. The origin and character of these passages will be discussed once the analysis of related material has been completed.

## Summary of Related Material

Fig. 4.7 summarizes common theme use in Abing's *erhu* pieces. Thus, a similar dominant-directed introductory passage occurs in both *Cold Spring Wind* and *Listening to the Pines*; a shared low-register, upper-hand-position theme cadencing to the tonic is found in *Second Springs* and *Cold Spring Wind*; a related middle-register, middle-hand-position theme with a dominant ending occurs within *Second Springs* and *Listening to the Pines*; a matching high-register, lower-hand-position theme with tonic cadence is heard in all three recorded performances; and a corresponding codetta theme with movement from first to fifth modal degrees appears in *Second Springs* and *Cold Spring Wind*.

| Piece | Introduction | Material | | | Codetta |
| --- | --- | --- | --- | --- | --- |
| | | Low register | Middle register | High register | |
| *Second Springs* | No | Yes | Yes | Yes | Yes |
| *Cold Spring Wind* | Yes | Yes | No | Yes | Yes |
| *Listening to the Pines* | Yes | No | Yes | Yes | No |

**Fig. 4.7. Presence or Absence of Shared Themes in Abing's Pieces for *Erhu***

### Locally Specific Variation Techniques

The comparative musical examples above illustrate the skill and variety with which Abing employed small-scale, musical-development techniques. At the most fundamental level was his use of ongoing melodic ornamentation or simplification through the insertion or omission of convenient fingered decorations. Aside from these, Abing also appears to have been adept at applying more complex modes of thematic expansion, insertion, repetition, contraction, omission, substitution, and transposition, each of these terms read with the above-mentioned qualification about their theoretical relativity held prominently in mind.

Thematic expansion or extension most typically results from the augmentation or repetition of a note or short figuration, or through the insertion of additional material. Abing's habit of immediately repeating and reworking part of a theme is most strikingly demonstrated in the high-register theme in *Listening to the Pines* (see fig. 4.5). This example simultaneously illustrates a variety of thematic contraction, in that the melody is performed at much faster tempo in *Listening to the Pines* than in either of the other two solos. More usually, melodic contraction involves the rhythmic diminution of part of a theme, often with a corresponding melodic simplification, or the shortening of a realization of a theme through the omission of part of the outline. Substitution of material is common in all three pieces, referring here to variation of a thematic outline through the inclusion of an alternate-pitch or phrase segment in place of a more commonly found note or passage. Transposition, movement of material from one register to another, is perhaps more important as a large-scale constructive technique but has some significance on a local level, for example in the extended forms of the codetta figure (see fig. 4.6). Frequently, more than one of these techniques is employed at the same time, indeed, it is possible to consider several of these techniques as related, or complementary. The insertion of new material or the repetition of notes and patterns often leads to the extension of a theme, while the omission of inessential melodic movement is in many respects akin to thematic contraction.

Abing's creative employment during performance of such small-scale variation techniques is an activity typical of a Chinese traditional musician in the development of a personal version of a tune or piece. Examples abound from the repertories of both instrumental and vocal music (see, for instance, the discussion of *tanhuang* in chapter 3), though necessarily in simultaneous group performance the scope for spontaneous structural adjustment is considerably limited. The aesthetic desire to vary the melodic surface of each performance of a memorized outline is also characteristic of many genres, such as the instrumental style Jiangnan *sizhu*.[8]

Use of paradigmatic forms of analysis, in which multiple versions of a melody are laid out for comparative purposes in vertical alignment, is a standard means of dealing with questions of thematic variation and improvisation in ethnomusicology.[9] The reductive outline appended to many of the music examples throughout this book is, I believe, a refinement of this mode of analysis. In the first place, the melodic skeleton proposed for each theme above is able to present information about the unfolding of each thematic element in a format which emphasizes common melodic motion rather than the idiosyncrasies of any one specific occurrence of the theme. The reduction thus functions as a kind of neutral, median form of the theme. A second benefit of this analytical format is the incorporation within it of a pitch hierarchy, from the essential structural level of beamed notes down to the less significant stratum of unbeamed note heads. This allows the analyst to demonstrate how themes act as directed musical motion from one modal pitch degree towards another.

There is ample justification in Chinese traditional music theory and practice for such an interpretation. Tonal hierarchies, directed musical motion, and ornamentation practices as found in the *Lament of Empress Chen* (*Changmen yuan*) for the zither *qin* are summarized by Joseph Lam as follows:

> First, *qin* music is tonal in the sense that its melodies progress towards particular pitches, a feature which can be experienced through listening, and which is attested to by numerous traditional Chinese writings on modes and their musical attributes. Second, the notes in *qin* music are unequal in significance, a difference which comes from the variety of tonal, rhythmic, timbral, and dynamic stress applied to individual notes. Such a hierarchy among notes finds theoretical support in the Chinese concept of *jiafa* [sic: *jia hua*] or "adding flowers". . . . "Flower notes" are structurally less significant than the notes on which they rest. Third, pitches in the *Lament* demonstrate distinctive patterns of organization.[10]

The analysis of such music becomes not so much the dry, after-the-event, descriptive dismemberment of an ossified musical product but rather a means of focusing attention on the progression through actual performance time of dynamic musical processes, an attempt to engage and empower the interpretative faculties of the listener. In some respects, an analysis enters into a dialogue with the composition it attempts to represent, proposing itself as a means of hearing the music in question. Thus, the analyst will ask whether he or she hears the music differently, having subjected it to analysis, and whether fundamental musical procedures are experienced more deeply as a result.[11]

In the instance of Abing's *erhu* music, my personal response tends towards the affirmative. Having through analysis exposed shared outlines unifying the majority of themes in *Second Springs, Cold Spring Wind*, and *Listening to the Pines*, I now find it difficult to listen to the unfolding of one theme without considering the contrasting treatment this same material receives elsewhere. Likewise, once the listener attends to Abing's *erhu* music as three contrasting workings of closely related melodic material, a new sense develops of the ordering of the various melodic elements into individual sections and complete performances.

### Large-Scale Constructive Techniques

By the term large-scale constructive techniques I refer to the creation by Abing in performance of finished musical structures from the various melodic elements at his disposal. Fig. 4.7 and the preceding thematic analyses made the point that all three *erhu* solos share a large amount of melodic material. However, the arrangement of this material differs from one piece to the next. In fig. 4.8 the thematic contents of *Second Springs* are listed by section, sectioning being based on the repetition of each set of themes. In total, the thematic core of low-register melody (theme A), middle-register melody (B), high-register tune (C), and codetta element (D) occurs six times, sometimes with certain additional material, either repeats of C and D, new material (E and F), or the high-register version of theme B, B' (see fig. 4.8). The specifics of each theme are given in fig. 4.9, an annotated paradigmatic analysis of the whole of *Second Springs*.

While the six-part sectioning of *Second Springs* given in figs. 4.8 and 4.9 is widely recognized, a different thematic subdivision within each section has been proposed by other analysts. For instance, Zhang Xiaohu and Yang Limei have suggested a two-part division within each line, theme A forming the "upper phrase" and elements B-D the "lower phrase."[12] Wang Zhongren, on the other hand, describes theme A as a transition, B an "upper phrase," and C-D a "lower phrase."[13] Although these analyses offer ways

| Section | Basic core | Additional elements |
|---|---|---|
| 1 | X, A, B, C, D; | |
| 2 | A, B, C, D, | C, D; |
| 3 | A, A, B, C, D, | C, D, E, B'; |
| 4 | A, B, C, D, | C; |
| 5 | A, B, C, D, | E, B', F; |
| 6 | A, B, C, D. | |

Fig. 4.8. Thematic Content of *Second Springs*.

of hearing *Second Springs*, neither explains the contrasting employment of common material in the other two pieces. Furthermore, if the themes labelled B-D or C-D were indeed considered a single "lower phrase" by Abing, why was he able, even in *Second Springs*, to repeat C-D immediately after the basic core of A, B, C, and D (sections 2 and 3) or insert theme C on its own (section 4)? If these are partial or complete repetitions of a structural "lower phrase," would not the listener be left with an unbalanced impression? Perhaps the additional contents of sections 2–5 are heard in an additive way, as extras following a basic thematic series rather than as (semi) repeats of a preceding "lower phrase."

Moving on to examine the construction of the other two *erhu* solos, and adopting similar thematic nomenclature as in fig. 4.8, it is immediately apparent that when related material is employed in these solos it is positioned quite differently (see fig. 4.10).

According to the thematic layout shown in fig. 4.10, the reiterative sectioning of *Second Springs* as a regular thematic core optionally followed by one or more additions, is not maintained in the other two pieces. Elements A, C, and D appear freely juxtaposed in *Cold Spring Wind*, while *Listening to the Pines* is distinguished by its triple statement of C. Assuming that one wishes to listen and respond to the music as a set of three solos rather than to *Second Springs* alone, thematic organization in these pieces, then, militates against both Zhang and Yang's bipartite phrase structure and Wang's postulation of theme A as interlude material. Since element D is independently employed in *Cold Spring Wind*, and C occurs without D in *Listening to the Pines*, it seems more fitting to consider D a separate melodic unit, even though in *Second Springs* it follows almost all occurrences of theme C.[14] Indeed, the contrasting employment of all related material in the three pieces suggests that each theme has a certain independence of function, one not completely revealed by the stricter patterning of *Second Springs*.

In fact, the structural looseness suggested by this preliminary look at *Cold Spring Wind* from the perspective of *Second Springs* may not be wholly accurate. Also, it is still necessary to analyze *Listening to the Pines* such that the positioning of related material amidst other thematic elements is clarified. Closer inspection of the role of cadential contrast in *Second Springs* and *Cold Spring Wind* leads to potential insights about the structuring of these two pieces, which, in turn, allows further thoughts to be raised on the topic of analyzing these *erhu* solos as performed improvisations. Finally, in the light of these findings, the unrelated material and overall form of *Listening to the Pines* is discussed.

Cadential contrast is an important facet of the design of Abing's solos and is straightforward and consistent in *Second Springs* and *Cold Spring Wind*, involving, with occasional exceptions, the alternating emphasis of do and sol. Themes A and C typically close on do, B and D on sol. In fig. 4.11, the melodic outlines of themes A-D are combined and further reduced, a process which underlines the alternating do-sol cadential emphasis of the core

Fig. 4.9. Paradigmatic Analysis of *Second Springs*.

of *Second Springs*, and makes more apparent structural parallels between themes A and C, and between B and D. Incidentally, note also the clarity with which Abing's movement from one register to another is depicted (see fig. 4.11).

While theme B is absent from *Cold Spring Wind*, reference to fig. 4.10 reveals that between occurrences of themes A and C, theme D takes the place of the absent theme B, reproducing the pattern of alternate cadences to the first and fifth modal degree. What is more, whenever it does so, it occurs in the registral area (and hand position) of theme B, cadencing onto d' rather than d". This point was noted during discussion preceding fig. 4.6 but its structural reason is only now explained. In one instance (measures 93–95) theme D in *Cold Spring Wind* even begins to resemble the surface detail of B from *Second Springs* (see fig. 4.12 and compare with the third stave of fig. 4.4).

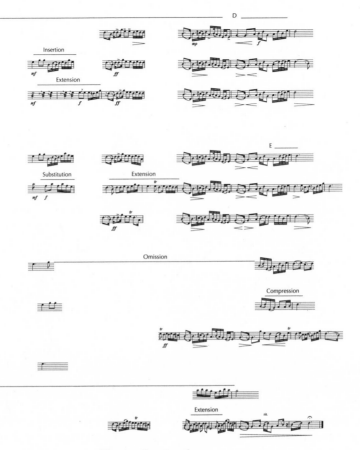

Fig. 4.9. *Continued.*

| Section | Contents | Measures |
|---|---|---|
| *Cold Spring Wind* | | |
| 1 | I, C, D, A, A, D, C, D, C; | 1–29 |
| 2 | I, I, C, A, A, D, X, A, D, C, D, C, C, A, D, C, D; | 29–81 |
| 3 | I, A, D, A, D, C, D. | 81–100 |
| *Listening to the Pines* | | 1 |
| 1 | I, X; | 1–11 |
| 2 | X; | 11–15 |
| 3 | X, B, C, C, C; | 16–46 |
| 4 | X; | 46–50 |
| 5 | X (with similarities to C). | 50–66 |

X material unrelated to that of *Second Springs.*

Figure 4.10. Comparative Thematic Content of
*Cold Spring Wind* and *Listening to the Pines.*

Fig. 4.11. Cadential Contrast in the Thematic Core of *Second Springs*.

Now, if theme D whenever it follows the low-register theme in *Cold Spring Wind* is recognized as equivalent to theme B in *Second Springs*, a more easily comprehended structural design emerges for this piece, one with considerable similarity to that for *Second Springs* (see fig. 4.13). A shared constructive technique for each section of both solos appears: a basic core of alternately cadencing elements A-D, before or after which additional material—most often the high-register theme C—may be inserted, with sections sometimes opened by an introductory passage (cadencing to sol, unlike the tonic cadences of themes A and C which follow).

The common sectional pattern with binary tonal emphasis which unifies *Second Springs* and *Cold Spring Wind* is intersected by a ternary alternation of register, or, perhaps more precisely, of left-hand position. Thus, the low-register theme A is performed in the upper hand position, the middle-register theme B is played in the middle hand position and the high-register themes C and D are executed in the lower hand position.[15] As fig. 4.11 shows, interchange between one theme, register, or hand position and the next are smoothed by a technique Zhang Xiaohu and Yang Limei refer to as *tong yin chengdi*, or "same note passes on," a constructive technique of Chinese folk music wherein the final pitch of one phrase is used or restated as the first pitch of the next.[16]

## Musical Structure as a Result of Performance Decisions

If the structural evidence presented above supports the contention that the transcriptions of Abing's solos now studied and reproduced by conservatory *erhu* players are the result of three recorded improvisations on similar themes, not three quite disparate, fixed compositions, it is possible to recast

Fig. 4.12. Final Occurrence of Theme D in *Cold Spring Wind*.

| Section | Contents | | | | |
|---|---|---|---|---|---|
| | Introductory | Inserted | Core | Inserted | Measures |
| *Cold Spring Wind* | | | | | |
| 1 | I | C, D, | A, A, B, C, D, | C; | 1–29 |
| 2 | I, I | C, | A, A, B, | X; | 29–51 |
| 3 | | | A, B, C, D, | C, C; | 51–68 |
| 4 | | | A, B, C, D, | | 68–81 |
| 5 | I | A, B, | A, B, C, D. | | 81–100 |
| *Second Springs* | | | | | |
| 1 | X | | A, B, C, D; | | 1–12 |
| 2 | | | A, B, C, D, | C, D; | 12–27 |
| 3 | | | A, A, B, C, D, | C, D, E, B'; | 27–49 |
| 4 | | | A, B, C, D, | C; | 49–62 |
| 5 | | | A, B, C, D, | E, B', F; | 62–78 |
| 6 | | | A, B, C, D. | | 78–89 |

Fig. 4.13. Revised Structural Plan of *Cold Spring Wind*, with Middle-Register Occurrences of Theme D (Now Described as B), Compared with Structural Plan of *Second Springs*.

structural analysis such that it reflects potential constructive choices during rehearsal and performance rather than actual performance results (as in fig. 4.13).[17] Such an analysis, focusing on musical process rather than musical product, would have the advantage of suggesting what could have occurred in renditions by Abing on other occasions, not simply what did occur at the recording session in 1950. Second, it draws further attention to the manner with which he combined his thematic elements as a stylistic technique in itself. To be sure, without access to Abing himself, or to as yet unknown recordings of him, any such analysis must remain conjectural, yet the format may prove valuable for the examination of creative processes involved in other improvisatory traditions (see fig. 4.14).

Progression through the analysis is from top to bottom, following the various routes from one thematic element to another. Each theme is enclosed by a shape giving some idea as to its cadential note: squares show themes with tonic cadences, circles those with dominant, and triangles the possibility of another cadence altogether. The choices available to Abing as he played each section are set out as lines connecting one theme to another. Solid lines indicate choices that were most frequently taken, dotted lines less common alternatives. Digits at the side of each route show the frequency with which Abing made each choice in the performance recorded.

Although the layout of the analysis is intended to show the chainlike formation of each section of *Second Springs*, much of it would remain unchanged if *Cold Spring Wind* had been the focus instead. The A-B-C-D thematic chain embodies the concepts of cadential contrast and variety of

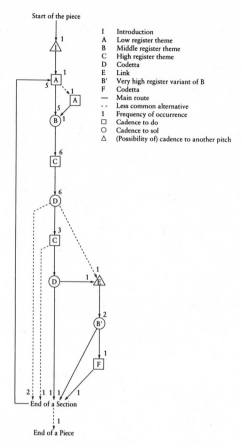

Fig. 4.14. Flow-Chart Structural Analysis of *Second Springs*.

register, and is extendible by the coupling of further elements to its rear, or in the case of *Cold Spring Wind*, before its start. It is also a musical structure allowing for the incorporation of the locally specific variations discussed above, since in order to create a coherent but varied musical section Abing needed only to keep in mind the order in which to perform his melodic elements, and where additional material could be inserted, not the exact details of each.

### The Case of *Listening to the Pines*
Unlike *Second Springs* and *Cold Spring Wind*, in which the great majority of melodic material is held in common, *Listening to the Pines* embraces, or at least appears to embrace, a significant amount of other thematic substance (CD track 2). This contrasting thematic substance is worth a brief examination, since much of it also shares basic characteristics of the common themes so far analyzed. According to fig. 4.10, after use of the introductory theme shared with *Cold Spring Wind*, Abing continued with an amount of

unrelated material. But, as demonstrated in fig. 4.15, it is also possible to hear part of this material as further development of the opening introductory thematic element.

The three trills which close fig. 4.15 have the function of reinforcing emphasis of the fifth modal degree, a middle-register, middle-hand-position melody cadencing on the first degree being about to follow (measures 11–15). Although this melody is not otherwise very similar in terms of melodic detail to the theme B or D tunes found in the other two solos, it is notably consistent in terms of cadential emphasis and register (hand position). Incidentally, this new theme is heard by most Chinese analysts and performers as being based on a fanfare-type call from Western military band music, the three trills preceding it representing rolls on the side drum. Such an interpretation is supported by the reappearance of "drumbeat" type music in measures 46–50, following the triple statement of theme C. It occurs to me that both readings may be correct, Abing working adopted features of military music into his standard cadential and registral patterns. Likewise, while the material which precedes this *Listening to the Pines* version of theme B differs in surface detail from a typical rendition of theme A in either of the other two solos, it does share with them the tonal goal of a tonic cadence and use of (primarily) the upper hand position and low register (see fig. 4.16).

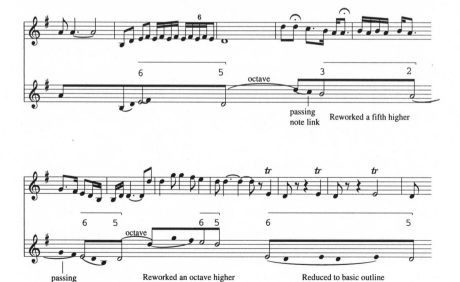

Time Signatures Omitted

Fig. 4.15. Analysis of Introductory Material in *Listening to the Pines*.

Fig. 4.16. Low-Register Passage in *Listening to the Pines*
Compared with Structural Outline of Theme A, Inserted Segments Noted.

In fact, quite significant portions of the melodic material in *Listening to the Pines* can be heard, in light of the analysis of constructive principles in the other two solos, as further varied forms of this same thematic stock. When the material shown in fig. 4.15 is heard as a extended development of the introductory theme, the middle-register material which follows as a form of theme B, and the low-register theme from fig. 4.16 an equivalent of theme A, the structural plan for *Listening to the Pines* can be redrawn as in fig. 4.17.

|  | | Contents | |
|---|---|---|---|
| Introductory | Inserted | Core | Inserted |
| I, | B, | A, B, C, | C, C, X (sim. to C) |

Figure 4.17. Revised Structural Plan for *Listening to the Pines*,
with Potentially Related Thematic Material Renamed.

## Conclusion

The analysis of small- and large-scale constructive techniques in these three solos reveals that Abing had a characteristic creative style. In each of his performed musical structures he reused a small number of adaptable themes, sought the regular variation of register by shifting hand position, and aimed to alternate cadential emphasis from do to sol. Through reliance on a chain of themes, each associated with a particular register, hand position, and cadential emphasis, it would have been both easy for the blind musician to create extended, coherent performances and convenient for him to concentrate on individual, locally specific variation techniques as he progressed.

Above, I have detailed the striking similarities between Abing's three recorded *erhu* pieces. I now propose that these similarities arise from the improvisatory process through which Abing composed his instrumental solos, and from the experience he had gained of traditional forms of musical creativity in Wuxi. In chapter 2, the controversy which exists over the names and naming of these pieces was discussed, and Zhu Shikuang's recollection that this music was neither named by Abing nor identified by him as three distinct pieces was cited. Chapter 3 introduced other traditional musical genres and techniques, and illustrated the improvisatory processes through which the melodic skeletons underlying such styles as Wuxi *tanhuang* drama were fleshed out during performance. In the case of the *tanhuang huang diao* aria structure analyzed in fig. 3.6, musical structure relies on alternation between emphasis of modal first and fifth degrees, as also in Abing's *erhu* solos. Likewise, a fundamental performance technique of Chinese traditional theatrical music was the reuse of common thematic outlines from one performance to another. Singers and accompanists were adept at restyling these, during rehearsal and performance, to fit a variety of metrical formats. Many writers have commented on Abing's skills as an improviser with his swift arrangement of news stories. Indeed, according to Cheng Ruxin, Abing himself devised a novel style, called *Ballad-Singing Tune* (see fig. 3.7). The brief study of instrumental styles such as *shifan gu* and *sizhu* in chapter 3 also introduced the aesthetic principle by which creative variation is valued above exact replication in these styles.

Given then, the existence in Wuxi of a large number of semi-improvisatory styles in which performers set out to dynamically realize during performance memorized musical elements, is it likely that Abing, in performing solo on the *erhu*, sought to exactly re-create three disparate, memorized compositions? Is it not more likely that the types of adaptation during performance described above were very much part of his personal style? Abing existed within a traditional musical culture in which the reworking of existing melodic elements during performance was a standard means of musical origination. Many genres in his home city presented him with examples of couplet or suite structures based on the combination of a handful of themes ensuring regular cadential contrast. Several of these genres also provided him with examples of how the same melodic skeleton could be restyled to suit multiple metrical contexts.

Flexible adaptation during performance may even have been a prerequisite of his typical performance context. When begging, whether as street singer or instrumentalist, Abing would have had an interest in spinning out material while his listeners remained attentive. On the other hand, as soon as they became restless, he needed to convincingly cadence and close to ask for money before the crowd dispersed. Of course, the context under which Abing was recorded in 1950 was atypical, with Yang Yinliu's team arranging three days in advance an evening recording session in a Wuxi school hall. Exactly how Abing might have performed on a street corner is now unknown; some *erhu* players today claim he played a little while moving through the town, but as soon as an audience was assembled he then sang or played requests as appropriate. Others say that he played instrumental solos predominantly in the evenings for leisure, and may indeed have had the opportunity to develop and rehearse extensive musical structures. In fig. 4.18 below, I present a complete transcription of another blind, fiddle-playing beggar's performance of *Second Springs*. For this street musician at least, a single section, rounded off by a second statement of theme A, comprised a complete musical performance (CD track 6).[18]

Learning to hear Abing's three *erhu* performances as creative processes—to borrow from the title of Bell Yung's study of Cantonese opera—rather than as the re-creation of disparate products, is important in that it allows greater insight into the relationship between one performance and another.[19] Recognizing these three solos as different results of a similar creative process, we are able to draw from Abing's *erhu* music more general conclusions about creativity in traditional Chinese music making. Such conclusions can then be compared with the situation in contemporary China, as in chapter

Fig. 4.18. *Second Springs,* Beijing Beggar's Version.

6, or with that characterizing music cultures in other parts of the world, many of which contain parallels that can further illumine our understanding of Abing's creative processes.

For example, music psychologist John Sloboda contrasts the skills of improvisation (an activity located at the interface of memorized model, habitual performance style, and improvisatory technique) and composition (the more self-conscious working out of a musical structure):

> I wish to argue . . . that what distinguishes improvisation from composition is primarily the pre-existence of a large set of formal constraints which comprise a 'blueprint' or 'skeleton' for the improvisation. The improviser can, therefore, dispense with much of the composer's habitual decision making concerning structure and direction. He uses a model which is, in most cases, externally provided by the culture, and which he embellishes and 'fills in' in various ways. Such models frequently have a recursive sectional form, so that the performer becomes very familiar with the structure of the basic section, which can, to a large extent, be considered independently from other sections. This means that the improviser does not have to be constantly referring back to the detailed working out of earlier sections as, it may be argued, a composer must. He can rely on the given constraints of the form together with his own 'style' to give the music unity.[20]

Sloboda's description of the improvisatory process, with its reliance on a basic sectional model performed successively in embellished forms by the musician, could almost have been written to summarize this analysis of Abing's *erhu* solos. Yet, had it been, it would have been necessary to balance its emphasis on the recurrent blueprint with the latter part of a comment of Alan Merriam, made two decades earlier in the context of a discussion of musical composition: "Among the Basongye, improvisation in xylophone music definitely follows clear-cut and predetermined patterns, and the xylophone player standardizes his 'licks' to such an extent that he can isolate and play oft-repeated phrases for the outside observer."[21]

Improvisatory musicians such as Abing not only rely on a simple, sectional outline or predetermined pattern, but, as the analysis above has shown, they also recognize and make use of standardized, memorized melodic elements. In forming an understanding of musical structure, it may be just as important to consider these stock themes, which have perhaps an inherent tonal function and specific technical "feel" (use of a specific hand position or bodily movement, for instance), as the larger structural outline into which they are slotted.[22]

Ethnomusicologists have sometimes taken a rather static view of these memorized and elaborated elements. For example, Song Bang-song discusses three factors which "contribute to the development of a personal style" among Korean instrumentalists for the genre *sanjo*, namely "preservation, elaboration, and creation."[23] Song describes these factors as "phases" a student performer works through over a period of at least ten years in order to create a new *sanjo* interpretation. However, it seems to me that Song's argument is then confused by his comparison of melodic phrases from a performance by "*sanjo* master" Sin K'we-dong with excerpts from that of Sin's teacher Paek Nak-chun. Applying Song's argument rigorously, the performer Sin, having worked his way through the long stylistic apprenticeship with Paek, must already have reached the third, creative phase. Thus, if Sin has decided to present certain phrases much as Paek taught him to, this decision is, in a performative sense, every bit as "creative" as the decision to depart from Paek's model.[24]

In fact, the root of the problem lies not so much in Song's translation of the stages of a diachronic learning process into synchronic analytical metaphor but more in his overly strict division of memorization (preservation), elaboration, and creative alteration. Likewise, it is necessary to refine the picture developed above of composition in performance as the patterned mixing of memorized (preserved) and spontaneously elaborated (creative) components to take account of findings from recent research on musical memorization and recollection. Very briefly, it now seems that recalling music from memory has been shown to be a creative process involving the active recombination of imagined sounds and learnt movement patterns. In the words of Nicholas Cook, "The distinction between recollection and improvisation is one of degree rather than one of kind."[25]

If this is so, there are major implications for the study of creativity in unwritten musics. Twenty years ago, during a discussion of Javanese *gamelan* music, Judith Becker commented, "Until recently, it was believed that oral performances were either memorized or improvised. In fact, they are neither."[26] Now, I think, we need to consider them as both. The relationship of musical creativity to the skills of composition, memorization, improvisation, and performance requires further cross-cultural examination.

This chapter has demonstrated how musical analysis can propose the hearing of Abing's *erhu* music as three improvisatory reworkings of the same thematic material. I have argued that this mode of listening to Abing's music may be closer to that he himself would have had in mind, and that it reveals more of his creative intentions than reifying, product-centered analyses. Contextual information supporting this analysis has been advanced, and an attempt made to link discussion of Abing's music to that of unwritten musical forms in general. In chapter 6 I return to the subject of Abing's *erhu* music, looking at the ways in which this music is performed, transmitted, and explained in contemporary China. First, however, I turn to examine Abing's three surviving solos for the lute *pipa*.

## Notes

1. Anthony Seeger, *Why Suyá Sing: A Musical Anthropology of an Amazonian People* (Cambridge: Cambridge University Press, 1987), xiii.
2. Du Yaxiong, for instance, states that *Listening to the Pines* "was composed in

1939"; Du Yaxiong, "Abing de san shou erhu qu," *Yuefu xinsheng*, 1985, no. 4:32–33 (32). Many Chinese commentators mention (but do not discuss) similarities between *Second Springs* and *Cold Spring Wind*; only Du Yaxiong has gone so far as to declare that these "are in fact two different ways of performing the same piece"; Du, "Erhu qu," 33. Mao Yuan, who analyzes each of Abing's solos, deals with them in a piecemeal manner, rather than relating one to another; Mao Yuan, *Abing meixue sixiang shitan* (Nanjing: Nanjing yishu xueyuan, 1983, [Mimeograph]).

3. Liang Mingyue, *Music of the Billion: An Introduction to Chinese Musical Culture* (New York: Heinrichshofen, 1985), 151.

4. For further on the romantic impact in twentieth-century China, see the discussion of the reception of Romain Rolland's *Jean-Christophe*—a super-romantic retelling of the Beethoven myth—in Richard Curt Kraus, *Pianos and Politics in China: Middle-Class Ambitions and the Struggle over Western Music* (New York: Oxford University Press, 1989), 71–72. A more specific articulation of another aspect of this same ideology is furnished by Shanghai Conservatory Professor of Composition, Mao Yu Run, who rounds off an article with the sentiment, "artistic creation is mainly an expression of one's free will"; Mao Yu Run, "Music under Mao: Its Background and Aftermath," *Asian Music* 22, no. 2 (Spring/Summer 1991): 97–125 (124).

5. See, for example, Cheng Ruxin, "*Er quan ying yue* yindiao yuanyuan tansuo," *Nanyi xuebao*, 1980, no. 2:48–52; Zhang Zhenji, "Abing wubiaoti erhu qu de yinyue neirong, sucai laiyuan ji qi yishu chuangzao," *Nanyi xuebao*, 1980, no. 2:53–64; Cheng Gongliang, "*Er quan ying yue* de yinyue sucai he jiegou tedian," *Yinyue yishu*, 1981, no. 1:36–40; Zhang Xiaohu and Yang Limei, "Lun *Er quan ying yue* de yinyue cailiao yu jiegou," *Zhongguo yinyue*, 1983, no. 1:16–20; Yu Siu Wah, "Three Er-hu Pieces from Jiangnan" (Queen's University of Belfast: M.A. Dissertation, 1985), 57–75; Wang Zhongren, "Shilun *Er quan ying yue* de daoyue tezheng," *Huang zhong*, 1990, no. 1:42–48.

6. In this and following figures, examples are identified by letter and number, "S" representing *Second Springs*, "C" *Cold Spring Wind* and "L" *Listening to the Pines*, while the number given is the measure number of the first note of the example. To allow more convenient comparison between each version, details of phrasing and ornamentation have been omitted. A complete transcription of *Second Springs* appears as fig. 4.9; *Cold Spring Wind* and *Listening to the Pines* are notated in Appendix 1. For further discussion of paradigmatic analysis, sometimes called distributional analysis, see Nicholas Cook, *A Guide to Musical Analysis* (London: Dent, 1987), 151–82; Nicolas Ruwet, "Methods of Analysis in Musicology," translated and introduced by Mark Everist, *Music Analysis* 6 (1987): 3–36.

7. With reference to medieval monodic song, Nicolas Ruwet has called the same phenomenon a "syntax of equivalence"; Ruwet, "Methods of Analysis," 32. Ruwet's discussions of modality and segmentation are valuable; however, in the case of Abing's music there already exists a Chinese modal theory allowing the immediate and unproblematic identification of a specific mode and associated pitch hierarchy. Also, the majority of the themes used by Abing are marked off from their neighbors by a change in left-hand position, thus providing a technical starting point for segmentation.

7. See, for instance, J. Lawrence Witzleben, *"Jiangnan Sizhu* Music Clubs in Shanghai: Context, Concept and Identity," *Ethnomusicology* 31 (1987): 240–60 (247–48); Alan R. Thrasher, "Bianzou—Performance Variation Techniques in Jiangnan Sizhu," *Chime,* no. 6 (Spring 1993): 4–20.

8. Romanian ethnomusicologist Constantin Brailoiu working in the 1930s was perhaps one of the first to use a version of this technique, "superimposing different versions of the same melody, recopying only those elements which are new"; Jean-Jacques Nattiez, *Music and Discourse: Toward a Semiology of Music,* translated by Carolyn Abbate (Princeton: Princeton University Press, 1990), 87. For Brailoiu's own description of this methodology, see Constantin Brailoiu, *Problems of Ethnomusicology,* ed. and trans. A. L. Lloyd (Cambridge: Cambridge University Press, 1984), 72, 74–76.

10. Joseph S. C. Lam, "Analyses and Interpretations of Chinese Seven-string Zither Music: The Case of the *Lament of Empress Chen," Ethnomusicology* 37 (1993): 353–85 (363, footnote reference omitted).

11. For further reflection on the relationship between analyst, analysis, and music, see Cook, *Analysis,* 228–30.

12. Zhang and Yang, "Lun *Er quan ying yue,"* 18.

13. Wang, "Shilun *Er quan ying yue,"* 43.

14. Several writers suggest the low-register theme is derived from a Wuxi opera *huang diao* instrumental transition: Cheng, *"Er quan ying yue* yindiao," 49–50; Zhang, "Abing wubiaoti erhu qu," 55, 58; Cheng, *"Er quan ying yue* de yinyue sucai," 36–37. However, examination of four collections of Wuxi opera excerpts reveals no instrumental passages exactly like those cited as evidence in these articles. In fact, the great majority of *huang diao* interludes are actually quite unlike Abing's low-register theme. See Zheng Hua and Cheng Ruxin, *Xiju qudiao jieshao* (Nanjing: Jiangsu wenyi chubanshe, 1954); Jiangsu yinyue gongzuo zu, ed., *Jiangsu nanbu minjian xiqu shuochang yinyue ji* (Beijing: Yinyue chubanshe,1955); Cheng Ruxin et al., *Xiju qudiao jieshao (xuji)* (Nanjing: Jiangsu wenyi chubanshe, 1956); Zhongguo yinyuejia xiehui, ed., *Jiangsu minjian yinyue xuanji,* (Nanjing: Jiangsu wenyi chubanshe, 1959). Nonetheless, if this attribution was proved correct, it does not necessarily follow that Abing used this material in his solos as a melodic interlude. The usage of certain melodic material in a *huang diao* aria structure and its structural function within Abing's solos cannot be assumed to be identical.

15. See chapter 3 for a discussion of *erhu* hand positions. Theme B' in *Second Springs* uses a hand position even lower on the *erhu* strings again than that employed for themes C and D.

16. Zhang and Yang, "Lun *Er quan ying yue,"* 18.

17. As many ethnomusicologists have pointed out, composition and improvisation are not alternative creative processes. See, for example, Bruno Nettl, "Thoughts on Improvisation: A Comparative Approach," *Musical Quarterly* 60 (1974): 1–19. For an assemblage of fourteen ethnomusicological definitions of improvisation, see Bernard Lortat-Jacob, ed., *L'improvisation dans les musiques de tradition orale* (Paris: Selaf, 1987), 67–70. A cross-cultural overview of research into improvisatory methods and models is provided by Jeff Pressing, "Improvisation: Methods and Models," in John A. Sloboda, ed., *Generative Processes in Music: The Psychology of Performance, Improvisation, and Composition* (Oxford: Clarendon Press, 1988), 129–78 (141–47).

18. Recorded in Beijing on 15 April 1990. Original pitch an augmented fourth higher, here transposed to allow more ready comparison with the other music examples in this chapter.

19. Bell Yung, *Cantonese Opera: Performance as Creative Process* (Cambridge: Cambridge University Press, 1989).

20. John A. Sloboda, *The Musical Mind: The Cognitive Psychology of Music* (Oxford: Clarendon, 1985), 139.

21. Alan P. Merriam, *The Anthropology of Music* (Evanston: Northwestern University Press, 1964), 179.

22. John Baily has emphasised the creative role played by "spatio-motor modes of musical cognition"; John Baily, "Some Cognitive Aspects of Motor Planning in Musical Performance," *Psychologica Belgica* 31, no. 2 (1991): 147–62 (150). See also John Baily and Peter Driver, "Spatio-Motor Thinking in Playing Folk Blues Guitar," *World of Music* 34, no. 3 (1992): 57–71.

23. Song Bang-song, "*Sanjo* versus *Raga*: A Preliminary Study," in Robert Falck and Timothy Rice, eds., *Cross-Cultural Perspectives on Music* (Toronto: University of Toronto Press, 1982), 101–16 (112).

24. Song Bang-song's specific example would appear further weakened in that the instance he gives of Sin's attempt "to preserve as closely as possible the original melody of his teacher" is immediately qualified by the remark "Sin's ornamentations are added to Paek's melody"; Song, "*Sanjo*," 113. How these decorations differ from those encountered during Song's second, elaborative phase is left unspecified.

25. Nicholas Cook, *Music, Imagination, and Culture* (Oxford: Clarendon Press, 1990), 112.

26. Quoted in R. Anderson Sutton, "Concept and Treatment in Javanese Gamelan Music, with Reference to the Gambang," *Asian Music* 11, no. 1 (Winter 1979): 59–79 (59).

# Chapter 5

# Music for *Pipa*

One of the most frequently mentioned techniques of composition is that which involves taking parts of old songs and putting them together to make new ones. Alan Merriam.[1]

The previous chapter examined the three surviving fiddle performances by Abing. More attention was paid to the analysis of thematic structure and potential performance process than to proposing origins of the individual themes employed by Abing, a major concern of previous Chinese analyses. In return, the contemporary Chinese professor of *erhu* performance will likely find much of the analysis in chapter 4 irrelevant, especially with its suggestion of an improvisatory basis for Abing's musical creativity and reference to exotic African or Indonesian percussion musics. This chapter looks at his three pipa solos, *Great Waves Washing the Sand* (*Da lang tao sha*, hereafter *Great Waves*),[2] *Zhaojun Crosses the Border* (*Zhaojun chu sai*, hereafter *Zhaojun*), and *Dragon Boats* (*Long chuan*). Identifying the folk themes employed by Abing in these pieces is more important than it was in the previous chapter, but primarily as a position from which to draw structural conclusions rather than as an end in itself. Again, my fundamental aim is to expose and discuss basic constructive principles. The manner in which contemporary musicians re-create this repertory is examined in the following chapter.

## Analysis

There are notable similarities between the situation of the *erhu* pieces and those performed on the *pipa*. In the first place, although all three *pipa* pieces have seemingly traditional titles, only one of the three is similar to another composition of the same name. Discussing this question with reference to *Great Waves*, Yang Yinliu writes:

> The origin of Blind Abing's piece is an enigma. Asked about his music's source he would say, "I can't remember." Even when one wanted him to think deeply, he would just casually say, "Perhaps I learned it from the Daoists," "Perhaps I learned it from the Buddhists," "Perhaps I learned it on the street," and so on. As a result, no definite source can be stated. . . . Although the ensemble repertory

has a *Great Waves Washing the Sand,* it is in the la mode, completely unlike this piece's sol mode. According to Abing, this piece is based on a Daoist *fanyin* ensemble *qupai,* which he played on the *pipa* with *pipa* techniques. . . .[3]

*Zhaojun Crosses the Border.* This piece is not found in current *pipa* scores; it has nothing in common with *Zhaojun's Regrets* [*Zhaojun yuan*] or *Borderland Piece* [*Saishang qu*]. According to Blind Abing, it was originally a *pipa* piece taught to him by Hua Xuemei [i.e. Hua Qinghe].[4]

Yang's conclusion is that these two pieces were Abing's own compositions. Lacking confidence, Abing graced them with traditional titles and ascribed them to other originators.[5] Perhaps this is so, although it is difficult to feel great confidence in any of Yang's reports about Abing after the exposure of the many problems riddling his original biographical narrative (see chapter 2). The third piece, which Yang recognizes as part of the traditional repertory, is *Dragon Boats.* His description of its organization is worth quoting at some length.

*Dragon Boats* was originally a popular piece amongst the people. In this piece the *pipa* imitates the sound of the dragon boat race on the 5th day of the 5th lunar month. From each boat comes the sound of *luogu* and singing. The opening section of this piece imitates the sound of the percussion; in the middle there can be many sections, each of which is a folk song or instrumental tune; and another imitation of the percussion music can be inserted between each section. The number of song or instrumental sections can be very many or very few, and the tunes used can be developed by the performer following his fancy. Following folk custom, the number of musical sections gives the number of dragon boats; for example, four sections, including four passages of folk song or instrumental music, was called four dragon boats. Blind Abing's performance of this piece is divided into four sections, and is four dragon boats. According to Abing himself, the four sections of *Dragon Boats* are three folk songs including *Playing Chess* [*Xia panqi*], and a section from the middle of the ensemble *All Things Harmonious* [*Sihe*]. When the popular forms of these tunes are compared with the melody he performed in this piece, it can be seen that the original tune has been much developed, and in some places Abing has inserted many measures of melody; when his performance of the percussion music is compared with the usual, it can be seen that before and after every percussion section, where the melody gives way to the percussion or the percussion to the melody, Abing knew how to freely use phrases he had composed himself as effective transitions.[6]

Whether or not Abing actually gave the names of the folk song *Playing Chess* and the *sizhu* ensemble *All Things Harmonious* to Yang Yinliu, there is certainly correspondence between these pieces and the former and latter melodic sections of *Dragon Boats.* As an illustration of this correspondence at its most marked, fig. 5.1 aligns the melody of one stanza of *Playing Chess* transnotated from *gongche* notation with the opening of section 2 of *Dragon Boats.*[7]

Uppercase letters identify the start of phrases

Upper stave: *Playing Chess,* text omitted, interlude phrases bracketed
Lower staves: *Dragon Boats,* articulation, etc. omitted

Fig. 5.1. *Playing Chess* and *Dragon Boats,* Section 2, Opening.

As fig. 5.1 shows, Abing's melody is similar in many respects to that
quoted by Jiang Tianyi for *Playing Chess*. Jiang's tune is published in an
early book of *gongche* notations for fiddle (1922), so we should not expect
it to concur with Abing's characteristic reiteration of the open D string of
the lute. Minor differences occur in the ordering of phrases and repetitions.

Both share an introductory phrase (marked "I" in fig. 5.1) but then go on to three phrases performed in slightly contrasting plans: A, A, B, C, B, C in the strophic folk song; A, A, B, B, C, L (link to next phrase) in the *pipa* solo. In the latter, further repetitions follow, each a little varied: A, A, B, B, C, (no link), and A' (partially expanded), A, B, B, L (leading into a "percussion" section). Although one phrase is treated with melodic expansion (see fig. 5.2), and Abing shows some variety in ordering phrases, this section of *Dragon Boats* does not demonstrate the same degree of melodic flexibility as *Second Springs*, perhaps a consequence of Abing's employment of a pre-existing folk melody in a context where it was expected to be recognizable as such.

Turning to compare the final melodic section of *Dragon Boats* with the ensemble piece *All Things Harmonious* reveals that there does indeed appear to be, as Yang Yinliu suggested, partial overlap between the two pieces (see fig. 5.3), although not as much as in the case of *Playing Chess*.[8] In fig. 5.2, I adjusted the barlines suggested by Cao Anhe, the original transcriber of Abing's performance, in order to emphasize the specifics of melodic contraction and repetition, but there is a problem in doing so which an examination of the final section of *Dragon Boats* makes clear. Cao's transcription (in this section) incorporates several changes of meter of just the kind suggested in fig. 5.2. These have the advantage of clarifying the small-scale patterning of individual musical elements. However, when a typical version of the parallel passage from *All Things Harmonious* is set beside *Dragon Boats*, we notice that such metric adjustments do not reflect the regular patterning of *All Things Harmonious*, its characteristic hemiola effects, and its syncopations (partially indicated in Cao's transcription with accents). Transcription, then, can both underline and undermine (see fig. 5.3).

Barlines in phrase A' adapted from those in Cao Anhe's transcription of *Dragon Boats* to emphasize melodic contraction (measure 3) and varied repetition (measure 4)

**Fig. 5.2. Phrases A and A', *Dragon Boats*.**

open strings sounded every eighth-note

Upper stave: part of *All Things Harmonious*
Lower stave(s): measures 8-17, final section, *Dragon Boats*, articulation omitted

**Fig. 5.3. Common Thematic Material in**
***All Things Harmonious* and *Dragon Boats*, Final Section.**

Returning to the melodic resemblance itself, the case is, in fact, not quite as simple as Yang Yinliu asserts. In his analysis of Jiangnan *sizhu* ensemble music, Alan Thrasher cites this very same theme as "the source of great unification" among the *sizhu* pieces *All Things Harmonious*, its variant form *Along the Street* (*Xingjie sihe*), and *Three-Six* (*Sanliu*).[9] Thrasher continues:

> . . . in the sizhu repertoire there is more than just stylistic continuity; many of these pieces are related in very direct thematic ways. *Sanliu* and *Sihe*, although thought to be of different origins, are melodically so similar that we must consider them as variants of a common musical prototype. . . .[10]

This melody, then, is characteristic of multiple, related *sizhu* pieces. To put it another way, the tune is one which traditional practice allows to be employed in a number of different musical contexts. Was Abing deliberately quoting *All Things Harmonious*, or indeed another of the ensemble pieces in which this theme occurs,[11] or was he instead making creative recourse to a preexisting stock melody, which from his experience of the *sizhu* repertory and style he knew to be effective in a variety of musical settings?

The two central melodic sections, according to Yang Yinliu, are based on (unspecified) folk song themes. The analyst Mao Yuan has proposed identities for these, namely the song *Yang Liuqing* for the second melodic section and *Eight-Segment Brocade* (*Ba duan jing*) for the third,[12] but examination of his suggestions reveals only a few matching measures in each case, and many measures of non-correspondence.[13] Wu Ben has identified these sections as arising from the folk songs *Wuxi Sights* (*Wuxi jing*) and *Eighteen Strokes* (*Shiba mo*) respectively.[14] Comparison of *Wuxi Sights* and the second melodic section of *Dragon Boats* reveals a fair degree of correspondence, approximately half the (sixteen-measure) folk song tune appearing in a broadly equivalent position in Abing's *pipa* solo.[15] The case of *Eighteen Strokes* is a little more complicated, since nothing in the notation of *Dragon Boats* immediately resembles it. Jiang Tianyi's fiddle version of this tune, however, notes that *Eighteen Strokes* is performed in the sol-re mode, i.e. the string more usually deemed as tuned to the first modal degree is treated as if (this same absolute pitch) was the fifth degree instead.[16] When a similar relative "transposition" is applied to the third melodic section of Cao's transcription of *Dragon Boats*, an intimate connection between Abing's solo and *Eighteen Strokes* appears (see fig. 5.4).[17]

As fig. 5.4 suggests, this section of Abing's *pipa* solo is derived from the melody *Eighteen Strokes*. This melody is performed five times, each a little varied, during this section of *Dragon Boats*. However, between the fourth and fifth renditions an additional "percussion" interlude is inserted. Yang Yinliu's description stipulates that the number of folk song themes gives the number of dragon boats but also states that percussion music is inserted between sections. Was Abing's return to a fifth rendition of *Eighteen Strokes* simply a performance error? Did he do this because he had not yet selected a new theme for the next melodic section? Or is there, in the fact that the pedal three-string reiteration accompanying renditions one to four is replaced in rendition five with a pedal D reiteration and use of a contrasting playing technique, enough evidence to suggest the possibility of a specific desire for a varied repeat on Abing's part? Was Abing perhaps striving against the constraints of the standard formal outline (one tune per boat, separated by a passage of percussion music) for pieces of this nature? If, as suggested in chapter 4, Abing was a creative improviser who tended to work preexisting, memorized themes or thematic outlines into an overall structural plan rather than recalling strictly memorized complete pieces, then the error scenario is certainly plausible. Rounding off what is effectively the fourth percussion section, Abing may have accidentally begun to play the same theme again, albeit with a different technique, and decided to

open strings continue

Upper stave: *Eighteen Strokes,* text omitted
Lower stave(s): *Dragon Boats,* excerpt from third melodic section (measures 272-87), articulation, etc. omitted and key signature (but not absolute pitch) adapted to reflect change of mode

Fig. 5.4. *Eighteen Strokes* and an Excerpt from *Dragon Boats.*

complete a full verse before going on to another percussion section and a new tune altogether.

These percussion sections are simple in melodic terms, though dramatic from the rhythmic perspective. The opening section of the piece, the most extensive percussion passage, basically twice alternates reiteration of the third (F#) and second (E) modal degrees, adding open-string strums or, in the case of E, lower-octave alternatives in a variety of additive patterns. The second percussion section is led to by a link which gradually moves from the melodic style of Abing's third rendition of *Playing Chess* towards reiteration of the second and then fifth (A) modal degrees. This section adopts patterns from the first, though it dispenses with elaboration of F#, introducing instead a new device which involves decoration of E with an upper auxiliary pitch G.

The third percussion passage is introduced by an abridged form of the same link passage used at the end of *Playing Chess*. Like the first, this section is quite extended, though its fundamental melodic plan alternates much more rapidly from emphasis of E to that of F# and back to E again, this in distinction to the opening section's more distinct prolongation of F#—E—F#—E in turn. The following percussion passage, that inserted within what Cao has transcribed as the third melodic section, uses the same rhythmic patterns and open-string strums to reiterate E, and the final percussion excerpt, that ushering in the *sizhu* ensemble stock theme, begins in like manner before alternating E and F# in the fashion of the third percussion section. It too is completed by reiteration of the pitch E.

In melodic terms, the percussion passages of *Dragon Boats* prolong the second modal degree (E), either elaborating it through alternation with F# or, as in the first passage, delaying the E through the insertion of repeated neighbor note passages in idiomatic *pipa* style on F#. Descent to the fundamental (D), is only established with complete force in the coda phrase to the final melodic section. The final seven measures are themselves a decorated descent from F# to D, acting in this sense as a summary of the piece as a whole as well as, on a more immediate plane, its rounding off.

Within this framework, the melodic sections are a little more varied. The first, *Playing Chess*, moves from the emphasis of the first (D) and fifth (A) degrees of the mode over an ostinato offbeat open D string to prolongation of A above offbeat open A's. The second is similar, though the fifth degree is less marked, both as a cadential pitch within the section proper and as a goal at the end of the link passage leading to the following percussion music section. The third and fourth melodic sections replace the earlier D-string drone with that of the three lower strings, the only periods of exception being the reprise of the third melodic section after the *luogu* interruption (performed to the accompaniment of the open D string) and the final coda (played without accompaniment until the final chord). The third melodic section, as noted above, is in a different mode from melodic sections one and two (sol-re rather than do-sol). Although the absolute pitches employed remain the same as those in other sections, phrases cadence onto a different pattern of pitches, principally E and A. In this manner, the third melodic section provides tonal contrast with the earlier sections. The final section shares this sense of modulation (temporarily exchanging the seventh degree for the first), moving from the opening do-sol mode to the la-mi mode. Do-sol orientation is re-established only during the coda itself.

*Dragon Boats* is formally equivalent to the *luogu* ensemble music discussed in chapter 3. Like that repertory, it consists of a suite of alternating sections of percussive and melodic music, although in this instance they are all performed on the medium of the *pipa*. Also, several of the sections of *Dragon Boats* share the tempo acceleration found in *luogu* and certain other ensemble styles. *Dragon Boats*, then, imitates percussion ensemble music on two planes: firstly, in its principles of structural organization and, secondly, in the specific synthesis of its rhythm-centered "percussion" sections.

Moving on to the other two solos, *Great Waves* actually shares its title with a *luogu* piece. However, as was noted, the percussion ensemble piece shares little with the music of the synonymous *pipa* solo, not even use of a common mode.[18] Certain sources have also posited a connection between the final section of *Great Waves* and another *luogu* melody, *The General's Orders* (*Jiangjun ling*), though, once again, examination of the scores in question casts some doubt on the ascription.[19] A further suggestion is Mao Yuan's derivation of *Great Waves* partially from the traditional melody and *pipa* solo *Autumn Moon over the Han Palace* (*Han gong qiu yue*, hereafter *Autumn Moon*), and partially from the ubiquitous Chinese folk melody *Eight-Beat* (*Baban*).[20] This proposal is examined in fig. 5.5 (CD track 3).

Fig. 5.5 is a composite of different sources, since Mao Yuan does not offer an analytical figure to support his identification of the opening part of *Great Waves* as a segment of *Autumn Moon* followed by a fragment of *Eight-Beat*. Nonetheless, assuming that the excerpts chosen are indeed those Mao intended, there is indeed a close degree of correspondence between *Great Waves* and *Autumn Moon*, particularly at the start. *Great Waves* appears to be a twofold expansion of *Autumn Moon*, although this difference may be illusory, resulting more from the comparison of a notated outline on the one hand and a transcribed performance extract on the other.[21] The proposal of *Eight-Beat* seems a little more problematic, since, in the first place, so few pitches are involved that overlap could be coincidental. Secondly, the phrases concerned are of dissimilar lengths, namely four measures in *Great Waves*, three in *Eight-Beat*. Thus, to accept that Abing extemporized the phrase from measures 10–13 of *Great Waves* out of material from *Eight-Beat*, we have to accept that he chose to use not a whole phrase but rather one-and-a-half phrases, altering his melody just before the original cadential pitch (d) to start a second version of the theme borrowed from *Autumn Moon* (but omitting the first two measures). In this case, such a scenario seems rather complicated, but this example should not invalidate our acknowledgment of the traditional Chinese habit of "taking parts of old songs and putting them together to make new ones."[22] Assemblage of material in this manner is found regularly in the *qin* zither repertory, Cantonese music, and *sizhu*, for example.[23]

Whatever the origin of this melodic material, its use in the first section of *Great Waves* is, in a certain sense, regular—little melodic material is found that cannot be found within measures 1–13 in fig. 5.5—and, in another sense, irregular—although the material from 1–13 is reused up until measure 70, few passages maintain exact repetition for more than a few beats in succession. The techniques employed by Abing in the variation of subsequent thematic renditions are similar in some respects to those found in the *erhu* solos, and could be analyzed at similar length. Instead, a single example of a subsequent appearance of this material is presented (fig. 5.6), which should be compared with measures 1–13 in fig. 5.5.

Staves 1 & 2: *Great Waves,* measures 1-13, articulation, etc. omitted
Stave 3, measures 1-6: *Autumn Moon,* measures 7-10: *Eight-Beat*

**Fig. 5.5. Opening of *Great Waves,***
**Compared with Two Tunes Suggested by Mao Yuan.**

In chapter 3, examination of the classical *pipa* repertory revealed characteristics shared by section 1 of *Great Waves,* most clearly the reuse and variation of short themes and phrases. A second attribute held in common by Abing's solo and classical lute pieces such as *Green Lotus* (see fig. 3.10) is cadential emphasis of the fifth (A) and first (D) modal degrees. Likewise, when its two-measure introduction is discounted, Abing's section weighs in at exactly the same beat count as that of *Green Lotus,* the traditional sixty-eight *ban*. Admittedly, one has, somewhat deviously, to count four triple-time measures as if they were duple to arrive at this count, so the similarity is one more of approximate proportion than exact correspondence.

Articulation, etc. omitted; repeated notes written out in full (measures 57 & 60)
Subscripted measure numbers suggest possible parallel measures in the earlier version
**Fig. 5.6. Reuse of Existing Melodic Material in *Great Waves*, Measures 49–61.**

The second and third sections of *Great Waves* together are shorter than section 1 alone, in terms of both total *ban* and overall duration. While the first section was performed at a slow tempo with a slight acceleration, in sections 2 and 3 Abing rapidly doubled speed until the deceleration of the final coda. These sections are alike in that each consists of additive phrases doing little more than alternately reiterate a pair of cadential pitches approached by step from above. From this perspective, it would be possible to consider these two sections as one. However, in section 2, emphasis is given primarily to E and A, much of this over a pedal open-string A, while in section 3, weight is concentrated on D and A. As in *Dragon Boats,* then, temporary modal shift (with C# largely replacing D) takes place before a return to the opening modality.

Abing's third recorded *pipa* solo is known as *Zhaojun Crosses the Border,* or *Zhaojun,* a title which refers to the popular Chinese tale of an imperial concubine given in ancient times as peace offering to a powerful Central Asian foe, a theme recounted in a number of Chinese traditional pieces and folk songs. Zhaojun herself is often depicted as a *pipa* player, though she actually lived a considerable period before the introduction of this instrumental form to China. As we saw, however, Yang Yinliu was unable to connect the melody of Abing's performance with existing pieces of similar titles.[24]

In fact, a connection of a kind between these pieces and Abing's solo has been implicitly made. Mao Yuan proposes that the opening and closing sections of Abing's *Zhaojun* are based on the popular *Eight-Beat* theme.[25] According to Ye Dong, this *Eight-Beat* model is itself the basis of the classical *pipa* composition *Borderland Piece (Saishang qu),* another piece associated with the image of the exiled concubine.[26] Further evidence arises from John Myers' analysis of the nineteenth-century Wuxi *pipa* collection, in which Myers shows five solos, "aside from the first few phrases of each piece . . . [to be] essentially variants of the same melody," i.e. *Eight-Beat.*[27] Possibly,

Upper stave: *Eight-Beat,* first phrase
Middle staves: *Zhaojun,* section 1, measures 4-7, articulation omitted
Lower staves: *Zhaojun,* section 3, measures 1-4, articulation omitted

Fig. 5.7. **Opening Phrases of Two Sections of *Zhaojun,* Compared with *Eight-Beat.***

then, Abing's rendition of *Zhaojun* is also of this nature, though employing the opening phrase of the basic *Eight-Beat* tune rather than, as in Myers' examples, inserting different phrases at the start, and then proceeding with variation of the *Eight-Beat* skeleton. Fig. 5.7 aligns the opening phrases of the first section (excluding a three-measure introduction) and third section of *Zhaojun* with that of the generic *Eight-Beat* tune (CD track 4).

Although correspondence looks convincing, a problem with the idea of explaining *Zhaojun* as a variant of *Eight-Beat* is that other than its opening phrase, very little of the *Eight-Beat* theme can be located within *Zhaojun*. To simply state that *Zhaojun* is based on *Eight-Beat*, then, leaves too much unsaid. Instead of pursuing alternate sources of material for this piece, as was helpful for *Dragon Boats*, it is interesting to compare the music of *Zhaojun* with that of *Great Waves*.

Abing's performance of *Zhaojun* falls into three quite distinct sections. As in *Great Waves*, the opening section is much the longest, beginning slowly and working through several free variations of the same material. The connection with *Great Waves* also extends to the specifics of the thematic material employed. An extended instance of this is shown in fig. 5.8 (see also fig. 5.6).

The second section of *Zhaojun* also has some affinity with its counterpart in *Great Waves*. For instance, in both solos the second section is linked to the first by octave reiteration of the pitch A. Offbeat, open-string A's are repeated throughout both these sections (although the ways in which they are performed and transcribed differ somewhat), and both second sections share the same characteristic of fast tempo with gradual acceleration. Finally, both second sections rely on simple melodic material of an additive nature which emphasizes a few pitches in turn. On the other hand, this section of *Zhaojun* is distinct from the shorter second section in *Great Waves* in that it returns to repeated octave A patterns at its end.

A similar sense of stylistic resemblance emerges from the examination of the third sections of *Zhaojun* and *Great Waves*. Tempo is fast in both, the A pedal from section 2 is replaced by periodic sounding of the open D string, and there is an amount of common melodic material. Rhythmic style is similar in each. An excerpt illustrating the correspondence between the third section of these two *pipa* solos by Abing is shown in fig. 5.9).

*Great Waves* and *Zhaojun* are closely related, sharing a three-part plan of an extended slow section composed from free variation of largely the same melodic material; a shorter, fast, and accelerating section of brief, repeated melodic motifs emphasising a few notes in turn over an offbeat pedal A; and a second short, stylistically unified fast-tempo section, again loosely based on similar thematic material. Nonetheless, the two pieces are not identical. For example, a few measures after the passage shown in fig. 5.9, *Zhaojun* ends on D, while *Great Waves* continues to a final cadence on the note A.

Upper staves: *Great Waves*, measures 19-33, articulation omitted
Lower staves: *Zhaojun*, measures 39-54, articulation omitted

Fig. 5.8. Parallel Thematic Material in *Great Waves* and *Zhaojun*.

Upper staves: *Great Waves,* measures 98-111, articulation omitted
Lower staves: *Zhaojun,* measures 132-43, articulation omitted

**Fig. 5.9. Comparison of Final Sections of Great Waves and Zhaojun.**

## Conclusion

Abing's recorded music for *pipa* is unlike his preserved *erhu* performances in several respects. Although striking similarities, including the use of shared thematic material, exist between the two shorter pieces, *Zhaojun* and *Great Waves,* these similarities are to be discerned most distinctly at the more abstract level of overall sectional and stylistic plan. In the *erhu* pieces, especially *Second Springs* and *Cold Spring Wind,* on the other hand, it was apparent thematic relationships which led to the uncovering of a common sectional procedure. This sectional procedure and the bulk of the same melodic material was also located, although to a less marked degree, in the third *erhu* solo, *Listening to the Pines. Dragon Boats,* the third *pipa* piece, however, does not appear to enter into this kind of mutual interrelationship with the other two lute compositions. Instead, it is formed from a succession of locally recognized folk song tunes interspersed with passages imitating percussion ensemble music, although there is in this solo too a penultimate melodic section in which tonal emphasis is temporarily shifted.

Two different styles of creativity are demonstrated by the three *pipa* pieces. On the one hand, through their free-variation opening sections *Great Waves* and *Zhaojun* may be seen as linked to the classical *pipa* repertory.

Through their use of a shared structural plan involving related material and the patterned occurrence of specific technical events, they are also close in spirit to the three improvised fiddle solos. On the other hand, *Dragon Boats*, with its deliberate employment of existing songs separated by free-time percussion interludes is related to the traditional *shifan luogu* repertory of suites for percussion and melodic instruments. Of course, in the case of a solo performance of such music on the lute, the selection of specific songs, their exact treatment, and the details of the percussion sections could be decided during performance.

Music psychologist Eric Clarke has characterized three possible patterns of relationship between small-scale musical units in improvisations. According to Clarke, there are performances in which a more-or-less preconceived hierarchical structure is followed, those in which units form an associative chain of interrelated elements, and those where a player proceeds by selecting preformed units from a repertory.[28] Adapting this model somewhat, it is possible to envisage all three of Abing's *pipa* pieces as relying on broadly considered structural plans. At a substructural level in *Great Waves* and *Zhaojun*, Clarke's second style of improvisatory progress appears dominant, the chaining of interconnected units. In *Dragon Boats*, however, Clarke's third improvisatory principle is operative, and units are chosen from a memorized repertory of folk song tunes.

Chapters 4 and 5 have sought to examine Abing's six surviving solos from an analytical perspective which takes no note of the conditions under which the pieces have been re-created and disseminated since the time of their original recording in 1950. If the analysis halted here, with the description of "the structure and performance of a certain genre or period,"[29] it would appeal only to those interested in the topic of improvisation as composition in Chinese traditional music or to those who wished to re-create "historically aware" performances of Abing's music. When the analysis is extended to explore the rise of the conservatory system, a window is opened on the ways and contexts within which Chinese musicians perform and explain Abing's pieces today, or what I have termed the Abing tradition. This is the theme of chapter 6.

## Notes

1. Alan P. Merriam, *The Anthropology of Music* (Evanston: Northwestern University Press, 1964), 177.
2. It has kindly been pointed out to me that a less ambiguous translation of *Da lang tao sha* would read *Waves Washing the Sand, the Large Version*, the implication being that one would expect a piece with this title to be an expanded form of the *qupai Waves Washing the Sand*. However, I retain the more open rendering *Great Waves*, which is easier to abridge, and because, as discussed below, Abing's piece does not appear to be an expanded version of the tune *Waves Washing the Sand*.

3. Fig. 3.8 shows two sections of a Daoist ensemble piece, the former being the *qupai Waves Washing the Sand*. This too is in the la mode. For complete transcriptions of Abing's three *pipa* solos, see appendix 2.

4. Zhongyang yinyue xueyuan minzu yinyue, ed., *Xiazi Abing qu ji* (Shanghai: Yinyue chubanshe, 1954), 7.

5. Zhongyang, *Xiazi Abing*, 8.

6. Zhongyang, *Xiazi Abing*, 7.

7. *Playing Chess* is derived from Jiang Tianyi, *Xiaodiao gongchepu* (Shanghai: Shanghai shijie shuju, 1922), 8–9.

8. *All Things Harmonious* is found in Jiang, *Xiaodiao*, 7–8.

9. Alan R. Thrasher, "The Melodic Structure of Jiangnan Sizhu," *Ethnomusicology* 29 (1985): 237–63 (257–58).

10. Thrasher, "Melodic Structure," 258.

11. In fact, comparison of Abing's melodic material in this section with that of the *sizhu* pieces *Along the Street* and *Processional Three-Six* (*Xingjie sanliu*) accounts for 7 additional measures of *Dragon Boats* immediately preceding the passage shown in fig. 5.3 and 5 more measures immediately following it; see Jiang, *Xiaodiao*, 6–7. The remaining 7 measures of *Dragon Boats* act as a coda: the pedal open-strings reiteration ceases and we hear a decorated descent from the third (F#) to the first modal degree (D).

12. Mao Yuan, *Abing meixue sixiang shitan* (Nanjing: Nanjing yishu xueyuan, 1983), 30–31.

13. Mao provides versions of only the matching measures in his study. A complete version of the former tune is presented in Sha Hankun, *Zhongguo min'ge de jiegou yu xuanfa* (Shanghai: Shanghai yinyue chubanshe, 1988), 36; Professor Dai Shuhong taught me a *di* version of the latter, reproduced in Jonathan P. J. Stock, *Chinese Flute Solos* (London: Schott, 1994), 5.

14. Wu Ben, personal communication, 5 February 1994.

15. *Wuxi Sights* is transcribed in Renmin yinyue chubanshe bianji bu, ed., *Zhongguo min'ge xuan* (Beijing: Renmin yinyue chubanshe, 1984), 358–59 and also in Zhou Chuanrong, *Zhongguo min'ge quanji* (Taibei: Li Ming wenhua shiye gongsi, 1978), 66.

16. Jiang, *Xiaodiao*, 10. This version is used in fig. 5.4.

17. My point about "transposition" is more clearly appreciated from versions of *Dragon Boats* transcribed in cipher notation than in stave notation, although the latter has been retained in fig. 5.4 in the interests of consistency. To give further explanation, Cao Anhe may have been correct to transcribe a certain note from *Dragon Boats* as a d' in absolute pitch terms, but incorrect to then rationalize that d' as "1" in the relative pitch terms of cipher notation. In this instance, a modal shift has occurred and d' is now the equivalent of "5." Incidentally, *Eighteen Strokes* seems to be another bawdy folk song (type), like *Intimate Companion* discussed in chapter 2; its specific identification may have been omitted from Yang Yinliu's introduction to the piece for similar reasons that he wished to discredit the *Intimate Companion* link. See Antoinet Schimmelpenninck, "Language and Music in the *Shan'ge* of Southern Jiangsu, China," (Leiden: Ph.D. Dissertation, forthcoming).

18. For a transcription of the outline melody of the *luogu* melody *Great Waves*, see Yang Yinliu and Cao Anhe, *Sunan shifan gu qu: datao qiyue hezouqu* (Beijing: Renmin yinyue chubanshe, 1982), 222.

19. See Zhongguo yishu yanjiuyuan yinyue yanjiusuo, ed., *Zhongguo yinyue cidian* (Beijing: Renmin yinyue chubanshe, 1985), 66, 189. A *pipa* solo of the name *The General's Orders* has been performed since the early nineteenth century; for discussion and partial transcription of one early version, see John E. Myers, *The Way of the Pipa: Structure and Imagery in Chinese Lute Music* (Kent, Ohio: Kent State University Press, 1992), 92–97. However, neither this piece nor another early version has much melodic affinity with Abing's *Great Waves*; see Cao Anhe and Jian Qihua, *Xiansuo shisan tao: (Qing) Ming Yi (Rong Zhai) chuanpu* (Beijing: Yinyue chubanshe, 1962) 3:99–105. For further discussion of this piece and the meaning of its title, see Stephen Jones, *Folk Music of China: Living Instrumental Traditions* (Oxford: Clarendon Press, 1995), 138–39.

20. Mao, *Abing meixue*, 26. *Eight-Beat* is an alternative name for *Old Six-Beat*, a tune found in many regional varieties and repertories, such as Jiangnan *sizhu*. For an English-language introduction to this important Chinese melody, see Huang Jinpei, "Concerning the Variants of '*Lao lioban*'," translated by Alan R. Thrasher, *Asian Music* 13, no. 2 (Spring/Summer 1982): 19–31. For fuller versions of themes of the *Eight-Beat* family, see fig. 3.9. The tune *Autumn Moon* in fig. 5.5 is derived (and transposed) from Ye Dong, *Minzu qiyue de ticai yu xingshi* (Shanghai: Shanghai wenyi chubanshe, 1983), 245.

21. In an earlier publication I compared two fiddle forms of *Autumn Moon* with this same *pipa* version, following Ye Dong in describing the fiddle tunes as twofold expansions of the *pipa* original; see Jonathan P. J. Stock, "Contemporary Recital Solos for the Chinese Two-Stringed Fiddle *Erhu*," *British Journal of Ethnomusicology* 1 (1992): 55–88 (64). However, this assumption may be incorrect. The *Yingzhou gu diao* collection of *pipa* scores from which Ye cites *Autumn Moon* dates from 1916; Ye , *Minzu qiyue*, 244; it would therefore very likely have been a *gongche* notation score. Notational practice in such scores has been decsribed as follows: "In terms of interpretation, the melodies shown in the gongche notation were often regarded by musicians as skeletal structures which were meant to be elaborated upon"; Myers, *Pipa*, 18. *Pipa* players, such as Abing, may then have been playing expanded versions of these melodies all along.

22. Merriam, *Anthropology of Music*, 177.

23. See Thrasher, "Melodic Structure," 252. In a further strand of his analysis, Alan Thrasher links *Autumn Moon* to the Cantonese piece *Autumn Moon over the Peaceful Lake* (*Ping hu qiu yue*), and both pieces to the folk song *Jasmine Flower* (*Molihua*) and the *sizhu* composition *Song of Happiness* (*Huanle ge*), Thrasher, "Melodic Structure," 251–54.

24. Zhongyang, *Xiazi Abing*, 7.

25. Mao, *Abing meixue*, 28.

26. Ye, *Minzu qiyue*, 221–32.

27. Myers, *Pipa*, 70.

28. Eric Clarke, "Generative Principles in Music Performance," in John A. Sloboda, ed., *Generative Processes in Music: The Psychology of Performance, Improvisation, and Composition* (Oxford: Clarendon Press, 1988), 1–26 (8–9).

29. Anthony Seeger, *Why Suyá Sing: A Musical Anthropology of an Amazonian People* (Cambridge: Cambridge University Press, 1987), xiii.

# Chapter 6

# Musical Creativity, Identity, and Meaning in Twentieth-Century China

> Music is at once an everyday activity, an industrial commodity, a flag of re-sistance, a personal world, and a deeply symbolic, emotional grounding for people in every class and cranny the superculture offers. Bourdieu offers a rea-son: music "says nothing and has nothing to say . . . music represents the most radical and most absolute form of the negation of the world, and especially the social world, which the bourgeois ethos tends to demand of all forms of art." . . . Ethnomusicology argues otherwise: it is not that music has nothing to say, but that it allows everyone to say what they want. It is not because it negates the world, but because it embodies any number of imagined worlds that people turn to music as a core form of expression.          Mark Slobin.[1]

In a sense, Pierre Bourdieu's position is not so much diametrically opposed to that proposed by Mark Slobin as its prerequisite: only through an ability to suspend mundane actuality could music conjure up multiple spheres of self-expression. At the very start of this book I briefly examined ethnomu-sicological views of the individual, drawing on Thomas Turino's idea of the cultural process as a multiplicity of individual variation to support my con-tention that the personal, the idiosyncratic, and the exceptional are very much part of the collective, the typical, and the ordinary. As I argued in chapter 2, the ordering of sense by every individual takes place within par-ticular social contexts, each of which encourages the promotion and nor-malization of certain interpretations and activities as opposed to others. Ac-cording to John Kaemmer, "power arrangements in a society strongly influence decisions concerning the kind of musical events that occur, and the developing regularities in these decisions constitute a major process in de-termining the nature of the resulting musical culture."[2]

Having discussed forms of collective cultural expression in chapter 3, I then progressed in chapters 4 and 5 to concentrate on Abing's actions as an individual musical creator, suggesting that the specific results of two peri-ods of transitory and improvisatory activity have endured as multiple, in-dependent solos. It is now time to look more closely at the question of how Abing's music acquires meaning in modern China. To do this, I begin by examining the conservatory tradition, focusing on the ways in which Abing's music is taught, performed, rearranged, and received by contemporary professional Chinese musicians and their audiences. The account thus continues the historical approach of chapter 1, fills in the ideological background to the creation of biographical narratives discussed in chapter 2, charts the impact of modernization on the performance of traditional genres like those introduced in chapter 3, and completes the musical analysis of chapters 4 and 5 by explaining why contemporary Chinese musicians envisage the Abing tradition in the way they do.

## The Conservatory Tradition

### Nationalist Establishment, 1920s–1949

The Chinese conservatory tradition was founded within Abing's lifetime. Indeed, Yang Yinliu, collector of Abing's solos, was himself one of the first generation of music conservatory staff.[3] In the early 1920s, as part of the wave of nationalistic sentiment accompanying the May 4th Movement (see chapter 1), a small number of Chinese academics had begun to establish music courses at a few universities and, from November 1927 onward, at the National Music College in Shanghai as well as at a handful of Western-run educational institutions.[4] Further courses were introduced to government schools. These music courses were predominantly Western in inspiration and content, but, through the activities of musicians such as the *erhu* players Liu Tianhua and Zhou Shaomei, some Chinese music was integrated into the new graduate curricula in music. Nonetheless, the Chinese element of these courses was not widely popular at first, with both Chinese music academics and students questioning the suitability of teaching such music in a modern, "scientific" educational context. In accounting for the resistance to indigenous musical traditions, and particularly those considered by the urban middle-class students and academics to be of low social status, Xiao Youmei (1884–1940), a principal figure at the Shanghai music college, apparently noted that, "The *erhu* had always been the peddler's tool or the smoking girl's plaything and was censured by the ancients as 'licentious in sound and injurious to virtue.'"[5] Liu Tianhua was also cognizant of this problem. His solution was first to attempt to distance the instrument from the music it was given to perform:

> [F]rom antiquity until today, there have always been those who consider fiddle music both coarse and lascivious, not in good taste. But this does not make clear musical sense. In fact, music's coarseness or elegance lies completely within the performer's expressivity and the makeup of the composition. The same musical instruments can express each of the "seven emotions"—how could the fiddle be an exception?[6]

A second part of Liu's agenda in the promotion of traditional instruments such as the two-stringed fiddle and *pipa* within the bounds of the new educational and social schemes was the parallel dissemination of a newly written or arranged repertory. This *guoyue*, or "national music" (see chapter 3), was nationalistic in the sense that it did not entirely reject past traditions; rather, it sought to harness existing elements to progressive ends. In some respects, a ready analogy was the concurrent replacement in official use of classical written Chinese by a form based on contemporary speech and Westernized punctuation symbols. *Guoyue* was Chinese, but it was perceived to be open to modification, professionalization, and development in a way that the specific traditions of individual regions were not.[7]

The search for a musical style that would be at once rational, modern, and nationally (as opposed to locally or regionally) representative was not confined to Chinese music reformers alone. Visiting Western musicians such as Alexander Tcherepnine [Tcherepnin] encouraged their Chinese pupils to use native traditions as a rich source of material and compositional inspiration.[8] More strikingly, similar concerns were voiced in other emergent nations. An example is furnished by post-Ottoman Turkey, where the Turkist Ziya Gökalp wrote a program for national music reform in 1923 closely akin to those of contemporary Chinese music educators:

> Our natural music . . . is to be born from a synthesis of our folk music and Western music. Our folk music provides us with a rich treasury of melodies. By collecting them and arranging them on the basis of Western musical techniques, we shall have both a national and a modern music.[9]

As will be imagined, the establishment of the conservatories, and the teaching of Chinese traditional instruments within Western-format schools and colleges, had a more profound effect than the writing of fiddle pieces with harmonized accompaniments. As Han Kuo-Huang points out:

> Musicians trained in Western style began to think and hear music in terms of Western intonation, harmony, tone color, range, and above all, standardization of musical instruments. The new generation of musicians who played traditional instruments were also influenced by the same way of thinking.[10]

In fact, arguably the central aspect of the rise of the conservatory tradition was the re-envisioning of individual compositions as enduring works, conceived, transmitted, and preserved in musical notation. This paradigm shift is illustrated by Liu Tianhua's *erhu* compositions, discussed in chapter 3. Liu's compositional style was fundamentally a synthesis of traditional melody, Western sectional structure, and adopted violin techniques, but the most essential point here is that his solos were from the outset treated as specific, fixed compositions.[11] In the conservatories, socially acceptable performance of this repertory demanded the ceding of creative primacy to the authoritative details of the written score, envisaged as legal surrogate for the individual composer's intentions. The publication in 1933 of detailed scores of Liu's pieces and technical studies for *erhu* and *pipa*, marks the formal adoption by conservatory-based national musicians of a written as opposed to oral ideal of musical transmission.[12]

Lydia Goehr refers to this ceding of creative primacy as the *Werktreue* concept, tracing its evolution in Western classical musical practice and thought. In Goehr's view, the work concept emerged around 1800, "when musicians began to reconstruct musical history to make it look as if musicians had always thought about their activities in modern terms."[13] However, as Goehr herself continues, and much ethnomusicological and musicological research confirms, this practical re-envisioning of the past is not an activity confined to European art musicians around, or since, 1800. Instead, it would seem a precondition of the rationalization of any tradition. An example from the field of Chinese music research is provided by Bell Yung. To Yung, the contemporary realization of *qin* zither music from old manuscripts suggests a concept of "historical interdependency," wherein knowledge of the present influences the perceived past.[14] Philip Schuyler's analysis of multidimensional Yemeni views of "tradition" also underlines this point: "Ultimately, it is not necessary that a tradition be a genuine historical relic, only that it appear to be so."[15]

Given that Chinese conservatory musicians from the very beginning saw their work as a refinement and enrichment of existing musical traditions, I feel that Antoinet Schimmelpenninck and Frank Kouwenhoven miss the mark when they describe the conservatory style as one "which is unrelated to the original tradition of the Chinese instruments but forms a new tradition in its own right."[16] The collection, adoption, and adaptation of Abing's music by conservatory musicians itself offers a prime example of the dynamic and self-conscious relationship between folk material and this alternate performance style. To look at this transformation immediately, however, would be to over-entangle the chronological thread. Instead, it is necessary to return to the history of the Chinese conservatory system.

Recapping briefly: a national conservatory had been formed in 1927, but there was still much resistance from the Chinese intelligentsia towards the sustenance of what they regarded as "low culture."[17] Perceived cultural inferiority, resting on the observation of China's economic and social imbalances, encouraged many young Chinese to embrace Western art music at this time. Liu Tianhua's answer was the fostering of a new repertory, one which interwove the positive symbols of modernization and nationalism. His work can also be considered as a manifestation of the late-nineteenth-century Chinese view of modernization as the retention of Chinese "essence" through Western "means."[18]

Liu himself was not able to provide an entire new repertory, but he encouraged his pupils to write their own pieces and arrange existing folk solos.

Among Liu's pupils, the most significant were perhaps Jiang Fengzhi, Chen Zhenduo, Lu Xiutang, and Cao Anhe. While Cao is known more as a teacher and music scholar, Chen Zhenduo produced an *erhu* method in 1941,[19] as well as collections of solos. Jiang Fengzhi and Lu Xiutang were also active as composers and transcribers in the preparation of new pieces at this time.[20]

These musicians were all familiar with *gongche* notation (see chapter 3) and also Western stave notation, but in the 1930s and 1940s they were among those who adopted cipher notation as a modern, scientific manner of prescribing musical sound.[21] Like *gongche* notation, cipher notation is fully transposable, using a series of simple characters to represent modal degrees. Unlike *gongche*, the basic character set is the Western digits: 1 (pronounced "do"), 2 ("re"), 3 ("mi") etc. These symbols are ordered horizontally from left to right rather than in vertical columns. Underscored lines mark rhythmic subdivisions, as in stave notation, and dots positioned above or below a symbol signify upper or lower octave variants. Cipher notation thus allowed Chinese conservatory musicians access to the rhythmic specificity of Western notation while retaining the advantages of a relative pitch system, such as the convenience of associating fingering patterns with relative modal degrees. Fig. 6.1 shows in parallel cipher and stave notations a passage from one of Lu Xiutang's *erhu* compositions, *Yearning for Home (Huai xiang xing).*[22]

The immediate impact of the work of Liu's pupils and other conservatory musicians was, however, limited by the political fragmentation of China, the

Fingering etc. omitted

Fig. 6.1. *Yearning for Home,* by Lu Xiutang in Cipher and Stave Notation.

Japanese invasion, and the ensuing war between the Nationalists and Communists. These factors stimulated other musical characteristics and considerations, including the development of new forms of music. Describing the rise of Chinese Communist culture from the experiments of the 1920s–1930s, Isabel Wong writes:

> By the 1940s . . . the results of this experimentation had been formulated into a comprehensive cultural policy whose tenets stood in sharp contrast to those of the May Fourth principles. For whereas the activities associated with the May Fourth Movement had been mostly urban and its manifestations, influenced strongly by the West, were produced by the educated for the educated, the revolutionary cultural products prescribed by Yan'an were predominantly rural and popular, produced for a mass audience and modeled after indigenous rural criteria.[23]

Thus, additional threads of musical activity during this period were the assembling by musicians of folk song melodies which were then reintroduced to the masses with new words, and the composition of new songs intended for general consumption supporting one political view or another. Conservatory musicians were associated with this movement in a number of ways, being prominent among the ranks of folk song collectors, and acting as composers of new, militant mass songs. The movement itself moved formally into the conservatories in Communist-administered areas during the Sino-Japanese war. The composer Xian Xinghai, sometime student at the Paris Conservatory, moved to Yan'an in 1938 to head the music department of the Lu Xun Arts Academy. There, Xian's activities included the training of cultural cadres in composition, and the organization and conducting of mass choral groups. He also composed a large amount of music for practical use in building communal spirit and maintaining morale. The bulk of this music was in song form, but Xian also wrote larger-scale pieces.[24]

Yan'an possessed few Western instruments, so Xian wrote in his larger works for a mixture of Chinese and European instruments. Use of Western harmonization demanded from the traditional instruments a standardization of performance practice and the adoption of equal-tempered intonation, underlining values expressed within the music of a decade earlier, such as Liu Tianhua's *erhu* solos. Calls were made for the revision and standardization of the manufacture of traditional instruments, and for their improvement along the lines of modern, scientific acoustics, as mentioned above by Han Kuo-Huang.

Although arising from the specific lack of a full Western instrumental ensemble at Yan'an, this trend towards the admixture of Chinese and Western instruments within the same performance group occurred elsewhere in China as well. Han Kuo-Huang has traced the development of the "national music" orchestra from the nucleus of the Jiangnan *sizhu* ensemble plus Western bass instruments.[25] The first appearance of such an orchestra was 1935, with Western-format concerts taking place from 1942 onwards. Significantly, the national music orchestra was established by the Chinese Central Broadcasting Station, which also maintained a Western-style ensemble, from whom the bass-line musicians were initially borrowed.

At the same time as the national orchestra's first concert-style performances, in May 1942, Mao Zedong presented his blueprint for future cultural production in China (see also chapter 1). Musicians, as other artists, were to keep in mind the irreducible social basis and political content of musical production. In order to give their work relevance to the masses, they were to experience rural conditions and traditions first hand, adopting and reforming these as necessary to further the revolution. This call resulted in the refocusing of the mass song movement, with greater emphasis placed on fitting revolutionary texts to well-known folk tunes. Direct communication with rural audiences was also the intention of travelling propaganda troupes who performed scenes of oppression and liberation to the music of local folk song or ballad singing. Representative of such works was the opera *The White-Haired Girl (Bai mao nü)*, written by Xian Xinghai's pupil Ma Ke (1918–76) and several associates.[26] In many respects, this piece encapsulates the characteristics of the Chinese conservatory style of the 1940s: it is a named work written by a team of named, formally instructed composers; it reflects the belief that a modern, national musical style would draw from both Western and Chinese traditions; and it acknowledges the intimate connection between the national music repertory and the sociopolitical causes of the day.

### Communist Consolidation, 1949–1994

By 1950, the Communists had defeated the Nationalists and introduced their cultural and political ideologies to the whole of the Chinese mainland.[27] New conservatories were opened, and links established with Eastern bloc nations; Chinese music students and performers visited these countries, and East European teachers came to China. Yet although foreign expertise was highly valued, indigenous peasant-worker-soldier culture was highly esteemed as well. The new Communist government promoted the ideal of a modernized, national, and working-class culture. Music specialists, the students and staff of the conservatories and professional performance units, were regularly detailed to visit the countryside, factories, or barracks, both to assist these people in their daily duties, to entertain them and educate them through musical performance, and to learn from them.

Other specialists were detailed to redesign traditional instruments, enhancing the acoustic properties and range of these instruments, as well as filling in chromatic steps and adjusting tone quality. Privately owned workshops were combined into collective factories. New sizes of instruments were constructed to provide the national music composer complete SATB families of Chinese wind, bowed, and plucked instruments. For instance, further frets were added to the *pipa*, and their spacing reconsidered, such that the instrument yielded an increased and fully chromatic range of equal-tempered pitches. On the *erhu*, steel strings—brighter in tone, more durable, less liable to slip during performance, and more reliable in the upper register—replaced those of silk (see photo 4).[28] Deeper-pitched fiddles were constructed, most notably the two-stringed *zhonghu*, or "mid-[pitched] fiddle," tuned a fifth below the *erhu*, and the four-stringed *gehu*, or "reformed fiddle," modeled on and tuned as the cello.

It was in this context that the collection and publication of Abing's performances took place. Whatever Yang Yinliu's personal motives for including two sessions with Abing beside his primary research into Wuxi percussion music, in order to understand how this material came to be interpreted by conservatory musicians, it is essential to recognize the progress-oriented musical value system of the period, in which appropriate music was invested with positive social function. While there were both romantic and modernist elements in the collection and dissemination of Abing's music, his solos were collected neither as part of a bourgeois, romantic fascination with exotic or quaint country folklore, nor as part of a modernist movement to preserve or document threatened traditions.

Among the conservatory musicians of the 1950s, already convinced of

Photo 4. Wu Zhimin Playing the Modernized *Erhu*.

the social role of music and of the centrality of their own progressive task in bringing technically improved music to the people, there can have been little initial reason to question the content of Abing's music. According to Yang Yinliu's biography, Abing was a blind folk musician from the lowest social echelons, and according to Mao Zedong, all music was imbued with the social background of its creator. Thus, Abing's music must have reflected the values of the lower classes, those theoretically most elevated in the new People's Republic. The performance of Abing's music, therefore, had distinct social advantages compared to the playing of solos by bourgeois, though admittedly patriotic and thus still acceptable, composers such as Liu Tianhua.

However, despite Abing's seemingly impeccable political credentials—Yang Yinliu had, after all, omitted all discussion of Abing's drug addiction and other potentially embarrassing habits from his biography—the conservatory musicians of the early 1950s were often themselves much closer to Liu Tianhua than Abing in musical ideology. Thus, the transcriptions of Abing's performances were interpreted by conservatory musicians as if they were written compositions, musical entities designed by the authoritative figure of a composer. They were played as if they were music of national relevance, the performance of which made a positive contribution to the establishment and maintenance of communist society. They were played by conservatory musicians on redesigned instruments, according to new standards of intonation and instrumental technique, in the modern contexts of the concert hall and the broadcasting studio.[29]

Abing's music was, above all else, music to be used, material suited to progressive re-creation in the new social and cultural context of its re-creators. Now, there may appear to be a contradiction between, on the one hand, my claim that conservatory musicians interpreted the transcriptions as prescriptive scores and, on the other, my assertion that they did so on the so-called "reformed" instruments with aspects of performance technique and standards of tuning foreign to the original. However, this potential incongruity disappears when consideration is given to a second strand of the nineteenth-century, romantic aesthetic on which much conservatory music making is founded. While the past provided models for present activity, it also offered the contemporary musician a series of musical masterpieces which transcended "temporal and spatial boundaries."[30] Through the assemblage of such pieces, a canon of great works was obtained. As far as the conservatory musicians were concerned, they still played Abing's great music, but as a result of their access to modernized instruments and training, they simply did it better than he.[31]

Henry Kingsbury's remarks on the dual nature of the relationship between musical scores and patterns of authority have already been mentioned and revolve around this same distinction. While the score, by nature of its perceived link with the intentions of the deceased composer, is claimed by performers as a resource "in negotiations of musical meaning, quality, and authority," further rhetorical appeals may be directed above and beyond the score to an asserted understanding of the composer's intentions. The performer argues that an interpretation reflects the fundamental spirit of the work, even when such a rendition requires inconsistent treatment of some detail of the notational code within which the composer attempted to encapsulate this musical spirit.[32]

The impact of this aesthetic system on the re-creation of Abing's music is considered further shortly. First, however, I continue to sketch recent Chinese history and the ongoing development of the conservatory tradition. Once ideological and historical contexts are in place, the particulars of musical re-creation become more meaningful.

In chapter 1 the Communist Party's campaigns of the early 1950s towards land reform and against superstition were introduced. These movements were, in fact, part of a larger systematic pattern reducing all non-Communist political power. Rural landlords were trimmed of surplus property through agricultural redistribution, urban businessmen were targeted by industrial and capital reform, religious influence was curtailed through campaigns which laicized many temples and churches, and clan networks were loosened by promulgation of a Marriage Law "which laid down equality between the sexes, banned arranged marriages, concubinage, polygamy and interference in the remarriage of widows, and greatly facilitated divorce."[33] New forms of social control were instituted, for example the neighborhood committee system, and vice laws struck at drug traffickers, prostitution, and secret societies.[34]

Conflict with the United States in Korea (1950–53) reinforced Chinese nationalism, and contrasted markedly with China's brusque humiliation there at the hands of the Japanese in 1894. Conservatory students were among those who volunteered for, and saw, service in Korea, several of the senior professors of the early 1990s having taken part in the war. Others, like the earlier musicians who had campaigned against the Qing Dynasty, took part in the many "Resist America, Aid Korea" activities of the time.[35]

New conservatories were opened in certain cities, and existing establishments were enlarged through the addition of extra departments. For instance, a national music department was added to the Shanghai Conservatory in 1956,[36] thus rationalizing the activities of existent individual teachers in these specialisms into specific degree curricula.[37] The collection and study of the music of folk songs and minority ethnic groups was further promoted from the institutional base of the conservatories and local cultural bureaus. Prominent folk musicians were invited to the music conservatories as visiting teachers and performers.[38] Instrumental ensembles, composed of redesigned instruments, were also augmented, and new repertory was composed and arranged for the combination. New solo pieces were also required by students taking degree-level qualifications in national instrumental performance at the growing conservatories.

Abing's solos suited these trends in three ways. On a practical level, publication of his six pieces increased somewhat the study material available to the growing number of conservatory students. Secondly, the performance of Abing's music was a useful example for elite conservatory musicians of their acceptance of the music of the working classes. Third, as was mentioned in chapter 2, *Second Springs* and *Listening to the Pines* provided music linked to a patriotic theme at a time when the integrity of China's borders appeared under threat.

As the 1950s progressed, the weighting of these themes altered to reflect the developing political situation and its impact on the priorities of the conservatory musicians. Thus, musical preferences veered from one position to another, reflecting the more open mood of the Hundred Flowers campaign, which encouraged public feedback on governmental policy; the narrower orthodoxies of the Anti-Rightist movement, in which the government struck back at those who had dared to offer criticism; and the production-dominated ideology of the economically disastrous Great Leap Forward (1958–59). When cosmopolitan values were most strongly emphasized, the mid–1950s and early 1960s, the study, performance, and continuation of the European classical tradition was considered the central concern of the conservatories. At other times, mass music making was stressed, and the promotion of newly written political songs and performance of nationally relevant works among the worker-peasant-soldier base of society ousted, or at least threatened to oust, more elitist interests.

The re-creation of Abing's music, within the context of a struggle between cosmopolitan and populist musical factions, suited neither category entirely well. Although the conservatories included Chinese music departments, there was among some conservatory leaders an air of denigration of traditional, monophonic music as compared to the richly harmonized and accompanied Western orchestral ideal.[39] On the other hand, the conservatory musicians' desire to re-create existing masterworks was clearly more supportive to the sustenance of Abing's solos than the accent placed by more populist musicians, often located outside the conservatories, on the creation of modern, mass works which would inspire and sustain social revolution. Yet, through its association with that most politically correct of Communist China's musical instruments, the *erhu*, and through appeal to the class standing of its originator, Abing's music had just the kind of direct, non-elitist allure that populist musicians desired for their own compositions. The harnessing of such allure to the revolutionary cause is illustrated by the following program note for *Second Springs* from a music book believed to date from 1958:

From its title, this composition seems to depict the scene of moonlight reflecting on the water of the world's second most famous spring [i.e. Second Springs] on

Hui-chuan [Huiquan] Mountain, Wusi [Wuxi] City. In reality, it is not based on a depiction of scenery. Using the lonely scenery of moonlight reflecting on the water, the composer portrays his own miserable life.[40]

Yang Yinliu's original account of *Second Springs* had more simply stated: "The meaning of the whole name is heavenly moonlight reflected in the Second Springs," and added that the name may have been applied by Abing to a preexistent piece for reasons of local color.[41] Lying between Yang Yinliu's account and that of 1958 is one of 1956, simultaneous with the liberal tone of the Hundred Flowers movement, in which the title's theme of pastoral tone painting is taken to reflect the literal musical content of the piece. This program describes the solo as "a piece of music depicting the moonlight scene of the world's second most famous spring at Hui-chuan Mountain, Wusi City."[42] In chapter 2, I quoted part of a description from 1963 of the same piece. The whole description actually synthesizes the 1956 and 1958 programs, claiming that the piece represents the beauty of the motherland, the composer's patriotism, and "the mutual life experience he and the people shared."[43]

It would be tempting to draw a teleological cultural progression from Yang Yinliu's 1954 citation of music with a locally referent title, through the 1956 presentation of the piece as a musical description of moonlit waters and the 1958 interpretation of it as autobiography through poetic metaphor, to the 1963 synthesis of music as patriotic realism. However, in light of Turino's reminder of the appearance of cultural coherence disguising a multiplicity of individual variation and Scott's description of cultural change, it is perhaps more probable that the latter three contrasting readings (and others besides) arose once Abing's music was disseminated and employed by different musicians in new contexts. Changes in the political character of the times helped fuel reconsideration of the music, and also brought these views into alternate prominence.

It is also possible to read the 1963 program as a rallying point for conservatory musicians wishing to perform this music. At this time, members of the populist music lobby were pursuing a major ideological offensive against pro-European conservatory leaders. For example, Richard Kraus details the 1963 campaign led by Yao Wenyuan, later prominent as a member of the "Gang of Four," to discredit Debussy and expose the bourgeois nature of impressionist music.[44] Both the 1963 program note and Yao Wenyuan's campaign hinge on the class content of their specified music, one pointing to Abing's life among the masses and the other to Debussy's middle-class connections. This is no coincidence. In September 1962, alarmed that the success of the more pragmatic economic policies replacing his disastrous mass mobilizations during the Great Leap Forward would lead both to his total eclipse as a national leader and to the return of bourgeois capitalism to the People's Republic, Mao Zedong called on the party leaders to remember the importance of class struggle.[45] Mao's supporters at a national level began to do likewise, with communist music aestheticians applying more rigorous modes of analysis to the concept of "musical image" (*yinyue xingxiang*). This broad concept, according to music historian Wang Liuhe, embraced issues of class content; historical and national contexts; questions of aesthetic representation and music's function within education and entertainment; and the emotional affect of music.[46]

Mao's insistence on class struggle led to bitter conflict in 1966, as rival factions contended for power at the start of what has become known as the Cultural Revolution. Conservatory leaders and professors who had previously argued in favor of foreign and bourgeois music were among the first to be purged, together with those known to prefer historical or religious music. Foreign music was all but banned, and traditional pieces, although free from foreign contamination, were largely discarded in the face of parallel movements against "old culture," which soon came to mean not only music created before 1949 but also that composed prior to 1966. Prominent interpreters of the now forbidden repertories (including Abing's music) were denounced and, in the case of the *erhu* teacher and composer Lu Xiutang, driven to death.

As mentioned in chapter 2, Abing's memorial tablet and stone were vandalized during the Cultural Revolution, and the musician recategorized locally as a ruffian purveyor of poisonous music. This evaluation relied partly on the assumption that since Abing had been active in pre-Communist times, his music must be imbued with the social spirit of those times, but also on the rumors in Wuxi, long suppressed in Yang Yinliu's official biography, of Abing's brothelizing, drug taking, and continued Daoist allegiance. In a musicological sense, further ammunition was provided for Abing's critics by the observation that although a patriotic and autobiographical program had been asserted for his best-known piece *Second Springs*, the piece did not conclude with the triumph of revolution over the forces of reactionary oppression. In this perception, the *erhu* solo was simply too passive for use in the Cultural Revolution. Perhaps it identified and characterized in sound the evils of pre-Communist society but, instead of inciting militant action, *Second Springs* functioned only to channel social pressure into fruitless cathartic release. The same reason was stated publicly for critical dismissal of Schubert's *Unfinished* Symphony at this time, as a 1974 newspaper review made clear:

> The opening phrase is sombre and gloomy. The whole symphony continues and expands on this emotion, filling it with petty-bourgeois despair, pessimism and solitary distress. At times the dreaming of freedom does come through but this too is escapist and negative.[47]

Although the scope of such critiques appears restricted to historical, class, and musicological domains, in a contemporary political sense, these judgments were highly significant, in that the Cultural Revolution was not only a period of great physical violence but also one of factional struggle by proxy. An assault on Abing, or Schubert, was an assault on those who performed, promoted, studied, and valued this music. Subsequent attempts to rehabilitate Abing, or Schubert, were often attempts to restore to authority those previously swept aside and dislodge those currently occupying positions of influence.[48]

The music conservatories gradually reopened in the early 1970s, though now with an emphasis on amateur and mass music making. New compositions and the performance of existing ones had to satisfy stringent revolutionary criteria, the failure to meet these leading to severe punishment. The ethos underlying musical work during this period is illustrated by a carefully worded paragraph opening a report on the recent activities of *erhu* exponent Min Huifen and *pipa* player Liu Dehai:

> Since the founding of the Chinese People's Republic in 1949, and especially since the Cultural Revolution initiated in 1966, revolutionary Chinese musicians inspired by the revolution in Peking opera have been carrying out Chairman Mao's policy of "making the past serve the present and foreign things serve China," and "weeding through the old to bring forth the new." In order to create new music which reflects the heroic images of the proletariat, our musicians have gone to live with the workers, peasants and soldiers and have composed many works reflecting current revolutionary struggles; at the same time they have been arranging large numbers of traditional pieces by critically assimilating their best points and introducing certain innovations. They have also improved the tonal volume, range and pitch of the traditional instruments created by various Chinese nationalities through the centuries, while preserving their distinctive features. The improved *erh-hu* and *pi-pa* for example, are now used not only as solo instruments but also in symphonic music and in the orchestral accompaniment for modern revolutionary operas and modern Chinese ballets.[49]

Wu Chou-Kuang continues to introduce a pair of solos performed by each of these musicians, stressing the class content, program, and process of revision under the direct guidance of the masses through which each piece (and soloist) had passed. The selection of music includes a newly written composition; two arrangements based on folk song tunes, one portraying "the sorrows of the laboring masses before Liberation," the other expressing "our revolutionary people's love and admiration for Chairman Mao";[50] and one revised historical solo depicting the triumph of a progressive general over his revisionary opponent.

Despite the inclusion of some revised pre-revolutionary pieces in Wu Chou-Kuang's set of acceptable music, Abing's music appears not to have been played in its original form at this time. Instead, pianist Chu Wanghua arranged a solo piano version of *Second Springs* (1972) where the original melody and structure were elaborated through "rich harmonization and

modulation . . . to produce a fully pianistic texture, which powerfully contrasts with the melody and better embodies the artistic conception of original composition."[51] An excerpt from this arrangement is shown in fig. 6.2,
the passage selected being the equivalent of themes B' and F in section 5 of
Abing's *erhu* solo (see also figs. 4.8 and 4.9; CD track 8).

Fig. 6.2. Chu Wanghua's Piano Version of *Second Springs,* Measures 49–52.

The revolutionary potential of the piano had been asserted by virtuoso Yin Chengzong (b.1941) at the start of the Cultural Revolution. At a time when many other pianists were under considerable pressure, Yin boldly "took the piano into the streets as a practical demonstration that it had a place in the Cultural Revolution."[52] The gesture caught the imagination of Jiang Qing, who saw Western instruments as more powerful expressive vehicles than those of China, even in their improved forms. After producing a version of the model opera *The Red Lantern* (*Hongdeng ji*) for two vocalists and piano accompaniment, Yin went on to rehabilitate Xian Xinghai's *Yellow River* Cantata (*Huanghe hechang*) in the guise of a piano concerto (1970).[53] By 1972, Yin was also producing arrangements of traditional pieces such as *Three Variations on Plum Blossom* and *Ambush on All Sides* (*Shimian maifu*; incidentally, a revised form of this *pipa* piece is among those discussed by Wu Chou-Kuang three years later), although it would seem that the piano transcriptions of these solos were not approved for performance.[54]

The public rehabilitation of the original *erhu* version seems to have occurred in 1976, the year of the death of Mao Zedong and the fall of the Gang of Four. This event was marked by the republication of Yang Yinliu's biography of Abing and a score of *Second Springs* in the journal *People's Music*.[55] Appearance of the material within this particular journal was significant, it being the official mouthpiece of the influential Chinese Musicians' Association. Endorsement of Abing and *Second Springs* there carried much greater political symbolism than had it occurred in any other journal.

The 1977 version of this biographical sketch is broadly similar to that first published by Yang more than twenty years earlier. Differences include an opening paragraph praising Chairman Hua, celebrating the downfall of the Gang of Four, and mentioning the reappearance of performances and broadcasts of *Second Springs*. As discussed in chapter 2, the scene of the moon's reflection moved from the Second Springs fount to a nearby lake. Yang Yinliu describes the program of the piece as being a description of the moonlit lakeside, though he grants that it also reflects the composer's love of the motherland and innermost emotions. More importantly for present purposes, Yang briefly mentions that a "string ensemble" (*xianyue hezou*) version of *Second Springs* has won the affections of the people.[56] Examination of the string version reveals more about the nature of the conservatory tradition. The version in question may actually be one of several, but it was very likely that of Wu Zuqiang (b.1927) prepared for string orchestra in 1976.[57]

Wu Zuqiang's harmonized and sometimes polyphonic arrangement largely follows the outline of Abing's piece. The introductory phrase is expanded through the composition of an additional four measures of music, and a one-measure link phrase is inserted before the final section, but Wu Zuqiang's major alteration is the omission of the third section of *Second Springs*, although a little of the cut material—the repetition of theme C—is inserted into the following section, just where Abing originally performed a shortened re-peat of theme C (see figs. 4.8 and 4.9). Apart from shortening the piece, Wu Zuqiang's cut has the effect of giving it a single climactic moment, when the extreme high register is opened up by thematic elements B' and F.[58]

Similar alterations have in fact been applied by *erhu* players and by ar-rangers for differing ensembles. An example is the string quartet arrange-ment prepared by Ding Shande (b.1911), vice president of the Shanghai Con-servatory both before and after the Cultural Revolution.[59] Ding Shande's version of *Second Springs* demonstrates in a specific way several of the fea-tures of the modernization of traditional music discussed elsewhere. As an art music composer, perhaps best known for his five-movement "Long March" Symphony (1962), Ding Shande recast Abing's *erhu* solo in the high-est status ensemble combination of the Western classical tradition. On the other hand, the composer's fingering instructions make it clear that he, like Wu Zuqiang in his version, expects the string players to add *erhu* style glis-sandi, although Ding, unlike Wu, dispensed with Abing's decorative use of C# (or D#, in that Ding's arrangement is pitched a tone above the *erhu* solo) in thematic element C, to fix the piece less equivocally into diatonic major tonality. The opening of Ding's arrangement is shown in fig. 6.3 (CD track 9).

The accompanying lines show that Ding frequently works in thematic and motivic imitations, but relies in the main on octave doublings and functional harmonies assembled primarily from the pentatonic set A, B, C#, E, and F#.[60] Octave doublings, often aurally disguised through the use of distinct rhythmic patterns in each part, may perhaps be seen as a resonance of the heterophonic performance style of traditional Chinese ensembles. However, unlike traditional heterophony, phrases of the main melody are typically al-ternated between the four instruments.

As we move on to consider the structural organization of the quartet, we notice that Ding cuts the final rendition's themes C and D. (This is presum-ably linked to his apparent desire to make Abing's solo conform more closely with a tonal ideal.) These themes ended in Abing's version with a cadence to the fifth degree of the scale. Instead, Ding Shande composes a chordal coda reiterating movement onto the A-major triad, with A in treble and bass. Ding also shortens the whole work, omitting themes C and D of section 1, and A and B of section 2. Section 3 is again cut, while section 4 follows in-tact. Section 5 is then presented with themes C and D from the previous sec-tion repeated over a new harmonization, followed immediately with themes B' and F (E is cut). Finally, themes A and B lead to the chordal coda. Ding Shande's version is, thus, like that of Wu Zuqiang, founded on a single rise to themes B' and F. It rationalizes Abing's six-section solo into a tighter four-section structure which corresponds rather neatly to the classical Chinese rhetorical mold of "introduction, elucidation, transition, and conclusion" (*qi-cheng-zhuan-he*).[61] Unlike Abing, whose creative model in this solo may have been the ongoing varied repetition of a chain of melodic elements, but

Fig. 6.3. Ding Shande's Arrangement of *Second Springs*
for String Quartet, Measures 1–8.

like many other contemporary performers, Ding carefully arranges the
themes and sections to correspond to an overall structural design.

Contemporary *erhu* performers, when they play Abing's solos, frequently
add accompaniments.[62] In the main, these are written for the *yangqin*,
though some employ larger forces, including concertino-type scoring for solo
*erhu* and national instrument orchestra. Terence Liu has completed a detailed comparison of several of the most prominent of these, which need not

be duplicated here. Liu's conclusions, however, are revealing about the aesthetic under which such new versions are produced and performed. On the one hand, conservatory musicians freely compose accompaniments, often in a functional harmonic style akin to that of Ding Shande. Also, they cut unwanted passages and move melodic elements from one section to another.[63] On the other hand, these musicians refrain from the addition of new material to the solo part.[64] To this, it may be added that conservatory players have also tended not to treat Abing's themes differently from one performance to another. Having established a favored arrangement of each solo, they aim to reproduce it each time. At the start of this section, I outlined the progressive attitude conservatory players maintain towards traditional solos like those of Abing, and their belief that the essence of this music can be re-created, at a higher grade of professionalism, in the new social and musical contexts of modern China (CD track 7). Other than its demonstration in the musical facts of the rearranged versions of *Second Springs* and the other fiddle pieces, this attitude is also made explicit in comments such as the following:

> Lan Yusong, professor at the Central Conservatory of Music, said Ah Bing had inherited and developed China's traditional style of folk music. People never tire of hearing it. However, judged by the standards of the 1980s, his music is not perfect. What makes it so moving is that Ah Bing knew how to express his feelings in melody, developing his own unique style which incorporated traditional and folk music, Professor Lan said.[65]

The reinterpretation of folk music in new contexts is a primary aspect of its maintenance in many parts of the modern world, and may follow similar paths in different nations. For example, Martin Stokes provides an illustration of the process in contemporary Turkey. There, urban musicians transform topical, improvised texts from the Black Sea region sung to *kemençe* fiddle melodic ostinati into fixed, orchestrated compositions with "rational," patterned stanzaic structures,[66] a description which accords with the transformations applied to *Second Springs* by contemporary Chinese musicians.

Philip Bohlman proposes the Middle Eastern bazaar as a metaphor which suggests the situation of folk music in the modern world, outlining its function as a meeting point for the old and the new, the urban and the rural, the traditional and the popular, the national and the minority.[67] Perhaps the music conservatory could itself be used as a second metaphor for the nationalization and professionalization of certain traditional musical styles in the twentieth century.[68] Bruno Nettl summarizes the values inhering within the conservatory system as follows:

> European teaching techniques characteristically involved the use of notation; the segregated instruction of instrumental and vocal technique, of repertory, theory, and history by specialists; wherever possible, teaching students in groups; the use

of some music whose purpose is only to aid learning and practicing. The teaching process was abstracted from the musical culture. Thus a teacher would present materials that would be incompatible in a concert, or he might extract units such as phrases, not acceptable as self-contained units in performance, for special pedagogical treatment. Western music teaching gives little if any attention to the relationship of music to the rest of culture.[69]

In our understanding of the process of "conservatorization," it matters little whether specific Western musical techniques, instruments, or genres are adopted, or if indigenous repertories are retained. What is significant is that the conservatory becomes a primary cultural institution at which musical change is effected and through which musical transmission takes place. The very notion of the music conservatory as a center for performance excellence carries with it the expectation that the music performed must itself be "excellent," able to stand, in the eyes of its practitioners and sponsors, beyond the purview of both the market place and the immediate context of its origin. Of course, exactly what is excellent is open to periodic redefinition, and may remain the subject of lengthy dispute; the conservatory system merely adds regulative force to the reproduction of a canon of works or performance styles and philosophies of music. The Western-inspired music conservatory is in these senses the alter ego of the Middle Eastern bazaar. It shares the bazaar's function as a meeting point for old and new, for urban and rural, for traditional and popular, for national and minority, yet it controls strictly the terms and scope of engagement between these polar opposites, fitting new material into modes of operation and valuing which arise, at least in part, from the Western romantic tradition.

## Musical Meaning

Since 1950 there have been major transformations in the way Abing's music is envisaged and re-created. In accounting for these transformations, I have examined the rise of the conservatory tradition in China, offering specific examples of the manner in which Abing's music is now performed. In previous chapters, I painted a portrait of Abing as city-dwelling folk musician well versed in the musical traditions and social developments of his time. Through detailed music analyses I tested the possibility that his six recorded solos were improvisatory in nature, relying on plans and techniques of musical creativity which Abing could use during performance. Conservatory musicians fix Abing's music in notation, add accompaniments to it, rearrange its structure, perform it on new or adapted instruments, and present it in new musical and social contexts; yet, for them, it is still Abing's music. These musicians provide Abing's music with titles, programs, and interpretations; yet, for them, it is still Abing's music. Identification of this music with perceptions of its originator clearly remains of importance to Chinese musicians and audiences. Yet, perceptions of Abing have also changed, resonating in different ways to developments in Chinese society and musicology. As we have seen, Abing has, at times, served as a tool in the redistribution of social power, most dramatically as a proxy during Cultural Revolution power struggles. Musicological dispute over the source, naming, and content of his compositions has not been concerned solely with the establishment of historical truth, but also with the establishment of a role for traditional music in a self-consciously modernizing society.

In a book embracing modern Chinese attitudes towards Beethoven's Ninth Symphony, Nicholas Cook cites Theodor Adorno's opinion that the political interpretation of music leads to its consumption;[70] the evidence of this study suggests the contrary, that political interpretations sustain music into new contexts and ages. Cook proposes that we need to reinterpret Beethoven's Ninth Symphony, Adorno's example, again and again, in order to prevent it "from being consumed by ideology"; I would argue that reinterpretation *is* the application of a fresh ideology to an existing musical product or practice.[71] Reinterpretation is possible, not simply in large scale works like Beethoven's Ninth but also in short, monophonic fiddle improvisations, because many of us as individual interpreters, Western and Chinese, currently believe that musical symbols are both suggestive and ambiguous. Our interpretations differ, even when we share similar cultural backgrounds, because our personal experiences of music differ. Musical sound resonates somewhat differently in each of us because of our contrasting needs to situate ourselves as individuals in broader society.[72] Only when no more stories can be spun from the multifarious, incongruous, and independent details of a musician's life, only when communal, individual, and imaginary worlds can no longer be established from the ambiguous suggestions of musical sound and cultural practice, only then will the music cease to be consumed, only then will the music cease to mean.

## Notes

1. Mark Slobin, "Micromusics of the West: A Comparative Approach," *Ethnomusicology* 36 (1992): 1–87 (57). Slobin quotes from Pierre Bourdieu, *Distinction: A Social Critique of the Judgement of Taste* (Cambridge: Harvard University Press, 1984), 19.

2. John E. Kaemmer, "Social Power and Musical Change Among the Shona," *Ethnomusicology* 33 (1989): 31–45 (31).

3. Yang, whose music studies with an American teacher began in 1914, graduated from the Wuxi No.2 Teachers' University in 1921. In 1936, he began to carry out research and teach Chinese music history at Yanjing University, Harvard's Beijing branch; Huang Xiangpeng, "Boda jingshen de yinyue yishu dajia—ji yinyue shixuejia, minzu yinyuexuejia Yang Yinliu," in Yi Ren, ed., *Youmei de xuanlü piaoxiang de ge—Jiangsu lidai yinyuejia* (Nanjing: Jiangsu wenshi ziliao, 1992), 130–32 (130).

4. Antoinet Schimmelpenninck and Frank Kouwenhoven, "The Shanghai Conservatory of Music—History and Foreign Students' Experiences," *Chime*, no. 6 (1993): 56–91 (59).

5. Zhao Pei, *Liu Tianhua zhuanji xiaoshuo* (Shanghai: Shanghai yinyue chubanshe, 1989), 273.

6. Zhao, *Liu Tianhua*, 228. The traditional set of seven emotions to which Liu alludes were joy, anger, sorrow, fear, love, hate, and desire.

7. The roles played by Zhou Shaomei and Liu Tianhua in the attachment of Chinese traditional instrumental music to the "New Culture Movement" of 1919 are detailed in Terence M. Liu, "The Development of the Chinese Two-Stringed Lute *Erhu* Following the New Culture Movement (c.1915–1985)," (Kent State University: Ph.D. Dissertation, 1988), 105–16.

8. See Alexander Tcherepnine, "Music in Modern China," *Musical Quarterly* 21 (1935): 391–400 (399).

9. Cited in Martin Stokes, *The Arabesk Debate: Music and Musicians in Modern Turkey* (Oxford: Clarendon Press, 1992), 33. For further discussion of Gökalp's musical ideology, see Walter Feldman, "Cultural Authority and Authenticity in the Turkish Repertoire," *Asian Music* 22, no. 1 (Winter 1990): 73–111 (98–100); Irene Markoff, "The Ideology of Musical Practice and the Professional Turkish Folk Musician: Tempering the Creative Impulse," *Asian Music* 22, no. 1 (Winter 1990): 129–45 (129–30). A second example is offered by consideration of the rise of "new folk songs" in early-twentieth-century Japan. Here, as elsewhere, graduates of a Western-style music conservatory sought to compose songs in an idiom consciously modeled on that of existing folk music. Likewise, they frequently added instrumental accompaniments (perhaps played on Western instruments), in which harmonic writing was preferred to traditional heterophonic or ostinato patterns. Nonetheless, the Japanese new folk song composers did not use preexistent folk tunes but instead wrote new tunes with a simpler melodic style than is found in the traditional repertory. See David W. Hughes, "Japanese 'New Folk Songs,' Old and New," *Asian Music* 22, no. 1 (Winter 1990): 1–49 (14–18).

10. Han Kuo-Huang, "The Modern Chinese Orchestra," *Asian Music* 11, no. 1 (Winter 1979): 1–43 (13).

11. Perhaps the solo *Birds Singing in the Deserted Mountains* is an exception to this, its special-effects sections being quite variously reinterpreted by certain subsequent performers, for instance Zhang Rui. Nonetheless, even in this case, the piece is still identified as Liu Tianhua's.

12. Liu Fu, ed., *The Musical Compositions of the Late Liu T'ien-hwa* (Beijing: Publisher not identified, 1933). Of course, oral transmission still plays a vital role, as in other "literate" traditions. On this topic, the score has been considered as a rhetorical device appealed to by teachers and interpreters; see Henry Kingsbury, *Music, Talent, and Performance: A Conservatory Cultural System* (Philadelphia: Temple University Press, 1988), 92. For further perspectives on musicological rhetoric, law, interpretation, the role of the *urtext* edition, and compositional intent, see Nicholas Cook, "The Editor and the Virtuoso, or Schenker versus Bülow," *Journal of the Royal Musical Association* 116 (1991): 78–95; Henry Kingsbury, "Sociological Factors in Musicological Poetics," *Ethnomusicology* 35 (1991): 195–219 (211–7).

13. Lydia Goehr, *The Imaginary Museum of Musical Works: An Essay in the Philosophy of Music* (Oxford: Clarendon Press, 1992), 245.
14. Bell Yung, "Historical Interdependency of Music: A Case Study of the Chinese Seven-String Zither," *Journal of the American Musicological Society* 40 (1987): 82–91.
15. Philip D. Schuyler, "Music and Tradition in Yemen," *Asian Music* 22, no. 1 (Winter 1990): 51–71 (52).
16. Schimmelpenninck and Kouwenhoven, "The Shanghai Conservatory," 82.
17. Isaabel K. F. Wong, "From Reaction to Synthesis: Chinese Musicology in the Twentieth Century," in Bruno Nettl and Philip V. Bohlman, eds., *Comparative Musicology and the Anthropology of Music: Essays on the History of Ethnomusicology* (Chicago: University of Chicago Press, 1991), 37–55 (43).
18. For an exposition of this ideology in late-nineteenth-century China, see Jonathan Spence, *The Search for Modern China* (New York: Norton, 1990), 225. The same ideology is operative still in the late twentieth century; see, for example, Jiang Jing's call for Chinese composers to "integrate the . . . techniques of western music into the Chinese national spirit and the quintessence of Chinese culture"; Jiang Jing, "The Influence of Traditional Chinese Music on Professional Instrumental Composition," *Asian Music* 22, no. 2 (Spring/Summer 1991): 83–96 (96).
19. Zhang Shao, *Erhu guangbo jiaoxue jiangzuo* (Shanghai: Shanghai yinyue chubanshe, 1989), 22.
20. For further discussion of Jiang and Lu, see Jonathan P. J. Stock, "Contemporary Recital Solos for the Chinese Two-Stringed Fiddle *Erhu*," *British Journal of Ethnomusicology* 1 (1992): 55–88 (64–66).
21. The form used was that developed as a sight-singing aid by Emile Chevé (1804–64). Today, it is generally held within mainland China that this form of notation was adopted by way of Japanese music education. It has, however, been suggested that this ascription may be an avoidance of mentioning the prior role of Christian missionaries in the dissemination of this notational form; see Richard Curt Kraus, *Pianos and Politics in China: Middle-Class Ambitions and the Struggle over Western Music* (New York: Oxford University Press, 1989), 52–53, 229.
22. Cipher notation in fig. 6.1 from Yih Mei, *Erhu quji di er ji* (Hong Kong: Yih Mei Book Company, 1987), 75.
23. Wong, "Reaction," 45.
24. Kraus, *Pianos*, 53–57. For further on Xian Xinghai, see David Holm, *Art and Ideology in Revolutionary China* (Oxford: Clarendon Press, 1991), 60–62.
25. Han, "Chinese Orchestra," 15–16.
26. Kraus, *Pianos*, 61–63.
27. For a brief description of these policies and their impact between 1949 and 1976, see Colin P. Mackerras, *The Performing Arts in Contemporary China* (London: Routledge and Kegan Paul, 1981), 9–37. Essential reading for this phase of Chinese music history includes the chapter "Science versus Revolution in the Modernization of Music" in Kraus, *Pianos*, 100–27.
28. For more information on the redesign of the fiddle see Jonathan P. J. Stock, "A Historical Account of the Chinese Two-Stringed Fiddle *Erhu*," *Galpin Society Journal* 46 (1993): 83–113 (102–4).

66. Stokes, *Arabesk Debate*, 61–69.

67. Philip V. Bohlman, *The Study of Folk Music in the Modern World* (Bloomington: Indiana University Press, 1988), 121–24.

68. In Europe, it was during the first half of the nineteenth century that specialist music institutions—conservatories, concert societies, and concert halls—were conceived and established on a large scale. The opening of these institutions was accompanied by the production of new histories of music, a new concert aesthetic, and by the expansion of the *Werktreue* ideal. See Goehr, *Imaginary Museum*, 239–42.

69. Bruno Nettl, *The Western Impact on World Music: Change, Adaptation, and Survival* (New York: Schirmer, 1985), 72.

70. Nicholas Cook, *Beethoven Symphony No. 9*, Cambridge Music Handbooks (Cambridge: Cambridge University Press, 1993), 100.

71. Cook, *Beethoven*, 105. For further discussion of the political nature of musicological interpretations, see Philip V. Bohlman, "Musicology as a Political Act," *Journal of Musicology* 11 (1993): 411–36.

72. Timothy Rice, *May It Fill Your Soul: Experiencing Bulgarian Music* (Chicago: University of Chicago Press, 1994), 299–302.

# Appendix 1: *Erhu* Music

## Cold Spring Wind

Performed by Abing (1950)
Original transcription, Cao Anhe,
adapted

## Listening to the Pines

Performed by Abing (1950)
Original transcription, Cao Anhe,
adapted

# Appendix 2: *Pipa* Music

## Dragon Boats

Performed by Abing (1950)
Original transcription, Cao Anhe,
adapted

Note:   performance techniques (such as various types of tremolo) omitted

## Great Waves Washing the Sand

Performed by Abing (1950)
Original transcription, Cao Anhe,
adapted

Note: performance techniques (such as various types of tremolo) omitted

## Zhaojun Crosses the Border

Performed by Abing (1950)
Original transcription, Cao Anhe,
adapted

Note:    performance techniques (such as various types of tremolo) omitted

# Glossary

This selected list of Chinese names, terms, and titles is divided into three parts. In the first, the names of the principal Chinese musicians mentioned during the course of this study are given, together with the simple-form characters now standard in mainland China and dates of birth and death, where available. The second listing concentrates on important instrument names, genres, and technical terminology. In the third, titles of significant compositions are listed, these in alphabetical order of the primary name used in the text, i.e. usually in English.[1]

## Chinese Personal Names

| | | |
|---|---|---|
| Abing | 阿炳 | properly Hua Yanjun, Wuxi folk musician (c.1890s–1950) |
| Cao Anhe | 曹安和 | musicologist, collector of Abing's music (b.1905) |
| Chen Zhenduo | 陈振铎 | *erhu* performer, teacher, and composer |
| Chu Wanghua | 储望华 | pianist, arranger of piano version of *The Moon Reflected on the Second Springs* |
| Ding Shande | 丁善德 | conservatory professor and composer (b.1911) |
| Dong Cuidi | 董催弟 | wife of Abing (1889?–1951) |
| Hua Qinghe | 华清和 | Wuxi Daoist believed to be Abing's father (d.1916?) |
| Hua Xuemei | 华雪梅 | literary name of Hua Qinghe |
| Hua Yanjun | 华彦钧 | see Abing |
| Jiang Fengzhi | 蒋风之 | *erhu* performer, teacher, and arranger (1908–86) |
| Liu Tianhua | 刘天华 | composer, teacher, and campaigner for *guoyue* (1895–1932) |

| Lu Xiutang | 陆修堂 | *erhu* teacher, performer, and composer (1911–66) |
| Nie Er | 聂耳 | revolutionary song composer (1912–35) |
| Wu Zuqiang | 吴祖强 | composer, arranger of string orchestra version of *The Moon Reflected on the Second Springs* (b.1927) |
| Xian Xinghai | 冼星海 | Communist composer (1905–45) |
| Xiao Youmei | 肖友梅 | musicologist, founder of China's conservatory system (1884–1940) |
| Yang Yinliu | 样荫浏 | musicologist, collector of Abing's music (1899–1984) |
| Zhou Shaomei | 周少梅 | musician and instrumental teacher (1885–1938) |
| Zhou Xuan | 周璇 | popular singer of pre-war Shanghai (1918?–57) |
| Zhu Shikuang | 祝世匡 | musician, collector of Abing's solos (b.1915) |

## Instruments, Genres, and Technical Terminology

| *ban* | 板 | wooden clapper; or metrical strong beat |
| *chuida* | 吹打 | generic term for wind and percussion ensemble music |
| *chuigu* | 吹鼓 | wind and percussion ensemble |
| *di* (also *dizi*) | 笛(笛子) | transverse bamboo flute |
| *diao* | 调 | mode; tuning; or tune |
| *erhu* | 二胡 | two-stringed fiddle |
| *fanyin* | 梵音 | collective term for Daoist and Buddhist ensemble music |
| *gongchepu* | 工尺谱 | traditional form of transposable notation |

| | | |
|---|---|---|
| *Guangdong yinyue* | 广东音乐 | Cantonese music, instrumental ensemble genre from South China |
| *guomen* | 过门 | instrumental introduction or interlude in operatic or ballad music |
| *guoyue* | 国乐 | "national music," generic term for progressive and professional music based on regional traditions |
| *guqin* | | see *qin* |
| *huang diao* | 簧调 | tune family used in *tanhuang* opera |
| *huqin* | 胡琴 | generic term for two-stringed fiddle |
| *jia hua* | 加花 | "adding decorations," traditional ornamental practice |
| Jiangnan *sizhu* | | see *sizhu* |
| *jingju* | 京剧 | "capital opera," Beijing opera |
| *kunqu* | 昆曲 | "Kunshan opera," literary and historical drama form from Jiangsu Province |
| *luogu* | 锣鼓 | "gongs and drums," percussion-dominated ensemble; or generic term for traditional percussion instruments |
| *minzu yinyue* | 民族音乐 | "national music," name now used for *guoyue* in mainland China |
| *pipa* | 琵琶 | four-stringed, pear-shaped lute |
| *qin* (also *guqin*) | 琴(古琴) | seven-stringed zither |
| *qingqu* | 清曲 | Yangzhou ballad singing |
| *qupai* | 曲牌 | "labelled tune," a melody adaptable to suit new musical purposes, its identity still intact |
| *sanxian* | 三弦 | three-stringed, long-necked lute |
| *sheng* | 笙 | mouth organ |

| | | |
|---|---|---|
| *shifan luogu* | 十番锣鼓 | "mixed gongs and drums," ensemble of percussion and other instruments from Wuxi |
| *sizhu* | 丝竹 | "silk and bamboo" instrumental ensemble tradition from East China; or generic term for such ensembles across China |
| *suona* | 唢呐 | oboe with flaring metal bell |
| *Suzhou* tanci | | see *tanci* |
| *tanci* | 弹词 | "performed poems," ballad style from Suzhou; generic term for ballad singing with plucked instrumental accompaniment |
| *tanhuang* | 滩簧 | rural drama style from East China |
| *xiao* | 箫 | vertical notched bamboo flute |
| *xiju* | 锡剧 | Wuxi opera |
| *yangqin* | 扬琴 | hammered dulcimer |
| *yunluo* | 云锣 | "cloud gongs," set of tuned gongs used in percussion ensemble music |

## Compositions

*All Things Harmonious*
四合          *Sihe*, Jiangnan *sizhu* piece, perhaps quoted within *Dragon Boats*

*Along the Street*
行街四合     *Xingjie sihe*, Jiangnan *sizhu* piece

*Autumn Moon over the Han Palace*
汉宫秋月     *Han gong qiu yue*, classical *pipa* solo

*Ballad-Singing Tune*
文书调        *Wenshu diao*, street-music tune attributed to Abing

*Birds Singing in the Deserted Mountains*
空山鸟语     *Kong shan niao yu*, *erhu* composition by Liu Tianhua

*Cold Spring Wind*
寒春风曲     *Han chun feng qu*, *erhu* solo by Abing

*Decorated Six-Beat*

花六板　　*Hua liuban*, ornamented variant of *Old Six-Beat*

*Dragon Boats*

龙船　　*Long chuan*, *pipa* solo by Abing

*Eight-Beat*

八板　　*Baban*, *qupai* related to *Old Six-Beat* found in many regional traditions

*Eighteen Strokes*

十八摸　　Wuxi folk tune found in *Dragon Boats*

*Full Moon and Blooming Flowers*

月圆花好　　*Yueyuan huahao*, 1930s film song by Yan Hua

*General's Orders, The*

将军令　　*Jiangjun ling*, traditional *pipa* solo

*Great Waves Washing the Sand*

大浪淘沙　　*Da lang tao sha*, *pipa* solo by Abing

*Song of the Green Lotus*

青莲乐府　　*Qing lian yuefu*, classical *pipa* solo

*Intimate Companion*

知心客　　*Zhixin ke*, bawdy folk song from Wuxi

*Listening to the Pines*

听松　　*Ting song*, *erhu* solo by Abing

*Moon Engraved upon Three Pools, The*

三潭印月　　*San tan yin yue*, Cantonese ensemble piece

*Moon Reflected on the Second Springs, The*

二泉映月　　*Er quan ying yue*, *erhu* solo by Abing

*Old Six-Beat*

老六板　　*Lao liuban*, *qupai* found in many regional traditions

*Offering a Toast to the Moon*

举杯邀月　　*Ju bei yao yue*, section of *Green Lotus in the Music Hall*

*Partridges Flying*

鹧鸪飞　　*Zhegu fei*, instrumental ensemble piece from Hunan Province

*Playing Chess*

下盘棋    *Xia panqi*, folk tune from Jiangsu Province found in *Dragon Boats*

*Three-Six*

三六    *Sanliu*, Jiangnan *sizhu* piece

*Three Variations on Plum Blossom*

梅花三弄    *Meihua san nong*, traditional ensemble piece also called *San liu*; or *qin* piece (different melody)

*Waves Washing the Sand*

浪淘沙    *Lang tao sha*, *qupai* found in various instrumental genres

*Wuxi Sights*

无锡景    *Wuxi jing*, Wuxi folk tune found in *Dragon Boats*

*Yearning for Home*

怀乡行    *Huai xiang xing*, *erhu* solo by Lu Xiutang

*Zhaojun Crosses the Border*

昭君出塞    *Zhaojun chu sai*, *pipa* solo by Abing

# Notes

1. To assist the non-Chinese-speaking reader, order of entries is strictly alphabetical by word-block; thus *guoyue* precedes *guqin*, even though the latter, begun by the character *gu*, would be found in front of the former, begun by *guo*, in a dictionary.

# Works Cited

Note: Chinese terms are ordered by separate character: Mao Yu Run precedes Mao Yuan, for instance.

Addison, Don. "Elements of Style in Performing the Chinese P'i-P'a." *Selected Reports in Ethnomusicology* 2, no. 1 (1974): 119–39.

Adshead, S. A. M. *China in World History*. London: Macmillan, 1988.

Agawu, V. Kofi. "Variation Procedures in Northern Ewe Song." *Ethnomusicology* 34 (1990): 221–43.

Anonymous. *All About Shanghai*, introduced by H. J. Lethbridge. Hong Kong: Oxford University Press, 1983. [Shanghai: University Press, 1934–35].

Baily, John. "Some Cognitive Aspects of Motor Planning in Musical Performance." *Psychologica Belgica* 31, no. 2 (1991): 147–62.

Baily, John and Peter Driver. "Spatio-Motor Thinking in Playing Folk Blues Guitar." *World of Music* 34, no. 3 (1992): 57–71.

Bergère, Marie-Claire. *The Golden Age of the Chinese Bourgeoisie 1911–1937*, translated by Janet Lloyd. Cambridge: Cambridge University Press, 1989.

Blacking, John. "Movement, Dance, Music, and the Venda Girls' Initiation Cycle." In *Society and the Dance: The Social Anthropology of Process and Performance*, edited by Paul Spencer, 64–91. Cambridge: Cambridge University Press, 1980.

———. "Tonal Organization in the Music of Two Venda Initiation Schools." *Ethnomusicology* 14 (1970): 1–56.

Bohlman, Philip V. "Musicology as a Political Act." *Journal of Musicology* 11 (1993): 411–36.

———. *The Study of Folk Music in the Modern World*. Bloomington: Indiana University Press, 1988.

Bourdieu, Pierre. *Distinction: A Social Critique of the Judgement of Taste*. Cambridge: Harvard University Press, 1984.

Brailoiu, Constantin. *Problems of Ethnomusicology*, edited and translated by A. L. Lloyd. Cambridge: Cambridge University Press, 1984.

Brown, Marshall. "Origins of Modernism: Musical Structures and Narrative Forms." In *Music and Text: Critical Enquiries*, edited by Steven P. Scher, 75–92. Cambridge: Cambridge University Press, 1992.

Cao Anhe. "Xuanlü zouchu shidai de qiangyin—ji zuoqujia, erhu, pipa yanzoujia Liu Tianhua." In *Youmei de xuanlü piaoxiang de ge—Jiangsu lidai yinyuejia*, edited by Yi Ren, 115–17. Nanjing: Jiangsu wenshi ziliao, 1992.

Cao Anhe and Jian Qihua. *Xiansuo shisan tao: (Qing) Ming Yi (Rong Zhai) chuanpu*, 3. Beijing: Yinyue chubanshe, 1962.

Capwell, Charles. "Marginality and Musicology in Nineteenth-Century Calcutta: The Case of Sourindro Mohun Tagore." In *Comparative Musicology and the Anthropology of Music: Essays on the History of Ethnomusicology*, edited by Bruno Nettl and Philip V. Bohlman, 228–43. Chicago: University of Chicago Press, 1991.

Chao Hua. "Has Absolute Music No Class Character?" *Peking Review* 17, no. 9 (1974): 15–17.

Chao, Paul. *Chinese Kinship*. London: Kegan Paul International, 1983.

Chen Dacan. *Chinese Taoist Music*. Shanghai: China Record Company, 1986. [Booklet accompanying music cassette HL–508.]

———. "Daojiao yinyue." In *Zhongguo dabaikequanshu: yinyue, wudao*, edited by Lü Ji et al., 113. Beijing: Zhongguo dabaikequanshu chubanshe, 1989.

Chen Yibing. "Xiju de xingcheng he fazhan." In *Xiju chuantong jumu kao lüe*, edited by Jin Yi et al., 9–20. Shanghai: Shanghai wenyi chubanshe, 1989.

Cheng Gongliang. "*Er quan ying yue* de yinyue sucai he jiegou tedian." *Yinyue yishu*, 1981, no. 1:36–40.

Cheng Ruxin. "*Er quan ying yue* yindiao yuanyuan tansuo." *Nanyi xuebao*, 1980, no. 2:48–52.

Cheng Ruxin et al. *Xiju qudiao jieshao (xuji)*. Nanjing: Jiangsu wenyi chubanshe, 1956.

Clarke, Eric F. "Generative Principles in Music Performance." In *Generative Processes in Music: The Psychology of Performance, Improvisation, and Composition*, edited by John A. Sloboda, 1–26. Oxford: Clarendon Press, 1988.

Cook, Nicholas. "The Editor and the Virtuoso, or Schenker versus Bülow." *Journal of the Royal Musical Association* 116 (1991): 78–95.

———. *Beethoven Symphony No. 9*. Cambridge Music Handbooks. Cambridge: Cambridge University Press, 1993.

———. *A Guide to Musical Analysis*. London: Dent, 1987.

———. *Music, Imagination, and Culture*. Oxford: Clarendon Press, 1990.

Coplan, David B. "Ethnomusicology and the Meaning of Tradition." In *Ethnomusicology and Modern Music History*, edited by Stephen Blum, Philip V. Bohlman, and Daniel M. Neuman, 35–48. Urbana: University of Illinois Press, 1991.

Ding Guobin. "Huju jiefang qian ge fazhan jieduan de changpian jianjie." *Shanghai xiqu shiliao huicui* 2 (1986):15–19.

Ding Shande. *Xianyue sichongzou: Er quan ying yue*. Beijing: Renmin yinyue chubanshe, 1984.

Ding Shande et al., editors. *Shanghai Yinyue Xueyuan jian shi 1927–1987*. Shanghai: Shanghai yinyue xueyuan, 1987.

Du Yaxiong. "Abing de san shou erhu qu." *Yuefu xinsheng*, 1985, no. 4:32–33.

———. "Abing zhuanlüe." *Nanyi xuebao*, 1981, no. 1:78–83.

———. "Recent Issues in Music Research in the People's Republic of China." *Association for Chinese Music Research Newsletter* 5, no. 1 (Winter 1992): 9–12.

Eagleton, Terry. *Literary Theory*. Oxford: Blackwell, 1983.

Fang Kun. "A Discussion on Chinese National Musical Traditions," translated by Keith Pratt, Introduction and Responses by Robert C. Provine and Alan Thrasher. *Asian Music* 12, no. 2 (Spring/Summer 1981): 1–16.

Feld, Steven. *Sound and Sentiment: Birds, Weeping, Poetics, and Song in Kaluli Expression*, 2nd edition. Philadelphia: University of Pennsylvania Press, 1990.

Feldman, Walter. "Cultural Authority and Authenticity in the Turkish Repertoire." *Asian Music* 22, no. 1 (Winter 1991): 73–111.

Gao Houyong. "The Unique Chinese Stringed and Woodwind Ensemble of the South of the Changjiang River." Paper distributed at the International Seminar on Chinese Music, Kingston-on-Thames, England, April 1988.

Geertz, Clifford. "Ideology as a Cultural System." In *Ideology and Discontent*, edited by David E. Apter, 47–76. New York: Free Press of Glencoe, 1964.

Goehr, Lydia. *The Imaginary Museum of Musical Works: An Essay in the Philosophy of Music.* Oxford: Clarendon Press, 1992.

Gray, Jack. *Rebellions and Revolutions: China from the 1800s to the 1980s.* The Short Oxford History of the Modern World, edited by J. M. Roberts. Oxford: Oxford University Press, 1990.

Hamm, Charles. "Music and Radio in the People's Republic of China." *Asian Music* 22, no. 2 (Spring/Summer 1991): 1–42.

Han Kuo-Huang. "The Chinese Concept of Program Music." *Asian Music* 10, no. 1 (Winter 1978): 17–38.

———. "The Modern Chinese Orchestra." *Asian Music* 11, no. 1 (Winter 1979): 1–43.

———. "Three Chinese Musicologists: Yang Yinliu, Yin Falu, Li Chunyi." *Ethnomusicology* 24 (1980): 483–529.

Hilmar, Ernst. *Franz Schubert in His Time*, translated by Reinhard G. Pauly. Portland: Amadeus Press, 1988.

Holm, David. *Art and Ideology in Revolutionary China.* Oxford: Clarendon Press, 1991.

Huadong wenhua bu yishu shiye guanli, editors. *Huadong difang xiqu jieshao.* Shanghai: Xin wenyi chubanshe, 1952.

Huang Jinpei. "Concerning the Variants of '*Lao lioban*'," translated by Alan R. Thrasher. *Asian Music* 13, no. 2 (Spring/Summer 1982): 19–31.

Huang Xiangpeng. "Boda jingshen de yinyue yishu dajia—ji yinyue shixuejia, minzu yinyuexuejia Yang Yinliu." In *Youmei de xuanlü piaoxiang de ge—Jiangsu lidai yinyuejia*, edited by Yi Ren, 130–32. Nanjing: Jiangsu wenshi ziliao, 1992.

Hughes, David W. "Japanese 'New Folk Songs,' Old and New." *Asian Music* 22, no. 1 (Winter 1990): 1–49.

Jeffery, Peter. *Re-Envisioning Past Musical Cultures: Ethnomusicology in the Study of Gregorian Chant.* Chicago: University of Chicago Press, 1992.

Jiang Jing. "The Influence of Traditional Chinese Music on Professional Instrumental Composition." *Asian Music* 22, no. 2 (Spring/Summer 1991): 83–96.

Jiangsu yinyue gongzuo zu, editors. *Jiangsu nanbu minjian xiqu shuochang yinyue ji.* Beijing: Yinyue chubanshe, 1955.

Jiang Tianyi. *Xiaodiao gongchepu.* Shanghai: Shanghai shijie shuju, 1922.

Jiang Xianji and Sun Yunnian. "Minjian yinyuejia Abing." *Taihu*, 1979, nos. 4–5:7–15.

Jin Zuli and Xu Ziren. "Shanghai minjian sizhu yinyue shi." *Zhongguo yinyue*, 1983, no. 3:28–31.

Jones, Andrew F. *Like a Knife: Ideology and Genre in Contemporary Chinese Popular Music.* Cornell East Asia Series 57. New York: Cornell University, 1992.

Jones, Stephen. "Daoism and Instrumental Music of Jiangsu." *Chime*, no. 8 (Spring 1995): 117–46.

———. *Folk Music of China: Living Instrumental Traditions.* Oxford: Clarendon Press, 1995.

Jones, Stephen and Xue Yibing. "The Music Associations of Hebei Province, China: A Preliminary Report." *Ethnomusicology* 35 (1991): 1–29.

Jones, Stephen et al. "Field Notes, 1991: Funeral Music in Shanxi." *Chime*, no. 5 (Spring 1992): 4–28.

Kagan, A. L. "Music and the Hundred Flowers Movement." *Musical Quarterly* 49 (1963): 417–30.

Kaemmer, John E. "Social Power and Musical Change Among the Shona." *Ethnomusicology* 33 (1989): 31–45.

Kaufmann, Walter. *Musical Notations of the Orient: Notational Systems of East, South, and Central Asia.* Bloomington: Indiana University Press, 1967.

———. *Musical References in the Chinese Classics.* Detroit: Information Coordinators, 1976.

Kingsbury, Henry. *Music, Talent, and Performance: A Conservatory Cultural System.* Philadelphia: Temple University Press, 1988.

———. "Sociological Factors in Musicological Poetics." *Ethnomusicology* 35(2):195–219.

Kraus, Richard Curt. *Pianos and Politics in China: Middle-Class Ambitions and the Struggle over Western Music.* New York: Oxford University Press, 1989.

Kwok, Theodore J. "Chinese Music Theses and Dissertations, A Preliminary List." *Association for Chinese Music Research Newsletter* 7, no.1 (Winter 1994): 18–33.

L. Y. "Ah Bing—A Name to Remember." *Beijing Review* 26, no. 43 (1983): 29–30.

Laloy, Louis. *La Musique chinoise.* Paris: Laurens, 1909.

Lam, Joseph S. C. "Analyses and Interpretations of Chinese Seven-String Zither Music: The Case of the *Lament of Empress Chen*." *Ethnomusicology* 37 (1993): 353–85.

Levy, Janet M. "Covert and Casual Values in Recent Writings about Music." *Journal of Musicology* 5 (1987): 3–27.

Liang Mingyue. *Music of the Billion: An Introduction to Chinese Musical Culture.* New York: Heinrichshofen, 1985.

Lieberman, Fredric. *Chinese Music: An Annotated Bibliography*, 2nd edition. New York: Garland, 1979.

Liu Dongsheng et al., editors. *Zhongguo yueqi tu zhi.* Beijing: Qinggongye chubanshe, 1987.

Liu Fu, editor. *The Musical Compositions of the Late Liu T'ien-hwa.* Beijing: Publisher not identified, 1933.

Liu Guangqing, editor. *Jiu Zhongguo de Shanghai guangbo shiye.* Beijing: Dang'an and Zhongguo guangbo dianshi chubanshe, 1985.

Liu, Terence M. "The Development of the Chinese Two-Stringed Lute *Erhu* Following the New Culture Movement (c.1915–1985)." Kent State University: Ph.D. Dissertation, 1988.

Loeb, David. "An Analytic Study of Japanese Koto Music." *Music Forum* 4 (1976): 335–93.

Lortat-Jacob, Bernard, editor. *L'improvisation dans les musiques de tradition orale.* Paris: Selaf, 1987.

Lui, Tsun-Yuen. "Pipa." In *New Grove Dictionary of Musical Instruments* 3, edited by Stanley Sadie, 115. London: Macmillan, 1984.

Mackerras, Colin P. *The Chinese Theatre in Modern Times: From 1840 to the Present Day.* London: Thames and Hudson, 1975.

———. *The Performing Arts in Contemporary China.* London: Routledge and Kegan Paul, 1981.

Manuel, Peter. *Popular Musics of the Non-Western World: An Introductory Survey.* New York: Oxford University Press, 1988.

Mao Yu Run. "Music under Mao: Its Background and Aftermath." *Asian Music* 22, no. 2 (Spring/Summer 1991): 97–125.

Mao Yuan. *Abing meixue sixiang shitan*. Nanjing: Nanjing yishu xueyuan, 1983.

Mao Zedong. *Talks at the Yenan Forum on Literature and Art*. Beijing: Foreign Languages Press, 1965.

Markoff, Irene. "The Ideology of Musical Practice and the Professional Turkish Folk Musician: Tempering the Creative Impulse." *Asian Music* 22, no. 1 (Winter 1990): 129–45.

Marks, Robert W. "The Music and Musical Instruments of Ancient China." *Musical Quarterly* 18 (1932): 593–607.

McDougall, Bonnie S., editor. *Popular Chinese Literature and Performing Arts in the People's Republic of China, 1949–1979*. Berkeley: University of California Press, 1984.

McGough, James P. "Deviant Marriage Patterns in Chinese Society." In *Normal and Abnormal Behaviour in Chinese Culture*, edited by Arthur Kleinman and Tsung-Yi Lin, 171–201. Dordrecht, Holland: D. Reidel, 1981.

Merriam, Alan P. *The Anthropology of Music*. Evanston: Northwestern University Press, 1964.

Myers, John E. *The Way of the Pipa: Structure and Imagery in Chinese Lute Music*. Kent, Ohio: Kent State University Press, 1992.

Naquin, Susan. "Funerals in North China: Uniformity and Variation." In *Death Ritual in Late Imperial and Modern China*, edited by James L. Watson and Evelyn S. Rawski, 37–70. Berkeley: University of California Press, 1988.

Nattiez, Jean-Jacques. "Can One Speak of Narrativity in Music?" translated by Katharine Ellis. *Journal of the Royal Musical Association* 115 (1990): 240–57.

———. *Music and Discourse: Toward a Semiology of Music*, translated by Carolyn Abbate. (Princeton: Princeton University Press, 1990).

———. "Simha Arom and the Return of Analysis to Ethnomusicology," translated by Catherine Dale. *Music Analysis* 12 (1993): 241–65.

Nettl, Bruno. "Biography of a Blackfoot Singer." *Musical Quarterly* 54 (1968): 199–207.

———. *The Study of Ethnomusicology: Twenty-Nine Issues and Concepts*. Urbana: University of Illinois Press, 1983.

———. "Thoughts on Improvisation: A Comparative Approach." *Musical Quarterly* 60 (1974): 1–19.

———. *The Western Impact on World Music: Change, Adaptation, and Survival*. New York: Schirmer, 1985.

Neuman, Daniel M. "Epilogue: Paradigms and Stories." In *Ethnomusicology and Modern Music History*, edited by Stephen Blum, Philip V. Bohlman, and Daniel M. Neuman, 268–77. Urbana: University of Illinois Press, 1991.

———. *The Life of Music in North India: The Organization of an Artistic Tradition*. Chicago: Chicago University Press, 1990 [1980].

Peng Xiuwen. "Chuida Music of Sunan," translated and introduced by Phoebe Hsu. *Asian Music* 13, no. 2 (Spring/Summer 1985): 31–38.

Perris, Arnold. "Music as Propaganda: Art at the Command of Doctrine in the P.R.C." *Ethnomusicology* 27 (1983): 1–28.

Pian, Rulan Chao. *Sonq Dynasty Musical Sources and Their Interpretation*. Cambridge: Harvard University Press, 1967.

———. "Text Setting with the *Shipyi* Animated Aria." In *Words and Music: The Scholar's View*, edited by Laurence Berman, 237–70. Cambridge: Harvard University Press, 1972.

————, translator. "My Life as a Drum Singer: The Autobiography of Jang Tsueyfenq (As Told to Liou Fang)." *Chinoperl Papers*, no. 13 (1984–85): 7–106.

Picken, Laurence E. R. "The Origin of the Short Lute." *Galpin Society Journal* 8 (1955): 32–42.

Picken, Laurence E. R. et al., editors. *Music from the Tang Court 1*. (Oxford: Oxford University Press, 1981).

Powers, Harold S. Review of *The Anthropology of Music* by Alan P. Merriam. *Perspectives of New Music* 4, no.2 (Spring 1966): 161–71.

Pressing, Jeff. "Improvisation: Methods and Models." In *Generative Processes in Music: The Psychology of Performance, Improvisation, and Composition*, edited by John A. Sloboda, 129–78. Oxford: Clarendon Press, 1988.

Qian Huirong. "Shanghai—xiju de faxiang di." *Shanghai xiqu shiliao huicui* 3 (1987): 43–44.

Qian Tiemin. "Abing yu daojiao." *Zhongguo yinyuexue*, 1994, no. 4:51–62.

Rees, Helen. "An Annotated Bibliography on Shuochang (Narrative Singing)." *Chime*, no. 3 (Spring 1991): 88–96.

Renmin yinyue chubanshe bianji bu, editors. *Zhongguo min'ge xuan*. Beijing: Renmin yinyue chubanshe, 1984.

Rice, Timothy. *May It Fill Your Soul: Experiencing Bulgarian Music*. Chicago: University of Chicago Press, 1994.

————. "Towards a Remodeling of Ethnomusicology." *Ethnomusicology* 31 (1987): 469–88.

Rodzinski, Witold. *The People's Republic of China: Reflections on Chinese Political History since 1949*. London: Collins, 1988.

Ruwet, Nicolas. "Methods of Analysis in Musicology," translated and introduced by Mark Everist. *Music Analysis* 6 (1987): 3–36.

Schak, David C. *A Chinese Beggars' Den: Poverty and Mobility in an Underclass Community*. Pittsburgh: University of Pittsburgh Press, 1988.

Schimmelpenninck, Antoinet. "Jiangsu Folk Song." *Chime*, no. 1 (Spring 1990): 16–29.

————. "Language and Music in the *Shan'ge* of Southern Jiangsu, China." Leiden: Ph.D. Dissertation, forthcoming.

Schimmelpenninck, Antoinet and Frank Kouwenhoven. "The Shanghai Conservatory of Music—History and Foreign Students' Experiences." *Chime*, no. 6 (Spring 1993): 56–91.

Schinz, Alfred. *Cities in China*. Urbanization of the Earth 7, edited by Wolf Tietze. Berlin: Gebrüder Borntraeger, 1989.

Schuyler, Philip D. "Music and Tradition in Yemen." *Asian Music* 22, no. 1 (Winter 1990): 51–71.

Scott, A. C. "China, §VI: Since 1949." In *The New Grove Dictionary of Music and Musicians* 4, edited by Stanley Sadie, 279–83. London: Macmillan, 1980.

Scott, Derek B. "Music and Sociology for the 1990s: A Changing Critical Perspective." *Musical Quarterly* 74 (1990): 385–410.

Seeger, Anthony. "Ethnography of Music." In *Ethnomusicology: An Introduction*. New Grove Handbooks in Music, edited by Helen Myers, 88–109. London: Macmillan, 1992.

————. *Why Suyá Sing: A Musical Anthropology of an Amazonian People*. Cambridge: Cambridge University Press, 1987.

Sha Hankun. *Zhongguo min'ge de jiegou yu xuanfa*. Shanghai: Shanghai yinyue chubanshe, 1988.

Shanghai yishu yanjiusuo and Zhongguo xijujia xiehui Shanghai fenhui, editors. *Zhongguo xiqu quyi cidian*. Shanghai: Shanghai cishu chubanshe, 1981.

Shen Qia. "Abing shikao yi er ji qita." *Nanyi xuebao*, 1980, no. 2:41–47.

———. "Minzu yinyuexue 10 nian." In *Zhongguo yinyue nianjian*, 338–55. Ji'nan: Shandong jiaoyu chubanshe, 1991.

Shen Yuan. "Wuxi pingqu." In *Zhongguo dabaikequanshu: xiqu, quyi*, edited by Zhang Geng et al., 416. Beijing: Zhongguo dabaikequanshu chubanshe, 1983.

Slobin, Mark. "Micromusics of the West: A Comparative Approach." *Ethnomusicology* 36 (1992): 1–87.

Sloboda, John A. *The Musical Mind: The Cognitive Psychology of Music*. Oxford: Clarendon, 1985.

Smith, Arthur H. *Village Life in China*. Edinburgh: Oliphant, Anderson, and Ferrier, 1990.

Solomon, Maynard. "The Rochlitz Anecdotes: Issues of Authenticity in Early Mozart Biography." In *Mozart Studies*, edited by Cliff Eisen, 1–59. Oxford: Clarendon Press, 1991.

Song Bang-song. "*Sanjo* versus *Raga*: A Preliminary Study." In *Cross-Cultural Perspectives on Music*, edited by Robert Falck and Timothy Rice, 101–16. Toronto: University of Toronto Press, 1982.

Soulié de Morant, Georges. *La Musique en Chine*. Paris: Ernest Leroux, 1911.

Spence, Jonathan D. *The Search for Modern China*. New York: Norton, 1990.

Stevenson, Robert Louis. *Dr. Jekyll and Mr. Hyde*. London: Penguin, 1994 [1886].

Stock, Jonathan P. J. "The Application of Schenkerian Analysis to Ethnomusicology: Problems and Possibilities." *Music Analysis* 12 (1993): 215–40.

———. *Chinese Flute Solos*. London, Schott, 1994.

———. "Contemporary Recital Solos for the Chinese Two-Stringed Fiddle *Erhu*." *British Journal of Ethnomusicology* 1 (1992): 55–88.

———. "Context and Creativity: The Chinese Two-Stringed Fiddle *Erhu* in Contemporary China." Queen's University of Belfast: Ph.D. Dissertation, 1991.

———. "An Ethnomusicological Perspective on Musical Style, With Reference to Music for Chinese Two-Stringed Fiddles." *Journal of the Royal Musical Association* 118 (1993): 276–99.

———. "A Historical Account of the Chinese Two-Stringed Fiddle *Erhu*." *Galpin Society Journal* 46 (1993): 83–113.

———. "Reconsidering the Past: Zhou Xuan and the Rehabilitation of Early Twentieth-Century Popular Music." *Asian Music* 26, no. 2 (Spring/Summer 1995): 119–35.

Stokes, Martin. *The Arabesk Debate: Music and Musicians in Modern Turkey*. Oxford: Clarendon Press, 1992.

Sutton, R. Anderson. "Concept and Treatment in Javanese Gamelan Music, with Reference to the Gambang." *Asian Music* 11, no. 1 (Winter 1979): 59–79.

Tan Longjian. *Sanxian yanzou yishu*. Beijing: Renmin yinyue chubanshe, 1989.

Tcherepnine, Alexander. "Music in Modern China." *Musical Quarterly* 21 (1935): 391–400.

Thrasher, Alan R. "Bianzou—Performance Variation Techniques in Jiangnan Sizhu." *Chime*, no. 6 (Spring 1993): 4–20.

——. "China." In *Ethnomusicology: Historical and Regional Studies*. The New Grove Handbooks in Music, edited by Helen Myers, 311–44. London: Macmillan, 1993.

——. "The Melodic Structure of Jiangnan Sizhu." *Ethnomusicology* 29 (1985): 237–63.

——. "Structural Continuity in Chinese Sizhu: The Baban Model." *Asian Music* 20, no. 2 (Spring/Summer 1989): 67–106.

——. "The Transverse Flute in Chinese Traditional Music." *Asian Music* 10, no. 1 (Winter 1978): 92–114.

Tian Liu and Zhang Yaozong. "Kaituo chuangxin, hongyang minyue—ji minyue yanzoujia, yinyue jiaoyujia Zhou Shaomei." In *Youmei de xuanlü piaoxiang de ge—Jiangsu lidai yinyuejia*, edited by Yi Ren, 87–90. Nanjing: Jiangsu wenshi ziliao, 1992.

Titon, Jeff Todd et al. *Worlds of Music: An Introduction to the Music of the World's Peoples*. New York: Schirmer, 1984.

Treitler, Leo. *Music and the Historical Imagination*. Cambridge: Harvard University Press, 1989.

——. "The Politics of Reception: Tailoring the Present as Fulfilment of a Desired Past." *Journal of the Royal Musical Association* 116 (1991): 280–98.

Tsao Pen-yeh. *The Music of Su-chou T'an-tz'u: A Study of the Structural Elements of the Chinese Southern Singing-Narrative*. Hong Kong: Chinese University Press, 1988.

——. "Structural Elements in the Music of Chinese Story-Telling." *Asian Music* 20, no. 2 (Spring/Summer 1989): 129–51.

Tsao Pen-yeh and Shi Xinming. "Current Research of Taoist Ritual Music in Mainland China and Hong Kong." *Yearbook for Traditional Music* 24 (1992): 118–25.

Turino, Thomas. *Moving Away from Silence: Music of the Peruvian Altiplano and the Experience of Urban Migration*. Chicago: University of Chicago Press, 1993.

Vander, Judith. *Songprints: The Musical Experience of Five Shoshone Women*. Urbana: University of Illinois Press, 1988.

Wang Can. "Xiju ji 'Shuang tui mo'." In *Zhongguo minzu yinyue da xi—xiqu yinyue juan* edited by Dongfang yinyuehui, 301–4. Shanghai: Shanghai yinyue chubanshe, 1989.

Wang Liuhe. *Zhongguo xiandai yinyue shi gang (1949–1986)*. Beijing: Huawen chubanshe, 1991.

Wang Zhongren. "Shilun *Er quan ying yue* de daoyue tezheng." *Huang zhong*, 1990, no. 1:42–8.

Waterman, Christopher A. *Jùjú: a Social History and Ethnography of an African Popular Music*. Chicago: Chicago University Press, 1990.

Watson, James L. "The Structure of Chinese Funerary Rites: Elementary Forms, Ritual Sequence, and the Primacy of Performance." In *Death Ritual in Late Imperial and Modern China*, edited by James L. Watson and Evelyn S. Rawski, 3–19. Berkeley: University of California Press, 1988.

Watson, Rubie S. "Remembering the Dead: Graves and Politics in Southeastern China." In *Death Ritual in Late Imperial and Modern China*, edited by James L. Watson and Evelyn S. Rawski, 203–27. Berkeley: University of California Press, 1988.

Wei Ren and Wei Minghua. *Yangzhou qingqu*. Shanghai: Shanghai wenyi chubanshe, 1985.

Wells, Marnix St. J. "Rhythm and Phrasing in Chinese Tune-Title Lyrics; Old Eight-Beat and Its 3–2–3 Meter." *Asian Music* 23, no. 1 (Winter 1991): 119–83.

White, Hayden. "Form, Reference, and Ideology in Musical Discourse." In *Music and Text: Critical Enquiries*, edited by Steven P. Scher, 288–319. Cambridge: Cambridge University Press, 1992.

Wichmann, Elizabeth. *Listening to Theatre: The Aural Dimension of Beijing Opera*. Honolulu: University of Hawaii Press, 1991.

Witzleben, J. Lawrence. "*Jiangnan Sizhu* Music Clubs in Shanghai: Context, Concept and Identity." *Ethnomusicology* 31 (1987): 240–60.

———. "*Silk and Bamboo" Music in Shanghai: The Jiangnan Sizhu Instrumental Ensemble Tradition*. Kent, Ohio: Kent State University Press, 1995.

Wong, Isabel K. F. "From Reaction to Synthesis: Chinese Musicology in the Twentieth Century." In *Comparative Musicology and the Anthropology of Music: Essays on the History of Ethnomusicology*, edited by Bruno Nettl and Philip V. Bohlman, 37–55. Chicago: University of Chicago Press, 1991.

———. "*Geming Gequ*: Songs for the Education of the Masses." In *Popular Chinese Literature and Performing Arts in the People's Republic of China 1949–1979*, edited by Bonnie S. McDougall, 112–43. Berkeley: University of California Press, 1984.

Wu Ben. "How Music is Transmitted in a Typical Chinese Folk Musical Group." *I.T.C.M. UK Chapter Bulletin* 21 (1988): 5–12.

———. "Pipa yinyue yu qi shehui beijing." *Zhongguo yinyuexue*, 1992, no. 2:57–67.

Wu Chou-Kuang. "The 'Erh-hu' and 'Pi-pa'." *Chinese Literature*, 1975, no. 1:100–5.

Xu Yihe. "Abing de shenghuo daolu yu yishu chengjiu." *Zhongguo yinyue*, 1983, no. 4:32–34.

———. "Abing shengnian kao." *Yinyue yanjiu*, 1989, no. 3:98–99.

Yang Mu. "Academic Ignorance or Political Taboo? Some Issues in China's Study of Its Folk Song Culture." *Ethnomusicology* 38 (1994):303–20.

Yang Yinliu. "Abing qi ren qi qu." *Renmin yinyue*, 1980, no. 3:31–34.

———. *Shifan luogu*. Beijing: Renmin yinyue chubanshe, 1980.

———. *Zhongguo gudai yinyue shi gao*. Beijing: Renmin yinyue chubanshe, 1981.

Yang Yinliu and Cao Anhe. "Er quan ying yue de zuozhe—Abing." *Renmin yinyue*, 1977, no. 6:32–33.

———. *Qing lian yuefu*. Beijing: Yinyue chubanshe, 1956.

———. *Sunan shifan gu qu: datao qiyue hezouqu*. Beijing: Renmin yinyue chubanshe, 1982. [Originally *Sunan chuida qu*, 1957.]

Ye Dong. *Minzu qiyue de ticai yu xingshi*. Shanghai: Shanghai wenyi chubanshe, 1983.

Yi Ren. "Zhongguo getan yi ke shanliang de mingxing—ji 'jin sangzi' Zhou Xuan." In *Youmei de xuanlü piaoxiang de ge—Jiangsu lidai yinyuejia*, edited by Yi Ren, 277–80. Nanjing: Jiangsu wenshi ziliao, 1992.

Yih Mei. *Erhu quji di er ji*. Hong Kong: Yih Mei Book Company, 1987.

Yin Yawei, editor. *Wu si yundong zai Jiangsu*. Yangzhou: Jiangsu guji chubanshe, 1992.

Yu Siu Wah. "Three Er-hu Pieces from Jiangnan." Queen's University of Belfast: M.A. Dissertation, 1985.

Yung, Bell. *Cantonese Opera: Performance as Creative Process*. Cambridge: Cambridge University Press, 1989.

————. "*Da Pu*: The Recreative Process for the Music of the Seven-String Zither." In *Music and Context: Essays in Honor of John Ward*, edited by Anne Dhu Shapiro, 370–84. Cambridge: Harvard University Press, 1985.

————. "Historical Interdependency of Music: A Case Study of the Chinese Seven-String Zither." *Journal of the American Musicological Society* 40 (1987): 82–91.

Zeng Xun. "*Ting song* yu 'Ting song'." *Mingqu xinshang yu yanzou*, edited by Zhang Rui et al., 12–13. Beijing: Jiefangjun wenyi chubanshe, 1987.

Zhang Shao. *Erhu guangbo jiaoxue jiangzuo*. Shanghai: Shanghai yinyue chubanshe, 1989.

Zhang Xiaohu and Yang Limei. "Lun *Er quan ying yue* de yinyue cailiao yu jiegou." *Zhongguo yinyue*, 1983, no. 1:16–20.

Zhang Xinxin and Sang Ye. "Her Past," translated by Delia Davin and Cheng Lingfang. In *Chinese Lives: An Oral History of Contemporary China*, edited by W. J. F. Jenner and Delia Davin, 31–8. Harmonsworth, Middlesex: Penguin, 1989.

Zhang Zhenji. "Abing wubiaoti erhu qu de yinyue neirong, sucai laiyuan ji qi yishu chuangzao." *Nanyi xuebao*, 1980, no. 2:53–64.

Zhao Pei. *Liu Tianhua zhuanji xiaoshuo*. Shanghai: Shanghai yinyue chubanshe, 1989.

Zhao Weiqing, editor. *Yang Yinliu yinyue lunwen xuanji*. Shanghai: Shanghai wenyi chubanshe, 1986.

Zheng Hua. "Xiju." In *Zhongguo dabaikequanshu: xiqu, quyi*, edited by Zhang Geng et al., 425. Beijing: Zhongguo dabaikequanshu chubanshe, 1983.

Zheng Hua and Cheng Ruxin. *Xiju qudiao jieshao*. Nanjing: Jiangsu wenyi chubanshe, 1954.

Zhongguo yishu yanjiuyuan yinyue yanjiusuo, editors. *Abing qu ji*. Beijing: Renmin yinyue chubanshe, 1983.

————. *Zhongguo yinyue cidian*. Beijing: Renmin yinyue chubanshe, 1985.

————. *Zhongguo yinyue cidian xubian*. Beijing: Renmin yinyue chubanshe, 1992.

Zhongguo yinyuejia xiehui, editors. *Jiangsu minjian yinyue xuanji*. Nanjing: Jiangsu wenyi chubanshe, 1959.

Zhongyang dianshi tai. *Xiazi Abing*. [TV Serial in eight parts, first broadcast March 1992.]

Zhongyang yinyue xueyuan minzu yinyue, editors. *Xiazi Abing qu ji*. Shanghai: Yinyue chubanshe, 1954.

Zhou Chang. "Abing (Hua Yanjun) de *Ting song* yu *Er quan ying yue*." *Changjiang gesheng*, 1983, no. 1:2–3.

————. "Lun Hua Yanjun chuangzuo." *Renmin yinyue*, 1963, no. 12:34–35.

Zhou Chuanrong. *Zhongguo min'ge quanji*. Taibei: Li Ming wenhua shiye gongsi, 1978.

Zhou Liangcai. "Tanhuangxi yu shidai de guanxi." *Shanghai xiqu shiliao huicui* 2 (1986): 9–15.

Zhu Jianming. "Tanhuang kao lun." *Xiqu yinyue ziliao huibian* 4 (1987): 13–16.

# Index